A Love Once Lost

A TIME TOWARD HOPE

JOVAN WILLIAMS

Eyedentified Publishing Solutions, SPRINGDALE, ARKANSAS

Eyedentified Publishing Solutions
PO Box 6892
Springdale, AR 72766-6892
www.eyedentifiedconsulting.com

Library of Congress Control Number: 2016938882

Publisher's Note: This is a work of fiction. Names, characters, places, and incidents are a product of the author's imagination. Locales and public names are sometimes used for atmospheric purposes. Any resemblance to actual people, living or dead, or to businesses, companies, events, institutions, or locales is completely coincidental.

Book Layout © 2015 BookDesignTemplates.com

Publisher's Cataloging-In-Publication Data
(Prepared by The Donohue Group, Inc.)

Names: Williams, Jovan.
Title: A love once lost : a time toward hope / Jovan Williams.
Description: 1st ed. | Springdale, Arkansas : Eyedentified Publishing Solutions, [2016]
Identifiers: LCCN 2016938882 | ISBN 978-0-9966649-6-7 (hardcover) | ISBN 978-0-9966649-4-3 (trade paper) | ISBN 978-0-9966649-7-4 (Kindle) | ISBN 978-0-9966649-5-0 (ePub)
Subjects: LCSH: Single fathers--Fiction. | Wives--Death--Fiction. | Man-woman relationships--Fiction. | Hope--Fiction. | Domestic fiction.
Classification: LCC PS3623.I55 L68 2016 (print) | LCC PS3623.I55 (ebook) | DDC 813/.6--dc23

A Love Once Lost/ Jovan Williams. -- 1st ed.
ISBN 978-0-9966649-4-3

DEDICATION

I would like to dedicate this book to two special people who are no longer with us. My dad, Delner Delmar Newsome and my lovely grandmother, Najama Ledbetter Williams.

Delmar: Man, I don't know how to thank for all you've ever done for me. I often think about the countless times you've stepped in and made a huge impact in my life. Yeah, we fussed and fought many times, but when it's all said and done, there was mutual love and respect we had for each other that made our bond strong. I miss you so much. I couldn't have asked for a better dad than you.
'Preciate you Cap'n!!!

Sogg: It's all your fault! You were the one that thrusted me into the arts. You gave me my first Sam Cooke record and my mother introduced me to Noel Pointer when I first started playing violin. After that, it was on and poppin'. You also introduced me to the old black and white films and always found a way to expose me to certain things whether it was physically or through your awesome storytelling. It's awesome to know that for a majority of the major events in my life: my birth, music performances, graduations from high school and college, witnessing me become the 1988 Drum Corps International World Champion, marriage, birth of children, and the list goes on and on. It's always been heartwarming to see you in the crowd or just knowing you were there.

Thank you for never leaving my side and always being willing to talk to me about everything no matter what. I miss our Thursday afternoon chats and miss you calling me Creature Boy Williams.

I'm so thankful that God allowed me to hear your voice in a dream after you passed away. I take it as an indication that you are still with me in my heart...and you'll be there forever. I love and miss you, Sogg Williams.

ACKNOWLEDGEMENTS

Words cannot express how happy I am to have my very first book published. I'm even more thankful for the countless number of people who have helped me and pushed me all my life to get me to this very moment.

First, I'd like thank God Almighty for giving me the idea/concept for the book. There is absolutely no way I could have come up with this and piece it all together without Him. I'm truly thankful that when I prayed and asked God for a book idea, this is what He gave me. I'm honored to have His work on display for the world to see and I give Him all the glory, honor, and praise for it.

To my wife, Sheronda: Thank you for seeing and catching hold of my vision from the start. You are one of the few people that have seen me go through this process from beginning to end. I'm thankful you will be able to see the finished product. Thank you for holding it down when things got rough. Your prayers and encouragement was greatly appreciated. I really means a lot to me and I love you for it.

To my mother, Rhonda Williams, what can I say? Thank you for giving me life. You've been a great mother in spite of. All of your hard work, dealing with adversity, doing all that needed to be done to make sure my big-headed self has the opportunity to do some awesome things in in my lifetime. I know I've been stubborn and wanted things to go my way. Thank you for telling me no and yes when it was possible. All you've ever done, and continue to do, have not gone unnoticed and I want to thank you from the bottom of my heart for taking really good care of me. Love ya like crazy!!!

To all my family, friends, and church family that have been in my corner from day one. You have no idea how much I love and appreciate you all. I'm not even going to attempt to name you all. It's too many of y'all!!! LOL!!! Your support, kind words, encouragement, and prayers have been appreciated then and now. One of the greatest feelings in the world is knowing there is a village of people that have my back. Every step of every journey I've had in life, you all have been right there for me and I'm forever grateful. To the family and friends that have gone on before me, thank you for paving the way so I can succeed. Thank you for being in my life in any and every way. Your memory will be forever alive in my heart. Thank you.

To many of my teachers (from elementary through college): If it were not for you ALL, I would not be who I am today. You pushed me in a way that I never realized until I got older and I love and appreciate you for doing that. You saw things in me that I didn't see and you took it upon yourselves to help me "get it out". Thank you to Mrs. Emma Perkins, Mrs. Joann Rogers, Mrs. Barbara Veasley, Mrs. Lois Bellis, Mrs. Joyce McBride, Mr. Robert Boedges, Mr. Terry Artis, Mrs. Barbara Moton, Ms. Joyce Center, Ms. Harriet Cuddy, Mr. Robert Camp, Mr. Patrick Jackson, Dr. London Branch, Ms. Rebecca Maltman (my lifesaver), Mr. Scott Stewart, Mr. Chris Thompson, Min. Jeffrey Rhone and Dr. Hilliard L. Scott. If I've omitted anyone (and I'm sure I did), please charge it to my head and not my heart. I am eternally indebted to all these awesome teachers/instructors for going above and beyond to ensure I succeeded. You all did it for me, now I have an obligation to pay it forward.

To my children, Jessica, Jared, Caleb, Kyla, and Kyle: You are my inspiration and motivation. Thank you for being who you are individually and I am honored and blessed to be your father. Please know that I love you with every fiber of my being and want you to experience God's very best in your lives. It's my prayer that whatever you endeavor to do in life, it all will manifest and you have great success. On days when I felt defeated and wanted to give up, God would flash your faces in my mind, my attitude would instantly change, and I'd get back on track. I love you to the moon and back, kiddos!!!

To my great team that worked hard to help me put out a great product:

Mrs. Terri Walker: What can I say? You are the bomb.com!!! Thank you so much for doing a super fantastic job at editing my book. Your skills are remarkable and I valued and appreciated your candid feedback. Thank you so much for all your hard work. Get some rest. Part 2 is on the way!

Mr. Jermaine Watts: Bro, you are an artistic genius. You truly have a gift and I'm glad we were able to collaborate. I remember those talks on the church parking lot about my book and having the opportunity see your brilliant work is a prayer answered. I appreciate your hard work and always knew you had mad skills. I'm glad the rest of the world can see it as well.

Mrs. LaTonya Jackson of Eyedentified Publishing Solutions: Thank you...Thank you...Thank you!!! We were connected at the perfect time. I had a billion questions and didn't know which way to go. Thank you for your guidance, feedback, and making me feel comfortable and at ease during this process. It has been an absolute pleasure to work with you. Let's do it again soon.

Mr. Anthony Adams of Creating Memorable Moments by Anthony: Thank you for the outstanding photos you took. I'm glad you captured my good sides. LOL! You have a great eye for photography and do Grade A work. Just to let you know, I will be writing more books and I will need a new photo for each one. You with me? Thanks, brother!!!

CONTENTS

CHAPTER ONE

Introduction

A Love Once Lost is a message of hope. This story is about a man who has, what seems to be, the absolute perfect life: a beautiful, healthy family; promising career; and the respect and admiration of his peers and community. What more could a man want?

Alex's perfect world comes to an end one dreadful night when he experiences sudden loss and adversity almost too much to bear. Now, he's left with raising a daughter and maintaining a household while still trying to keep up with his professional responsibilities. He feels that all hope is lost, until one day... someone surfaces and changes his world completely. Then, all hope is restored. What he thought was lost has now been found. What he thought he would never see nor feel again, he now sees and feels; but the journey to this point has not been easy. It's been a frightening and frustrating journey for Alex, but on his way to restoration, he has also experienced some surprisingly hilarious moments, which allowed him to survive the process.

CHARACTERS:

Alexander Michael Reed ("Alex"): Alex is the kind of guy that everyone wants to be around. Even though he's extremely smart and successful, he is a very humble person.

Alex was born in Charlotte, North Carolina, into a single- parent home with his mother Regina Maxine Reed. Alex's grandparents, whom he and his mother lived with, played a major role in his upbringing and he had a lot of fun living with them. He and his mom were not poor, but there was a struggle at times since his mom brought in the only income. The living situation took a big load off of her because she didn't have to worry about paying rent. She did, however, give her parents money every paycheck to "help out." Unbeknownst to Regina or Alex, her parents kept all the money over the years and saved it with the intent of helping them put a down payment on a house of their own. Unfortunately, that never happened because Regina passed away when Alex was just sixteen years old. Thankfully, through this tragedy, he had the love and support of his grandparents.

During his childhood, Alex was always observant of his surroundings and asked a lot of questions to get an understanding of people or situations. He loved to read and very much enjoyed a heated debate with someone; hence his passion for law and the opportunity to prove someone wrong.

Alex's grandparents made sure he had all the tools to succeed and all the love and support he needed, while instilling in him a strong work ethic. After graduating valedictorian from high school, Alex went on to study pre-law and then law school on scholarship at Harvard University.

His grandparents continued to support him in life even after he left the nest. The money that they had been saving up for he and Regina's down payment was given to him as a down payment for his first home. They were there for him at every major milestone. Alex loved and admired them dearly and appreciated everything they had ever done for him. He, of course, made sure that once he reached a level of success, they were well taken care of.

After graduating from law school, Alex went to work for the law firm of Goldberg, Oswald, & Danielson, where he is now a successful corporate attorney. He's been with the firm for fifteen years and has labored hard to move his way through the ranks. He has been one of the senior partners for five years. Other firms have courted him and made very lucrative offers, but he felt "in his gut" that this was the firm he was destined to work, and it has paid off beyond belief.

Alex has been married to the love of his life, Gabrielle, for ten years and they have one daughter, Jasmine Alexis, who is eight years old.

He is a member of Alpha Phi Alpha Fraternity, Inc. and the National Bar Association. He is also a deacon at New Grace Church and a coach with a junior football league team. Alex is someone who receives love from everyone he encounters and loves even harder. He gets it from all he's received from his family growing up—it's something that's always stuck with him. Some say that loving hard can either be a blessing or a curse. Whatever the case, Alex will love no matter what.

Gabrielle Simone (Wallace) Reed ("Gabby"): Gabby was born in Savannah, Georgia. She is the youngest of three children (she has two older brothers) born to the union of Rev. Charles G. Wallace and Mrs. Rosemary M. Wallace. Rev. Wallace is the pastor of the Prince of

Peace Missionary Baptist Church and Mrs. Wallace is the organist, minister of music, and Sunday school teacher.

Being the only girl, Gabby was the apple of her father's eye; but not a spoiled brat. Having two older brothers taught her how to be tough, but her mother taught her how to be a good, godly woman. She loves singing, playing the piano, going to church, and cooking. As a girl, she loved school and math was her favorite subject. After graduating valedictorian of her high school class, she went on to study finance at Georgia State University and later went on to earn an MBA in Finance from Duke University. Currently, Gabby is vice president of finance at the Federal Reserve Bank of Charlotte.

Gabby met Alex through a mutual friend at a Christmas party and they hit it off immediately. They dated for six months, falling madly in love. Soon after, they had a fairy tale wedding and honeymooned in the Bahamas. Together, they have one daughter, Jasmine Alexis.

Gabby is a member of Alpha Kappa Alpha Sorority, Inc., board member of Girl's Inc. of the Greater Charlotte, and a Sunday school teacher.

Jasmine Alexis Reed ("Jazzy"): Jazzy is an eight-year-old cutie and a lot of fun to be around. She has the personalities of both of her parents but with a sense of sass. Once would say that she has "been here before." Jazzy loves her parents, family, school...life in general. Like her mom and dad, even though she is an only child, she isn't spoiled at all. She has learned to be thankful for what she has and appreciates everything she receives.

Jazzy is a very intelligent third grader at Garfield Elementary School. Although she has the aptitude of a fourth grader, her parents thought that keeping her in the third grade would be best because they didn't want her academics to fall short in the event that the classes would be too hard. They didn't want to see her fail.

She enjoys singing and dancing and is very active with the puppet ministry in her church's youth department. She can be a bit of a comedienne. She has a quick wit and always seems to make people laugh. Jazzy has the ability to light up a room with her beautiful smile and awesome attitude.

Since Jasmine has the personalities of both parents, it's funny how she is able to interact with them. For example, when her mother, Gabrielle, is cooking, she is there to help and watch so she can learn. She has great taste in clothes and knows how to coordinate to make a stylish outfit, and she can also spot a bargain a mile away. Mama has trained her well.

She knows all about sports, especially football and basketball; and probably knows more than Alex. When she goes to games with her dad, you would think that she is one of the coaches because she gets completely involved (and even argues with the referees on bad calls). Jasmine also has the skills to debate, which she got from her father (since he is a lawyer). She will "tell it like it is" and not back down.

Dr. Vanessa Denise (Cortez) León: Vanessa was born in Dallas, Texas, to a Mexican father and an African-American mother. She is a professor of English at Johnson C. Smith University and has been there for twenty years. She holds a bachelor of arts in Applied Behavior Sciences from Texas A&M University, and a master's and PhD in English, both from Duke University.

She has been married to Guillermo León for twelve years and they have one son, Enrique "Ricky," who is fourteen-years-old and a high school freshman.

Guillermo Jesus León: Guillermo was born in Miami, Florida, and moved to Midland, Texas, at a young age. After graduating high school, Guillermo attended Texas A&M majoring in architecture. It was there that he obtained his bachelor's degree and met the woman of his dreams, Ms. Vanessa Denise Cortez. They met and became sweethearts almost instantly. After graduation, they obtained jobs in Charlotte, married, and relocated there to begin their lives together.

Guillermo is employed as an architect with Finch & Associates, located in uptown Charlotte, and has been there for twenty years. He's responsible for a majority of the major contracts with the city and is well known in the business community.

Enrique "Ricky" León: Ricky is a fourteen-year-old freshman in high school. Although he is a very smart young man, he is at the age where he is trying to find himself and figure out what he wants to do with his life. He is on the freshman football team and is one of the team's leading wide receivers.

Ricky is a joy to be around and has a great time with his friends, but deep down inside, he has the desire to be a big brother and is tired of being an only child. He's been asking his parents for years but it's never happened. Unfortunately, his mother had two miscarriages and to prevent disappointment and heartbreak for Ricky, she's never disclosed any of this to him.

CHAPTER TWO

The Beginning

It's late summer in Charlotte, North Carolina, on a beautiful Wednesday morning. Birds are chirping loudly and big, puffy white clouds are scattered throughout the vast of the blue sky. The sun is shining bright, providing endless light, which seems to be a perfect start to the day.

It's 6:00 a.m. and Alex wakes up before his family to begin his daily routine of exercise. Being a little over six feet tall, weighing two hundred fifty pounds, and having demanding roles as an attorney, husband, and father, he has to stay in tip-top shape. He goes into his basement, turns on the television and DVD player, and pops in the day's scheduled Insanity® to get a rigorous workout from Shawn T. After about forty-five minutes of a complete ass whooping, Alex goes back upstairs to get the rest of the family up, shower, and go about the day.

After his shower, he climbs into bed and gives his beautiful wife, Gabby, a soft kiss on her face, then her neck, and finally an ear, attempting to lovingly wake her up.

"Good morning sleeping beauty," he says, softly in her ear while tickling her.

"NOOOOOOO...leave me alone. It's not time to get up yet," Gabby moans, while clutching onto the bed covers in the fetal position.

"Yes baby. It's that time," Alex says. "Come on, now. Let's get this party started. Move it, move it, move it!!!" Alex says like a drill sergeant.

"OK, OK, OK!!! I'm getting up. I'm up. I'm up!" she says while throwing a pillow at him for fun. "Since you're so bright-eyed and bushy-tailed, why don't you go get Jazzy up?" Gabby yells to Alex.

"Yes ma'am!" Alex yells back.

Alex goes down the hall to Jazzy's room to wake her up and finds her sleeping soundly, almost in a hibernation-like state. Alex stands in the doorway and whispers,

"Good morning Jazzy. Time to get up."

She does not budge. He says it again a little louder while standing in the doorway,

"JAZZYYYYY! Come on, baby girl. Let's get moving! It's time to make the donuts!"

Jasmine pulls the covers over her head and yells from underneath, "I don't even like donuts. Plus, it's Saturday, why am I up so early?"

Alex laughs and says in response, "Girl, get your butt out the bed and get ready to go to school, it's NOT Saturday. Let's go baby!"

Jazzy says, "AWWWW!!! You're not supposed to say butt. Mama says that's a bad word."

She's still under the covers and grabs them even tighter. Now laughing even harder, Alex yanks the covers off and grabs her by the feet and slowly drags her out of the bed. Jasmine is trying to kick her feet from the grasps of her father, but she is unsuccessful.

"Come on, now. Get your butt, booty, buttocks, whatever you want to call it, out of this bed before the Tickle Monster comes out."

He tickles her and she erupts into laughter as she tries to break free. Alex picks her up.

"Good morning, Daddy!" Jasmine says, kissing Alex on the cheek.

"EWWWW! You got dragon breath! Go brush your teeth!" Alex says. They both burst into laughter as Alex lowers her to the floor and she goes off to get ready for her day.

Meanwhile, across town, the León family begins to prepare for their day. Vanessa—the wife, mother, and matriarch of the family—has already been up since 5:00 a.m. getting in half an hour of exercise on the treadmill and half an hour of yoga before getting her husband, Guillermo, and son, Enrique, up from their deep slumbers to go about their day.

After taking a relaxing, hot shower, Vanessa climbs into bed with Guillermo, shakes him to wake up, and whispers into his ear, "Papi...buenos dias mi marido, guapo fuerte." (Good morning my very handsome husband.)

Guillermo slowly opens his eyes, smiles at Vanessa and says, "Buenos dias, Mami! Mi hermosa, queridu esposa." (Good morning my beautiful, sweet wife.)

They exchange a kiss as Guillermo grabs Vanessa and pulls her into the bed with him to hold her close.

"I don't want to go to work today. Stay home with me."

"Oh honey. I wish I could but I have a lecture today and I have to be there," Vanessa says apologetically, while rubbing his chest.

"Damn lectures!" Guillermo yells jokingly. "I was hoping you could stay home with me. We could watch TV, make a baby, go to sleep, wake up, make another baby..."

They burst into laughter and Vanessa gives him a shove as she gets out of bed.

"As much as I would love to stay and make babies with you, I've got to get breakfast started and get Ricky out of bed."

"I'll get Ricky out of bed while you get breakfast started," Guillermo offers.

Vanessa yells back, "Good luck with that!" as she heads out of the bedroom and into the kitchen.

Guillermo gets out of bed and heads toward Ricky's room. He knocks on the door.

"Ricky! Good morning! Time to get up and get going."

He doesn't hear any movement, so he knocks on the door a little harder and yells a little louder.

"Ricky! Chop chop! Let's go!"

He still hears no movement. He opens the door and notices Ricky still in the bed with his headphones on his ears and music blasting. Guillermo goes over to Ricky's iPod and cranks up the volume on the device...he still does not move. Now getting more frustrated, Guillermo goes over to his bed and begins to shake him saying, "Ricky! Vamos! Let's go! You don't need to be late."

Ricky, unfazed by his father's attempts, rolls over onto his back and begins to snore louder than he was before.

"You've got to be friggin' kidding me," Guillermo says under his breath. "Is this kid even alive?"

Now he's to the point where he is about to explode, "Vanessa! Why won't this boy get out of bed? Please help!"

Vanessa comes into the room, sees what has happened (or not happened), laughs, and says to Guillermo, "Let me show you how it's done."

Vanessa goes over to the side of Ricky's bed, sits beside him on the edge, rubs the side of his head, and whispers ever so softly and sweetly, "Ricky. Good morning, sweetheart. Time to wake up."

All of a sudden, Ricky's eyes pop open and he immediately jumps out of bed as if there is an earthquake taking place, realizes who is in the room, and says,

"G'mornin' mami and papi!" Ricky mumbles as he walks past them headed towards the bathroom.

"Hurry up, Ricky! I don't want you to be late," Vanessa says.

"Yes ma'am!" Ricky yells back.

Looking at Vanessa with a puzzled look on his face, Guillermo says, "That's a damn shame! I swear that kid is from another planet."

Vanessa laughs, "I see I still got it." She snaps her finger, turns around, and walks away. Guillermo shakes his head and walks out of the room.

Before anyone leaves the house, it's customary for Guillermo to offer a word of prayer covering his family for the day and for a safe return home:

"Father, we thank you and we love you. We are nothing without you. We count it all joy that you love us the way you do. We are in awe of your goodness and mercy and would never take any of that for granted. Lord, I thank you for my beautiful family. Protect us as we leave this place going in our own separate directions and please give us the grace to come back together to this loving home. En nombre de Padre, de Hijo, y de Espiritu Santo (In the name of the Father, Son, and the Holy Spirit). Amen.

Guillermo kisses Vanessa as she grabs her tumbler of hot tea. She kisses Ricky on his forehead and darts out the door for work and to beat the congested Charlotte traffic. Guillermo and Ricky exchange hi-fives and a hug. Ricky grabs his things and heads to the bus stop while Guillermo gets into his car to head to work.

In the Reed home, it's also customary for Alex to offer a word of prayer for his family. So, standing in a circle, holding hands in the living room, Alex prays:

"Heavenly Father, we thank you for all your many blessings. We thank you for allowing us to see this brand new day. Father, we can't thank you enough for what you have done for us even when we feel when we don't even deserve it. Please Lord, cover this family when we're together and apart and please see to it that we are brought together better that we were when we left. I can't thank you enough for my family; my beautiful wife and daughter. You knew exactly what I needed in my life and I got it and I'm eternally grateful. We thank you for the love you share with us each and every day and pray it spills onto others we encounter. We thank you and praise you, giving you the honor, glory, and praise. In Jesus' name. Amen."

After their morning prayers, Alex walks Gabrielle to her car and they exchange a kiss. She gets in the car and drives off to work. Jasmine gets into the front seat of Alex's car and buckles her seat belt for her ride to school.

CHAPTER THREE

Celebration Time

Gabby is finishing up a conference call when she hears a knock on the door.

"Come on in," she says, "I've just finished up on a call."

"Gabby, do you have a minute?" In walks her boss, Bill Ingram, with an angry look on his face.

"Hey Bill! Sure. What's going on?" Gabby was unsure how to interpret his facial expression.

"There is a situation that has been brought to my attention that we really need to discuss. I need you to meet me in Conference Room One in ten minutes."

He turns around and walks off saying nothing else. Gabby is puzzled by his unusual behavior and wonders what could be so urgent. She sits and thinks for a few minutes, grabs her portfolio containing a legal pad and her pen, and heads for the conference room. Upon entering, she sees Bill and another well-dressed gentleman seated at the end of the long table in the conference room.

"Come in and have a seat, Gabby," Bill speaks sternly, still with an angry look on his face.

Gabby sits down, opens her portfolio, and takes out her pen in case she needs to write something.

"There's no need for paper and pen. We're just here to talk," Bill says.

"About what, sir?"

"First, let me introduce you to Mr. Raymond Ledbetter," Bill says. Mr. Ledbetter stands up and reaches out his hand to Gabby, "Pleasure to meet you, Mrs. Reed."

Gabby stands and shakes his hand, "Pleasure to meet you as well, sir. You may call me Gabby."

Before Gabby can start any conversation with Mr. Ledbetter, Bill quickly intercepts, "Gabby, a lot of calls have been forwarded to me regarding your performance here and that's why the three of us are meeting."

"Performance? What's wrong with my performance when I've had outstanding performance appraisals since I've been here? Why all of a sudden is there an issue now?"

Gabby has gone from puzzled to angry.

Bill and Mr. Ledbetter look at each other and all of a sudden burst into laughter. Gabby is not pleased at all with this exchange.

"Gentlemen! Please excuse my bluntness, but what's so funny and what the hell is going on?"

Bill stands up, laughing very hard, but now with a sweet expression in his eyes.

"Gabby, please sit down. Nothing is wrong. I promise."

Gabby sits down and gives an evil stare to both the men. After the men regain their composure, Bill explains,

"Mr. Ledbetter is the CEO and publisher of the Charlotte Business Journal and has some very exciting news for you. Mr. Ledbetter, the floor is yours."

"Thank you Bill," Mr. Ledbetter explains his reason for being present. "We've been talking to a number of senior managers and executives in the area, Bill being one of them, and your name came up a number of times. They all had remarkable things to say about you so we had to check you out. Since you've been here with the Federal Reserve, you've been a rising star in your own right and an outstanding leader in this community. And for your top-notch leadership, the Charlotte Business Journal has selected you, Gabrielle Simone Reed, to be honored as one of Charlotte's 40 Under 40 Outstanding Leaders."

Mr. Ledbetter begins to clap, Bill starts to clap, and suddenly the door to the conference room bursts open with people from the office coming in with balloons, cheering and clapping. Gabby is speechless and can do nothing but stand in utter amazement and try to soak up in her mind what is taking place. Bill and Mr. Ledbetter walk over to her side of the table. Mr. Ledbetter shakes her hand, "Congratulations Gabby! Sorry we gave you a scare. That was Bill's idea."

"Thank you, sir! Gabby says. "For once, I don't know what to say."

Mr. Ledbetter gives her a reassuring look, "The work you do speaks volumes, young lady. You deserve it."

Bill then comes along and shakes her hand and gives her a big hug and says, "I gotcha!" Bill declared while playfully grabbing her shoulders and shaking her hand. "Please forgive me, I couldn't help myself. I wanted to set you up for the surprise."

Gabby finally gathers her thoughts and emotions enough so that she can finally laugh it off. She harbors no ill towards Bill for his trickery. As reality sets in, she looks around the room at the faces of her colleagues and absorbs all of the happiness and support that is being expressed just for her.

Suddenly, all of the people in the room began to chant "Speech...Speech...Speech..." Bill motions everyone to quiet down so that Gabby can express herself.

"This is such an honor and an amazing surprise. Seriously, I feel speechless, but you all know that I am rarely at a loss for words. I do want to say that I come to work every day to make a quiet difference. Meaning, I'm not looking for any pomp and circumstance or looking to outshine anyone. I'm a team player and want to see others on this team succeed and do well. Never in a million years would I have thought that I would be honored like this. I am eternally grateful and honored. Thank you."

Everyone in the room cheers and applauds again.

"Alright, alright! Everyone get back to work. This show is over." Bill laughs, turns to Gabby, and says, "Gabby, stay here a few minutes longer. Mr. Ledbetter wants to give you some more information."

They all sit and Mr. Ledbetter begins to speak.

"Gabby, again, congratulations on your nomination. There will be an awards banquet honoring you and the other awardees on September twelfth at seven o'clock in the evening at the Ritz-Carlton. You'll be allotted a certain amount of tickets for your guests. Someone from my office will be contacting you later in the week to square away all of the details and to schedule a photo shoot so we can..."

"A photo shoot?!" Gabby asks, feeling like a celebrity.

"Yes, your photo is needed in the program and in our publication, as well as on the big screen during the banquet when you are announced." Reaching out to shake her hand, he continues, "Congrats again. I can tell you're well liked and respected around here. This honor is well deserved."

"Thank you Mr. Ledbetter," Gabby replies. I look forward to the call from your office and seeing you on September twelfth. I must get back to my office and tell my husband this great news and, of course, get some work done." Gabby turns to Bill, "Bill, I'll be talking with you later I'm sure. And I forgive you for pulling my leg."

"Good! Congratulations, and again, you deserve this. I'm proud of you."

Gabby goes back to her office, closes her door, and exhales as she sinks comfortably into her chair. Before she realizes it, she's weeping tears of joy and begins to pray, "Lord, I am so thankful right now. You are so amazing and I love you. I don't know what I did to deserve all this but I sincerely thank you. Please keep me humble and deeply grounded and rooted in you. I pray the same for my family. In Jesus' name, Amen. Thank you, Lord. Thank you."

Once she regains her composure and wipes away her tears, she picks up the phone to call Alex at work.

Alex is in such deep thought and total concentration typing on his computer that he doesn't hear the phone ring. The phone rings again but he still doesn't realize it's ringing because he's so engrossed in what he is doing. Not too soon after, his email notification pops up on his screen. He sees it's from Gabby, so he stops what he's doing, and opens the e-mail:

Alex, are you there? Answer the phone, Knucklehead!!! ☺

Alex's phone rings again and this time he quickly picks up.

"Hey baby! So, I'm a knucklehead now, huh?"

They both laugh.

"I've been trying to call you for the longest but you never answered."

"I'm sorry, sweetness. I was so into typing this brief that I didn't even hear it. What's up? How's your day going?"

"I am doing exceptionally well, my love. Especially since I've been nominated this year as one of Charlotte's 40 Under 40 Outstanding Leaders by the Charlotte Business Journal."

"Are you serious?!" Alex asks in excitement. "Baby, that's awesome!!! When did all of this take place? This is super exciting."

"I just got word of it today and it was a total shock."

"I bet it was. I am so proud of you, sweetheart. I just might have to give you some boo-tay tonight," Alex jokes as they both laugh.

"The awards ceremony is going to be held on September twelfth at the Ritz-Carlton."

"Oh, so you're a big baller, shot caller now. I hear ya' baby. Are they going to roll out the red carpet too?" Alex asks laughing.

"They need to, and throw out rose petals too!" They both erupt into laughter.

"Seriously baby, this is a true blessing. I never expected this. I'm still in awe."

"You deserve nothing but the very best God has for you. The best part is that He ain't done yet. So just get ready! You've worked very hard and this is well deserved. I'm blessed and proud to be your husband."

"Awww, that's sweet. Thank you, love!" Gabrielle smiles from ear to ear, blushing. "I can invite guests to the ceremony so I've got to let the crew know so everyone can clear their schedules to be there."

"Why don't you send out an e-mail to everyone reminding them of our monthly get together at Petey's and mention that there will be a special announcement when we meet. But don't go into too much detail."

"That's exactly what I will do," replies Gabrielle. "Let me get off of the phone and send this e-mail out and get back to work."

"OK baby," Alex says. "Oh, by the way, don't forget Jazzy and I are going to the Carver High football game today with the team, so we'll be a little late getting home."

"No prob. I didn't forget," Gabrielle says. "Y'all have fun and see you when you get home. Love you!!!"

"Love you too, baby. Bye."

The second she hangs up the phone, Gabrielle turns to her computer, pulls up her e-mail, and composes a message:

Dear Friends,

I pray this message finds you all well today. This is just a friendly reminder about our monthly get together at Petey's this Saturday at 7:00 p.m. It would be in your best interest to be there AND be on time to hear a very important announcement. Trust me, you don't want to miss this!!! ☺ See you Saturday!!!

Love Y'all,

Gabby

Meanwhile, Guillermo has just finished an important conference call with his staff and a longtime client who wants Guillermo's firm to be a part of a new project. As Guillermo sits at his desk going over notes from the meeting, he gets a call from his assistant, Pamela.

"Yes ma'am," he answers.

"Sir, I have a Mr. Juan Santos with the Latin American Chamber of Commerce here to see you and he says it's very urgent. He apologizes for coming on short notice," Pamela explains.

"No problem," responds Guillermo. "Please send him in."

After a few seconds, there is a soft knock on his door and Pamela escorts Mr. Santos into Guillermo's office.

"Señor León! Buenos días. My name is Juan Santos and I am with the Latin American Chamber of Commerce here in Charlotte. It's a pleasure to finally meet you.

"Buenos días, Señor Santos!" Guillermo shakes his hand. "It's a pleasure to meet you, as well. Please have a seat."

"May I offer you some coffee or water, Señor Santos?" Guillermo asks.

"No sir," Juan replies. "I am fine. Gracias!"

"De nada."

"Señor León, please accept my apologies for the unannounced visit. I hope I'm not imposing on your time. I promise to be as brief as I can."

"This is OK. How may I help you?" Guillermo asks.

"Well Señor León, we at the Chamber love to search out those individuals that not only do a lot for the Latino community but have made a lasting impression in the city of Charlotte. You have been on our radar for quite some time now and I'm pleased to say that we are impressed with what you have accomplished over the past few years, especially with the renovation of the Blumenthal Performing Arts Center. That was an amazing feat and you and your firm made it seem easy. That is to be commended."

"Why thank you," Guillermo says. "We work hard to make sure that every client is completely satisfied and that we produce a high quality product. That's our mission."

"Well, that's the reason for my visit," adds Juan. I'm honored to let you know that you have been recognized by the Chamber as a true leader and want to award you the prestigious Outstanding Leadership Award."

Guillermo slumps back in his chair and sits in utter amazement, his mouth slightly ajar.

"Oh my God, are you serious?" Guillermo asks. "This is absolutely amazing. I don't know what to say."

"Congratulations mi amigo! It is well deserved," Juan smiles brightly. "God bless you for what you do for our community. Muchas gracias!"

"Wow!" Guillermo laughs. "No. Thank you and the Chamber for such a great honor. I'm very thankful and humbled."

"And you have every reason to be," says Juan. "We are hosting a banquet for all our honorees at the Ritz-Carlton on September twelfth. It's going to be a grand evening."

Juan reaches into his leather briefcase, pulls out a packet of information, and hands it to Guillermo.

"Here is some information for you regarding that evening. Please take a moment to review it at your leisure. Someone from our office will be contacting you within the next day or two to get some additional information from you and to set up a time to take some photos of you. If you have any additional questions, please don't hesitate to contact me. All of my information is in the packet."

"Thank you so much, Juan," Guillermo says. "This is such a great honor. Thank you from the bottom of my heart."

"You're very welcome. We'll be in touch very soon. Oh, by the way, please invite your family and friends so they can share in this special occasion with you."

"Yes sir, I will. I'm sure they will enjoy it just as much as I will."

Both men stand and shake hands again.

"Adiós mi amigo! Have a great rest of the day!"

"Adiós Juan!" Guillermo replies.

After Juan leaves, Guillermo tells Pamela to hold his phone calls for about fifteen minutes and closes his office door. He immediately gets on the phone and calls Vanessa. He knows this is one of her big lecture days and is hoping and praying that she is done at this point, but the phone rings and rings. He hangs up and calls again, all the while tapping his foot on the floor and his fingers on the desk. Finally, she picks up.

"This is Dr. León. How may I help you?" Vanessa answers.

"Oh, mi amor! I'm glad you picked up," Guillermo says excitedly. "How are you? How is your day? Are you sitting down or standing up? I'm sorry sweetheart," Guillermo apologizes. "Am I rambling? I think I am."

Vanessa, very nervous and concerned, responds, "Honey! Slow down. Breathe. What's wrong? Is everything OK? Talk to me."

"I don't mean to startle you, everything's just fine. I'm just very excited right now. A gentleman from the Latino Chamber of Commerce just left my office and informed me that I've been selected to receive the Outstanding Leadership Award on September twelfth. Isn't that great?!"

"Oh my goodness, honey! That is awesome!" Vanessa says enthusiastically.

"More details are coming soon, but I have some information to look over now."

"I am so proud of you! Oh my. What will I wear? How will I wear my hair? I need new shoes."

Guillermo laughs and cuts her off, "Honey. Now you slow down. Relax. Breathe. We have plenty of time. I'm sure you'll get all of that worked out."

"I'm so proud of you, papi. I'm going to fix you a meal tonight that is fit for a king," Vanessa says with a smile on her face. "God is really smiling down on you and this family."

"Yes He is," replies Guillermo. "I am so grateful. You all are so wonderful. What more could a guy ask for? OK, I have to go now. Don't forget Ricky has a game tonight."

"Is that tonight?" Vanessa asks. "Dang it! I almost forgot. Well, I guess we will have to have your feast another night, Your Highness."

"Ha ha. You are so funny," Guillermo says. "We can have something light. That will be fine. We can do something this weekend to celebrate. Te llamo (I love you)!

"Te amo, mi amor. Con todo mi corazon." [I love you my love, with all of my heart.]

Later that day, Alex gets off work a little early and picks up Jasmine from school to head straight to Carver. Both are dressed and ready to witness some good football between Carver High and Central High. They wait at the field for all of the members of the team Alex coaches to arrive so they can go in and all sit together. Once everyone arrives, they all get plenty of snacks to enjoy (hotdogs, popcorn, nachos, water, and Gatorade) and then they file into the stadium before the game starts.

As soon as the game begins, Alex and Jasmine begin their analysis comparable to ESPN sportscasters broadcasting the Sunday afternoon NFL game—guessing what plays will be called next, critiquing players, and, for Jasmine, yelling at the referees after a bad call or penalty. One of the players who gets a lot of attention is a freshman wide receiver from Carver, number seven, Enrique "Ricky" León. He is having an amazing game. He runs for over seventy-five yards and has twelve carries and two touchdowns. This is a very impressive outcome for such a young player. The final score is Carver High–35, to Central High-14.

Once the game is over, everyone begins filing out of the stadium like a herd of cattle. Alex and Jasmine notice the Carver High team huddled around talking with the team coaches and Ricky on the outside of the huddle. Jasmine breaks away from Alex and runs toward Ricky. She taps him on the back and as soon as he turns around, she grabs his hand and shakes it hard while greeting him. "Hey number seven! Great game today! You looked really good out there, but make sure you keep the ball close to your body when you run. I thought for sure the ball was going to pop out of your hands a few times."

Ricky looks up at Alex, who has caught up with Jasmine, and laughs as Alex shakes his head.

"Please forgive my daughter," Alex says. "She's very passionate about football and can be quite critical at times, as you can see." Alex reaches out his hand and introduces himself to Ricky.

"I'm Alex Reed and this is my daughter Jasmine. We call her Jazzy."

"Pleasure to meet you sir, and you too Jazzy," replies Ricky.

"The pleasure is alllll mine!" Jasmine says as Ricky and Alex laugh.

"I'm one of the coaches of the Wildcat football team and we'd love to have you or the team come by one of our practices and talk with the players. It would be good for them and they would really enjoy it. Your coach and I are good friends and I will get that arranged soon."

"Sure, that sounds cool, I'd love that," Ricky replies. "Sorry to cut this short, but I see my parents and I've got to go. It was a pleasure meeting you...and a pleasure to meet you too, Ms. Jazzy," Ricky gives her a fist bump and jogs to his parents.

"See ya!" Jazzy admiringly watches Ricky run off as she waves goodbye to Ricky.

Alex also turns and waves to Ricky and his parents, then makes sure all of the Wildcats are headed off safely home.

CHAPTER FOUR

Reflection and Thanksgiving

Alex and Gabby have wonderful friends who provide lots of love and support. They are a very interesting bunch, but their uniqueness makes them loveable. They all get together quite often, mostly as a group, but sometimes the men and the ladies separate to do their own thing. Whatever the case, there will be deep conversations and potential drama. The group consists of a good mix of single and married couples, so you know there is bound to be a lot of heated debates and differing viewpoints. The awesome thing about this band of friends is that whenever they get together, whatever is said between them stays between them. Here they are:

Craig Spencer: IT Programmer, single, class clown, and extremely anti-relationship. He will not commit to a relationship to save his life. He chooses to be the "hit-it and quit-it" kind of guy.

Nia Rogers: The Diva. Sales executive, single, very attractive, classy, and a bit of a beauty queen. Not interested in relationships either; she claims she doesn't need a man. She prefers to be wined and dined instead of committing to anything serious.

Craig and Nia have both experienced bad relationships in the past, which has contributed to their resistance to entering into another relationship. They are always at each other's throat but still have a mutual respect for one another.

Foster & Alicia Ellis: Happily married for six years and live successful lives. Foster is an accountant and Alicia is a pharmaceutical sales representative.

Elijah & Corrine Corruthers: Married for ten years and have a love/hate relationship. Elijah is a retired Air Force Master Sargent but is into real estate part-time. Corrine is an office manager at a pediatrician's office.

Bradley (Brad) & Hannah Maguire: Newlyweds. Brad is a marketing executive and Hannah is a kindergarten teacher.

Juni Leong & Keiko Sun: Owners of a very successful daycare and preschool in Charlotte. They have been in a committed relationship for three years and they are seriously thinking about getting married.

They currently live together.

On Saturday night at seven o'clock, Alex and Gabrielle join their group of friends at Petey's for their monthly get-together. (This is an outing everyone looks forward to as a chance to get out and have a good time with each other.) Petey's has long been their go-to hangout. For one, it's got one of the tastiest menus in town; two, the eatery often has enjoyable live music; and three, it's one of the few places in town that suits everyone.

After eating a good meal and enjoying some good conversation coupled with laughter, they begin on dessert and cocktails. Then suddenly, Craig begins to take the conversation in a totally different direction.

"I am done with relationships!" he declares with disgust.

"Oh Lord! What has happened now?" Gabrielle asks with a slight giggle.

"Just when I was seriously thinking about settling down with one chick, she ends up going crazy on me and I ain't got time for foolishness," Craig says.

"So tell us what happened, man," Alex interjects.

"Just when I was about to dismiss all my side chicks, tear up my little black book, and get rid of my playa's card, these chicks think they own me and can run all over me. The Kid don't play that."

"Whatever, fool!" Nia chimes in. "I'm surprised you haven't caught anything yet the way you are just out there sleeping with all those different women. You need to cut it out before you come across the wrong chick and have a "Fatal Attraction" on your hands. Then what you gonna do?"

"Fool?" Craig replies. "I got your fool! Like I said, ain't no chick gonna get me trapped. Plus, why are you all up in my business? Where is your man, huh? Or are you just mad because you have not been able to get with this?" Craig teasingly asks as he points to himself. "You know you want me. Why are you frontin'?"

"Negro please!" says Nia with an attitude. "There is nothing on you I want. I don't want to sit next to you. I'm afraid whatever you may have caught from one of your hood rats might jump off on me. And don't you worry about who I'm with. I'm doing fine all by myself. I don't need a man. Y'all ain't nothin' but some damn dogs anyway...with y'all trifling asses."

"Well hell, y'all made us that way," Craig responds. "If you all would learn how to treat us; we wouldn't be having this discussion. You heifers are just as bad as we are."

Nia stands up in anger, throws her napkin at Craig and says, "Heifer? Oh, I got your heifer with your dusty ass!"

They continue to go back and forth shouting insults at each other until Elijah and Corrine break them up and calm them down. Everyone else is laughing hysterically while enjoying the drama unfolding. With those two, it's almost expected that something is going to transpire... and it's usually something bad.

"Y'all about to get us kicked out of here with this foolishness," Elijah laughs. "You both act like two old people. Why don't you all just go ahead and become a couple."

Elijah's wife, Corrine, chimes in, "Personally, I think you would make an attractive couple."

Craig and Nia look at each other, frown, and simultaneously shout, "HELL NO!" They brush off what was said and continue on with the evening.

The group always looks forward to this time so they can all catch up from the last time they were together. Everyone tells the group about new developments in their lives—careers, business goals, promotions, love interests, and family changes— or they find an opportunity to argue and fight.

"Well, Mrs. Gabby," Alicia says, "what's this big news you've been so quiet about? Go ahead and spill it, girl."

"Well, you all know I absolutely love what I do and don't look for any type of recognition, right?"

"Yeah, yeah," Foster interrupts. "We know all that. What do you have to tell us, woman?"

"Calm yourself down, Sergeant! I'm getting to that. I have recently been told that yours truly has been recognized as one of Charlotte's top 40 Under 40 Outstanding Leaders by the Charlotte Business Journal."

The group lets off a simultaneous loud gasp, then a loud cheer, followed by a round of applause. Gabrielle gushes and continues, "The ceremony is going to be held on September twelfth at the Ritz and it would really mean a lot to me if you all would be my honored guests."

"Girl, you know we will be there. We got you!" Alicia says.

"Oh yeah. We will be the best-looking couple in the place," Foster chimes in as he erupts into laughter.

"We'll be there as well," Brad replies. "I'm not traveling and will actually be in town for a change."

"Hallelujah!!!" Hannah shouts, lifting her hands to Heaven as if she's in church. They all laugh again.

"Even if we did have something going on, we would cancel and be there for you, Gab," Keiko says.

"Yeah, what could be more important than supporting one of Charlotte's finest? We're there!" Juni answers.

"Aww hell!" Elijah says. "Now Corrine has another excuse to go shopping for some more damn clothes." He turns and looks at Corrine, "Hopefully, you will just look in the closet and rediscover what you already have. I'm sure there's something in there that still has the tags on it."

"Now there you go with your cheap ass. You act like I live in the stores," says Corrine. "I only shop when it's necessary. You don't complain when I buy stuff for you, do you?" she asks with a piercing stare. Elijah is quiet, looks back at Corrine, and says, "We ain't talkin' 'bout me. We're on you right now."

They both continue to go back and forth arguing with each other while the rest of the group enjoys a really good laugh. Alex interrupts, "Alright you two. Calm down before we get kicked out of here for real. On a positive note, we're happy and blessed to have great friends like you and so glad you have our backs. Let's make a toast."

Everyone raises his or her glass in the air.

"To my beautiful wife. Words cannot express how proud of you I am. We all are. Here's to your continued success because when you succeed, we all succeed. So here's to great success. Salud!"

"Here! Here!" everyone shouts. Alex clinks his glass with Gabrielle's and kisses her on the lips.

"I love you guys so much. I really hope you know that," Gabrielle says. "All of this is still a bit overwhelming and unexpected but I'm thankful at the same time. Thanks for all your love and support throughout the years. It really means a lot to us."

She continues on, "Don't y'all drink too much tonight. I'd better see your butts at church in the morning. Craig, I'm speaking to you," she says with a laugh.

"I'll do my best. It depends on who is staying over tonight. Who knows, I might just bring her with me," Craig says only half-jokingly. No one really pays him any attention as they say their goodbyes and go their respective ways.

While Guillermo and Ricky are away at a game, Vanessa stations herself in the kitchen to begin preparing some of Guillermo's favorites dishes to eat so they can celebrate his nomination. She gets to work on some cheesy chicken enchiladas, spicy beef empanadas, and rice and beans.

While she's getting the chips and salsa ready as an appetizer, Guillermo and Ricky walk into the house. They are stopped immediately once they reach the threshold of the door at the aroma of Vanessa's delicious food. Both of them stand completely mesmerized.

"Hey guys!" Vanessa yells from the kitchen. "Go get washed up and ready for dinner."

"OK baby!" Guillermo yells back. "Ricky, go ahead and get cleaned up. I'll be there in a second."

"OK papi!" Ricky says as he heads towards the bathroom. Guillermo walks into the kitchen and sees all the delicious food Vanessa has prepared. He feels like he's died and gone to Heaven. He walks towards Vanessa, gives her a kiss on the lips, and says, "Well now. What's the special occasion?"

"Well, my dear," the special occasion is that my sweetie is receiving such a prestigious award and deserves a meal fit for a king."

"Gracias, mi amor. I feel very regal right now...and very hungry."

"Go on and get washed up so we can eat," Vanessa says.

Guillermo walks over to the kitchen sink to wash his hands and joins the family at the dinner table.

"Wow. This looks delicious. What did I do to deserve such a feast?"

"You being nominated for this award is a big deal for this family," Vanessa explains. "It's not every day that you're viewed as an outstanding contributor in the city or state. That's an awesome honor that needs to be celebrated. Enough talk; let's eat. Please bless the table."

They grasp hands, bow their heads, and Guillermo proceeds to say the blessing. Once he is finished, they joyfully partake of the delicious meal together as a loving family—talking, laughing, and eating, as they so commonly do.

As everyone is finishing up dessert, Guillermo puts down his spoon, places his elbows on the table and his hands in a fist as he rests them against his mouth. He gazes at Vanessa without saying a word. Guillermo and Vanessa give each other a puzzled look, look back at

Guillermo, and then back at each other. They both shrug their shoulders and Ricky says, "What's on your mind, Dad?"

Guillermo doesn't respond right away, but he takes a deep breath, wipes tears away from his eyes, clears his throat, and replies, "I'm OK. I'm just sitting here thinking about and looking at how God has been so good to us. I work very hard. Always have and always will. I want nothing but the very best for this family because you deserve it. I am a very humble man and don't look for any fancy awards, I just make sure I'm giving my all to what I do and produce quality work. You all are my inspiration and my life. I appreciate you all for sticking by me."

Vanessa and Ricky's eyes fill with tears in response to Guillermo's sentimental words. They get up from their chairs, go over to Guillermo, and embrace in a group hug, telling him how much they love and are proud of him.

Sunday mornings are always interesting at the Reed and León households. Getting ready for church is a constant chore. No one wants to get out of bed, and once they do, everyone drags around. Unfortunately, clothes are usually not ironed or put out the night before, and anything that could go wrong, sometimes does. Shoe heels break off, someone spills something on their clothes, wardrobes malfunction—you name it, it happens. This particular Sunday was the exception. In both houses, everyone gets up on time, clothes have already been put out, and there are no accidents or mishaps. Everyone eats breakfast and gets out the door on time, without rushing.

The Reeds attend New Grace Church where Bishop Eli Palmer is the pastor. The León's are members of Grace Tabernacle Church where Javier Carlos Mendoza is pastor. As each family files into their sanctuary, they take their seats and prepare to receive a powerful and wonderful message from the pastor. Praise and worship is high at both places and the presence of God is felt. As the pastors of both churches approach their pulpits, the congregations have their full attention and are completely captivated by what they have to say. Before both pastors begin with their sermon, they say the following words almost verbatim (with perplexed looks on their faces):

"Good morning children of God. I'm not quite sure what someone needs today spiritually, but the message I was prepared to preach will not be shared today. The Holy Spirit has been dealing with me all weekend about another message and I couldn't understand why. I yielded and He changed my entire message. I pray that whomever this is for, that it ministers to you right where you need it. Let us pray."

As they begin to pray, there is an overwhelming sense of anticipation throughout both congregations and everyone is waiting on pins and needles for them to finish so they can proceed with the message. Even though they speak with different words, they speak the same message.

"Family and friends, I'm grateful to God to be here and to see you. I'm thankful we have a place to run to when we need it. I could stand here all day just telling you about how good God has been and how faithful and true He is, but that's not my assignment for today. Every single one of you could testify of the goodness of God and all He has done. But with that in mind, what if we lost all of that? How would we feel if we had every good thing we could think of? Enjoying it day in and day out and all of a sudden, it's gone. How would we feel if someone told you that the good thing you have would be lost, but soon after, you would get something better? Something even better than what you lost? What would you say? What would you do? This morning, we are going to read a lot of scripture. I pray you will be patient and really focus on the texts and how they relate. Starting with the book of John, in the thirteenth chapter, let's start with verse one."

The pastors read the entire chapter.

"Next, in John, Chapter 8, verses twenty-eight through thirty-one, it reads..."

The pastors continue, "The title of today's sermon is, What's Good in a Loss?"

"Many of us have either played a sport or watched a sport on television, especially during the championships. This is the time where the last two teams are battling for the title, and unfortunately, someone has to lose. The teams fight—or play—like they've never fought before. And when they get down to the last few seconds and the buzzer sounds, the final score is displayed. Only one team comes out victoriously as the winner.

Or maybe you've been on your job for five, ten, fifteen-plus years; you've worked very hard, been promoted, been recognized for all of your accomplishments and all of a sudden, you get a pink slip and told that your services are no longer needed. For the athlete, the words of consolation are, 'Better luck next year' or 'Next year, we'll win it all.' And for the employee, 'There's another company that will hire you.

You'll be fine.' But at the time of each of those losses, the main questions that are running through their minds are, Why? How did we lose that game? What is going to be better next time? What better chance will I encounter next time?

After all, both accomplished a great deal and made significant strides in their respective areas, so they have to wonder, Why didn't I come out number one? What am I to do now?

In the thirteenth and fourteenth chapters of John, we see how the disciples felt when Jesus informed them that his time on Earth was coming to an end. I can only imagine what they were thinking or saying: 'Why do you have to leave? Why can't we go with you? Things are going well, why change? What will we do without you?' Think about it. They had been with Jesus for three years and experienced some miraculous things and all of a sudden, he wants to leave. OMG-stop the presses."

The congregations laugh.

"What is he thinking? He reassures them that even though he's going away, he's sending someone to replace him, someone that will be even better. Who could possibly be better than Jesus himself? I'm certain they were asking this. But he promises them that they will be in good hands."

As the congregations are listening to their pastors attentively, Alex grabs Gabrielle's hand and Vanessa grabs Guillermo's hand, they look into their eyes, give a smile, and turn their attention to the pastors as they come to the end of the sermon.

"In closing, no matter what's been lost, God is able to restore. That job you lost, don't worry. God will restore. That most prized possession you had. Don't worry, God will restore. Some of you may be feeling like you're losing your mind. I've said it before and I'll say it again. Don't worry. God will restore. No matter how great the loss is, God will give it back to you greater than you could ever imagine; greater than our finite minds can fathom. So don't put all your focus and energy into the loss. Just know without a shadow of a doubt, God will bless you with something greater. Amen."

The pastors pray a benediction and church is dismissed. Each family gets into their car and drives home. While the Reed family is driving home, everyone in the car is quiet as they look out of the window, listening to a CD; with the exception of Jasmine. She has fallen fast asleep. After several minutes of silence, Alex grabs Gabrielle's hand again and says, "That was really a good message Bishop Palmer preached today, huh?"

"It sure was," Gabrielle agreed. "The entire service was great."

While still holding her hand, Alex continues, "You know, while I was listening to him, I began to think of all the things I could possibly lose, like my job, this car, our home, or anything I own. If we lost it all today, I would be OK because I'm reassured that God has our back. But, there are two things that I could lose and I would be totally devastated."

"What's that, babe?" Gabrielle asks.

"You and Jazzy," Alex replies. "I tell you, if anything were to happen to either of you, someone would have to have me committed into a mental institution. I would lose my mind."

"Awww, sweetheart!" Gabrielle replies. "You won't have to worry about that because we're going to be around for a long, long time. Plus, we've got too much to do, so ain't nobody gonna lose nobody."

They both laugh.

"Yeah, you're right. We've got a long, prosperous life ahead of us. We don't have time to lose. I love you, baby."

"I love you back."

Alex kisses the back of her hand and continues to hold it for the remainder of the drive home.

The León family is headed to a relative's house for dinner. Vanessa turns in her seat so she can get a good look at Guillermo and says, "You know, papi, I was thinking about the sermon Pastor Mendoza preached today and it got me thinking. Life is too short and we should be thankful for what we have today because it's no guarantee that we will have it tomorrow."

"You're right, sweetie," Guillermo says.

"I appreciate you, my love. You are an excellent husband, father, and a very hard worker who provides for this family and you take really good care of Ricky and I. What more can a girl ask for? You are a wonderful man and I am truly thankful that God saw fit to bring us together. I love you so much."

"Wow! Thank you, sweetie!" Guillermo says. "That's very sweet of you to say. I love you too, with all my heart. I don't know where that came from but I'm honored to be in the lives of you and Ricky. You are my world and I would do any and everything to make sure you are both provided for. That's my responsibility and I take it very seriously.

I love my family with all that's within me."

Vanessa kisses the back of his hand and they continue on until they reach their destination.

From there on out, everyone continues with their regular routines: Alex argues cases, Gabrielle makes numerous presentations, Jasmine is Jasmine, Guillermo presents new construction plans to clients, Vanessa facilitates lectures, and Ricky continues playing football and excelling in academics. Life is good for all.

CHAPTER FIVE

Changing Winds

September twelfth arrives and Alex and Gabrielle are consumed with getting ready for the night of celebration. Alex has just gotten out of the shower, is drying off, and all of a sudden, he hears Gabrielle scream, "No, no, no, NO!"

Alex ties his towel around his waist and runs into the bedroom where Gabrielle is.

"Baby, what's wrong?" Alex frantically asks.

Gabrielle is in tears as she holds a ripped dress in her hands.

"I was trying on my dress and it ripped under the arm and the stupid zipper broke. What am I going to do now? I'll just have to call one of the girls to see if they have something. But then I have to find jewelry to coordinate with whatever I get from someone. This is horrible. Absolutely horrible. Where's my phone? I need to make some calls."

Alex laughs.

"Honey, I can't believe you're laughing at me. This is serious. How can I receive an award with no dress?"

Alex can hear the anger and frustration in Gabrielle's voice.

"Sweetheart, I've got you covered. Go ahead and get in the shower. I'll take care of everything."

"And how do you plan to do that on such short notice?" Gabrielle asks. "Where are you going to go? Who are you going to call?"

"Don't worry your pretty little head about that. I'll have the perfect solution for you when you get out the shower. Trust me."

"I don't know how you're going to do it, but OK," Gabrielle replies as she goes into the bathroom to shower.

When Alex hears the bathroom door close, he waits until her

hears the water running in the shower before he goes into his closet and pulls out a garment bag, a shoe box, and two small powder blue boxes tied with white bows. He unzips the garment bag and takes out a beautiful black La Femme strapless gown and black pair of Jimmy Choo sandals with four-inch heels. He lays the dress out on the bed and stages the shoes next to it. He then begins to get himself dressed for the evening by putting on some of his clothes, but not completely.

When Gabrielle gets out of the shower, she immediately asks, "OK. So what did you come up with?"

Before she can say another word, she looks on the bed and lets out a gasp followed by a scream, and runs to the bed to see up close and personal the goodies Alex bought for her. Alex stands off to the side with his arms crossed, laughing, and enjoying his wife act like an excited child on Christmas morning.

"Well, don't just stand there. Try that stuff on," Alex says.

She takes off her bathrobe and carefully unzips the dress so she can try it on. She motions for Alex to come over and assist her with zipping up her dress from behind. Once she has it on, she looks into the mirror and smiles.

"Oh honey!" Gabrielle says. "It's beautiful and perfect. How did you do it? When did you do it?"

"Awww...it was nothing," Alex humbly dismisses her praise.

"No, really. How did you find this in such a short period of time? Did you already have it?"

Alex tries very hard not to laugh but eventually bursts into laughter and still doesn't answer Gabrielle's question.

"I see you have a lot to laugh about tonight, mister," Gabrielle says with her hands on her hips. "Thank you, thank you, thank you." She rushes over to give Alex a tight hug.

"The dress is absolutely beautiful. Now I have to find some accessories to go with it."

Gabrielle goes through her vast collection of earrings to see what will match. Each pair that she picks up and holds to her ear doesn't seem to be the right fit and she begins to get frustrated.

"Ugh!" Gabrielle grunted out. "None of these will work.

Ugh!"

"Baby, relax," Alex says calmly. "Come here and sit down."

She walks slowly towards Alex and sits in a chair by the mirror.

"Relax. Breathe. Everything is all right. Close your eyes. Think happy thoughts and relax. Don't open your eyes until I tell you to."

Gabrielle closes her eyes, takes a deep breath, and puts her hands in her lap. Alex reaches his hand into his pocket and pulls out the smaller of the two blue boxes. He asks Gabrielle to hold out her hand. When she does, he places the box that's tied with the white ribbon in her hand. Her eyes open quickly and she sits there amazed with her mouth open. She looks at the box again, recognizing that it's from Tiffany and Co., and her hand begins to shake.

"Oh my goodness...oh my goodness...oh my goodness!" Gabrielle says as her hands are shaking even more than before. She unties the ribbon, opens the box, and sees a beautiful, sparkling pair of Tiffany Aria Drop earrings that are made of pearls and diamonds. She is elated and puts them to her ears.

"Thank you, dear!! They are beautiful and go perfectly with my dress! Now I just have to look for some pearls or a nice necklace to wear with my outfit to make it complete," Gabrielle adds. She wants to look perfect.

"I'm glad you said that," Alex says. "Close your eyes and hold out your hands again."

"What are you up to now, Mr. Reed?" Gabrielle asks.

"Don't worry about it. Just close your eyes and hold out your hands."

Gabrielle smiles, takes another deep breath, closes her eyes, and holds out her hands again. Alex grabs the second box and takes out a matching Tiffany Aria necklace, also made with pearls and diamonds, which complements the earrings he purchased. Alex walks behind her and places the necklace around her neck. His actions surprise her and she jumps. But once she sees the beautiful necklace around her neck, her eyes light up and she displays one of the biggest smiles ever upon her face.

"Oh sweetie!" Gabrielle says. "I'm speechless. This is absolutely gorgeous. All of this is just too much, yet so wonderful. When did you find the time to go shopping without me?"

Alex laughs. "Well, when you first told me about the award, I knew I had to do something special. I looked online at some pieces and when I laid my eyes on what you now have, I knew you would love it. I called Tiffany to see if they were in stock and they were. I also looked on Nordstrom's website for some dresses and it didn't take long to spot the perfect one for you. I got off early that day and picked everything up before Jazzy and I went to the game. Ha! You didn't know I had skills like that, huh?"

"Well, you did an awesome job, sweetie. I may need to hire you as my personal shopper and stylist."

They burst into laughter.

"Thank you so much, baby, for my wonderful outfit!" Gabrielle continues. "I feel like a queen."

"Well, baby, you are my queen and you deserve nothing but the finest. No matter the cost," Alex says. "This is your special night and I had to do something very special."

"Sweetie, you always take such good care of us. You are the one that needs to be treated like a king."

"As long as I have you and Jazzy, I'm the most blessed person on the face of the earth. I'm blessed to have you all in my life and I don't know what I'd do if you were not."

Alex and Gabrielle share a kiss and resume getting ready for the evening. After they are ready, they go into Jasmine's room to help her finish getting ready.

"Ooooh! Mama and daddy, you look very nice," Jasmine says.

"And you look very lovely yourself, baby girl," Alex replies. "Hey, let's all take a selfie with my phone."

They all gather together and Alex takes out his iPhone to take the picture.

"Aww! That's a cute picture," Jasmine says after viewing the image.

"Yes it is, baby," Gabrielle replies.

"Absolutely!" says Alex. "I can use this as my new screen saver.

Looking at his watch, Alex realizes that they need to be on their way. "OK, all! It's about that time. We'd better get going."

They all get into the car and head uptown to the event.

Vanessa is fully dressed, combing her hair. Ricky is almost dressed and listening to music and dancing. Guillermo, on the other hand, is having problems getting dressed. His nerves are shot because he is so nervous.

"Vanessa!" Guillermo yells. "Have you seen my cuff links?"

"They're right here on the dresser, dear!" Vanessa says in a very calm voice.

"Gracias!" Guillermo says. A few minutes later, he lets out another yell.

"Vanessa! Have you seen my tie?"

Vanessa giggles and says, "Papi, the tie is next to the cuff links. Is there anything else you are looking for? Do you have your shoes? Or what about your underwear? You're not going to be going commando are you?" Vanessa adds jokingly.

"Ha, ha, ha! That's not funny!" Guillermo says. "I'm sorry to be a pest but I am so doggone nervous. My hands are shaking and it's obvious I can't even think straight."

"It's OK, Papi. This is a big day for you and you should be very excited. There's nothing to be nervous about. We will be right there with you."

"Thank you, my love! Thank you so much. I feel better already."

Guillermo leans over and gives Vanessa a kiss on the lips just as Ricky walks in.

"Ugh! Gross! Are you guys ready yet?" Ricky asks. "I hope they have some good food. I'm starving. I know I look good and all but I need some food to go with all this good-lookingness."

Everyone gets a good laugh.

"I see that I'm holding up progress. Let me get these last few things on and we can get out of here. This is going to be a great night," Guillermo confidently says with a smile on his face.

"Yes, indeed it will," Vanessa responds. Guillermo finishes getting dressed and they all get into the car to head over to the Ritz-Carlton.

Tonight is one of the biggest nights in Charlotte. People from all over the city and surrounding areas are coming together to celebrate the successes of a number of very deserving, individuals. The Charlotte Business Journal is holding their event in The Great Room of the Ritz, and the Latin American Chamber of Commerce event is being held in the Ballroom Perfection Room. Both events are filled to capacity.

In the Great Room, Gabrielle's boss, Bill Ingram, is called to the podium to present her award.

"Thank you so much for that warm introduction. It is my esteemed pleasure to present this next award. When I was approached by the Journal about making a nomination, this was a no brainer. I knew immediately who I would nominate. Gabrielle Reed is an exemplary associate. I wish I had a thousand more like her. From the first day she walked through the doors of the Federal Reserve Bank of Charlotte, I knew she was something special. In my many years at the Reserve, I've never seen anyone with her work ethic, drive, and determination. Every deadline I give her; she gets it to me way ahead of time. I've even tried to trip her up and give her a task I thought was impossible."

The audience laughs.

"Well, she shocked me and got it done with no problem. I'm so very proud of her and what she's been able to accomplish up to this point. I know there's a lot more we're going to see in the very near future. Lastly, what I'm about to say can be said with honesty and truth. If there were any person within our organization that I would feel comfortable transitioning into my role or even heading this company, I'd put my full faith in Gabby, hands down; and I hope she does. So ladies and gentlemen, please welcome to the stage one of Charlotte's '40 Under 40 Outstanding Leaders Award' recipients, Mrs. Gabrielle Simone Reed."

Gabrielle receives a standing ovation along with applause as Alex helps her out of her chair. He gives her a kiss on the lips and she passionately returns the kiss and runs her right hand over his left cheek as she whispers, "I love you."

She then turns to Jasmine, who gives her a big hug and kiss. As Gabrielle leaves her chair to receive her award, the applause gets louder and people begin to cheer. It's obvious that Gabrielle is becoming emotional because she's smiling and crying at the same time. As she gets closer to the podium, she wipes away tears and regains her composure. Once she's arrives to the podium, Bill gives her a hug, congratulates her, and hands her a huge, crystal plaque that reads:

The Charlotte Business Journal Proudly Salutes
Gabrielle Simone Reed
In recognition of your impeccable leadership at the
Federal Reserve Bank of Charlotte
and your commitment to community service.
Your tireless devotion has not gone unnoticed.
Congratulations on being selected as one of Charlotte's
40 Under 40 Outstanding Leaders.
September 13, 2014
Charlotte, North Carolina

Bill hands Gabrielle the plaque and stands off to the side as she takes her place behind the podium. She does not speak immediately because she is choked up and trying not to burst into tears as she looks out amongst the room and sees not only her loving family and friends, but the multitude of people still on their feet applauding her accomplishment. After she wipes more tears away and clears her throat, she begins to speak,

"Thank you. Thank you. Thank you. Again, I'm at a loss for words; and that's rare for me. First of all, before I go any further, I want to give honor and praise to my heavenly Father for divinely orchestrating my existence and my life up to this point. I thank and praise God for giving me all that I need to do what

He's called me to do. For that, I'm eternally grateful for His goodness and mercy. I want to thank the Charlotte Business Journal for honoring me with such a prestigious award. I never thought in a million years that I would be recognized for what I do. Thank you to my boss and good friend, Bill Ingram, for thinking enough of me to nominate me for this," Gabrielle says, as she looks over and smiles at Bill.

"I'll be honest, I come to work every day just wanting to do the best job I can possibly do and work hard at being a positive role model to those precious girls at Girl's, Inc. I don't look for the spotlight but look to be the light to all who I come in contact with. I want to say a huge thank you to my awesome friends that have always had my back no matter what. I really appreciate you all very much.

And to my precious family, what can I say? You all are my inspiration and my rock. Jazzy, my little mini-me, I have enjoyed seeing you develop into a beautiful young lady. From the minute I laid eyes on you I knew you were a special little girl. I know without a shadow of a doubt you are going to be a success and the sky is the limit. Everything you set your heart to do will be a success. I love you, baby.

Last, but definitely not least, to my husband, Alex, my king, my protector, and the love of my life. You are the air that I breathe. With you by my side, I've always felt I could take on the world. Not only do you encourage me and lift me up in prayer but also I know you love me. Not a day goes by that you don't tell me or show me; and I feel that you love me more than anything. You are an amazing man and father. I'm thankful to God that He thought enough of me to prepare me especially for you. If you were not in my life, I don't know where I would be. From the bottom of my heart, sweetheart, thank you. I love you with every fiber of my being. Whew! Let me stop here before I start crying again and I refuse to mess up my makeup. I spent too much time getting it together." The crowd bursts into laughter. "Again, thank you for such a great honor. God bless you, and goodnight."

Everyone stands and gives Gabrielle another standing ovation and cheers louder than before. She makes her way back to her table and is greeted with hugs and kisses form her family and friends. After she takes her seat, the rest of the program continues.

Meanwhile, in the next banquet room, the awards ceremony for the Latin American Chamber of Commerce is taking place. After dinner, dessert, and coffee, Juan Santos approaches the podium and begins the awards presentation.

"Buenos tardes! Thank you all so much for attending and supporting our annual Outstanding Leadership Award ceremony. This is a time where we honor and recognize the leaders in the Latino community that are making an impact in this city. We are honored and privileged to have a gentleman with us that not only lives up to what we look for in a leader, but also does a great job at making the city of Charlotte look good. As one of the premier architects in this city, you've seen his work around town such as the Blumenthal Performing Arts Center, Bank of America Stadium, and the Charlotte Convention Center—just to name a few. Our distinguished honoree is responsible for that. Ladies and gentlemen, please join me in honoring Señor Guillermo León as this year's Outstanding Leadership Award recipient."

Everyone in the room stands and gives Guillermo a standing ovation. He rises from his chair, gives Vanessa a kiss on the lips, and slaps a high-five with Ricky. As he comes to the stage, he shakes hands with Mr. Santos, who reaches out to uncover a large crystal plaque. Mr. Santos shows the plaque to the audience and Guillermo, and begins to read the inscription, which states:

This award is presented to
Sr. Guillermo Jesus León
for his leadership and service to the
city of Charlotte and the Latino community.
Your untiring work has not gone unnoticed. For this, we're

pleased to honor you as an
Outstanding Leader of Charlotte, North Carolina,
on behalf of the Latin American Chamber of Commerce
September 13, 2014

Juan hands Guillermo the plaque and he takes his place behind the podium to give his speech.

"Thank you all so very much. This is such a great and very unexpected honor. You know, I come to work every day and ask myself, 'What can I do to make a difference?' 'What can I do to brighten someone's life?' I close my eyes, say a prayer and put my best foot forward and make sure I produce the best products for my clients and work diligently to make a difference and put a smile on people's face. I'm honored and blessed to receive this amazing award. I'm also blessed to work with a dynamic team at Finch and Associates. You guys rock and I share this award with all of you. Last, but not least, I'm the luckiest man on the face of the earth to have a family like I have. Vanessa. Ricky. You guys are my world and my life would be nothing without you. God answered my prayers when I asked for a wonderful, loving family. He exceeded my expectations and gave me the best. I love you all so much for your love and support. It warms my heart to know that no matter where I go or what I do, you are in my corner and give me so much love. Gracias. Gracias. Gracias."

Guillermo shakes Juan's hand again and goes back to his seat. The audience gives him another standing ovation as he goes back to his table to be greeted by more hugs and kisses from Vanessa and Ricky as the program continues.

After the award ceremonies are over and everyone starts to go their separate ways, Gabrielle's family and friends stick around to congratulate her on her accomplishment. Jasmine comes up to her, gives her a hug and says, "Congratulations Mama! You're the best mother in the world! I'm soooo proud of you. I love you!"

Jasmine pulls her mother's arm for her to come down to her level. She then hugs Gabrielle's neck, gives her a kiss on the cheek, and hugs her neck again.

"Thank you, baby girl. I love you too. You have a bright future ahead of you and I'm looking forward to seeing it."

Jasmine smiles.

"Elijah and Corrine, thank you so much for letting Jazzy spend the night with you guys. We really appreciate it," Gabrielle says.

"Girl, don't even worry about it," Corrine replies. "She's a good girl and we're going to have a lot of fun."

"It's not going to be fun for me," Elijah says. "They're going to take over my bed and I'll either end up in the other room or on the couch."

They all burst into laughter.

"Nah, we're going to have a great time," Elijah admitted.

"You really are an inspiration to us all, Gabby," Juni says.

"Yeah. We can't think of a person that's more deserving of this award than you. I'm proud to know you," Keiko says.

"Oh you guys!" Gabrielle responds. "You all are going to make me cry all over again. I love you all!"

"Awwwww!" Everyone chimes in as they all embrace in a group hug filled with kisses and I-love-yous.

"I really appreciate you all for sharing this night with me," says Gabrielle. "I have the best friends in the world and I sincerely love you guys."

"We love you too, girlie!" Craig says.

"You know we have your back," Nia continues.

"Thanks again, y'all!" Gabrielle says. "Jazzy, you be good and don't cause any trouble."

"Mama, you know I'm not the one you need to worry about. You know you have to keep your eyes on Uncle Elijah."

Everyone laughs in agreement with Jasmine. They all say their final goodbyes and head home.

"Wow! This has been an amazing evening," Gabrielle comments to Alex.

"Yes ma'am it has," he replies. "It's been an amazing evening for an amazing woman. I am so proud of you."

"Aww! Thank you, honey. I couldn't have accomplished what I have without my amazing husband."

"Well, all I know is that my life is absolutely nothing without you. You are my heart and soul and I can't fathom my life without you," Alex says.

He grabs her left hand and brings it to his lips to give it a gentle kiss. As Alex continues to hold her hand, Gabrielle turns on the iPod and their favorite song, "Endless Love" by Lionel Richie and Diana Ross, plays as they begin singing along.

Still in the hotel lobby, Guillermo, Vanessa, and Ricky are surrounded by family, friends, and co-workers congratulating Guillermo on his recognition.

"Thank you so much for all your support," Guillermo says. "It really warms my heart to see my family and good friends come out and share in the evening with me. I'm sure there are a million other places you could have been tonight. But the fact that you chose to be here with me really means a lot."

"I'm sure I can speak for all of us when I say that we wouldn't have missed this for the world," Vanessa says to Guillermo.

"Yeah man," says Guillermo's colleague, Marshall. "You're a rock star in the firm. Why wouldn't we be here?"

"Gracias, mi amigo!" Guillermo says to Marshall as he shakes his hand and gives him a hug. Then Ricky chimes in, "Yeah papi! You are the MAN! We had to be here."

"You are very deserving of this great honor and we are so proud of you, honey," Vanessa adds.

Guillermo and Vanessa exchange a small kiss before saying goodbye to their guests.

"Ricky, be on your best behavior at Mr. Carlos' house," Guillermo instructs Ricky.

"No need to worry," says Carlos. "Once I beat him really bad at video games, I'll make sure he gets to bed real early."

"I don't know about him beating me," Ricky says. "But because of his old age, he might fall asleep early."

Everyone laughs.

"Thanks again for coming," Guillermo says. "Enjoy the rest of your evening. Ricky, we'll pick you up tomorrow."

"Yes sir!" Ricky replies.

"No need to rush. He'll be fine," says Carlos. "I don't have anything going on. We'll hang out. You love birds enjoy yourselves. You deserve it."

"OK. Call us if you need us," Vanessa says.

They all say their parting words before getting into their cars and leaving.

Once Guillermo and Vanessa get in their car, they drive off. After a few minutes of silence, Guillermo says, "Wow! What an amazing evening."

"Yes indeed, it has been. It's been an amazing evening for an amazing man. I am so proud of you."

"Thank you, sweetheart. I couldn't have accomplished what I have without my amazing wife," Guillermo adds.

"Well, all I know is that my life is absolutely nothing without you," Vanessa says, looking deeply at Guillermo. "You are my heart and soul and can't fathom my life without you."

Guillermo grabs her left hand, kisses the back of it, and continues holding it during their drive back home.

Vanessa turns on the radio and their favorite song, "Endless Love" by Lionel Richie and Diana Ross, is on. They begin to sing along as they continue to drive.

Meanwhile, in a tavern not too far from the Ritz-Carlton, two gentlemen who are noisy, irate, and drunk are thrown out by management. As they stumble out of the tavern, one of the owners comes out behind them and tells them that they are not welcome in his establishment anymore and suggests that they wait there until he calls a cab. His words fall on deaf ears and the two men yell obscenities at him. They get into a Ford F-150 and drive off, almost hitting every parked car on that street. They turn the radio on, blasting heavy metal music. The driver is speeding along, but also stopping and slamming the brakes...just being a completely reckless drunk driver. Unfortunately, no police officers are around to end this reckless behavior.

As Guillermo and Vanessa are still driving and enjoying each other's company, Vanessa discovers she doesn't have her purse.

"Oh no, oh no, oh no!!! Vanessa yells.

"What's the matter, baby?" Guillermo asks.

"I left my purse at the Ritz. We've got to go back."

"No worries, my love," Guillermo says. "We're not that far. We'll go back."

Guillermo turns the car around and heads back to the Ritz.

While Gabrielle and Alex are driving and singing, Gabrielle gets a thought and interrupts, "Hey. I've got a crazy idea."

"Oh yeah? What is it?"

"Since we're not too far from the downtown area and have never stayed at the Ritz, let's get a room and enjoy ALL it has to offer."

"Hmmm...that's not a bad idea. Problem is, we still need to go home and get a change of clothes and come back out."

"No we don't," Gabrielle responded. "We can go to that twenty-four hour Wal-Mart we just passed and get some very inexpensive clothes, shoes, and whatever necessities we need. It'll just be something to throw on in the morning and we can go about our day doing whatever."

"That's a splendid idea, baby. Let's make it happen."

Alex changes direction and drive back towards the Wal-Mart.

When Guillermo and Vanessa get close to the Ritz, she tells him to pull in the front of the hotel and let her out so she can run in to get her purse.

"Oh, Mrs. León!" the front desk attendant says. "I'm so glad you came back. We were trying to locate a number to inform you that your purse had been brought to the front desk. Would you please check your purse to make sure your items are still there?"

"I'm sure that it is; but I'll check anyway," Vanessa says.

Once she checks her purse and finds that everything is still there, she thanks the attendant and the hotel manager for their service and integrity.

"That was quick," Guillermo says as Gabrielle gets back into the car.

"Yes it was. They actually had the purse waiting on me when I got there. They have the best service. We should stay there one weekend. I think it would be a nice, romantic staycation for us."

"Well, our anniversary is coming up. I'll look into it and get planning," Guillermo says.

"Hey! I've got an idea," Guillermo says.

"What?" Vanessa asks.

"I heard on the radio that there was a really good reggae band playing at Antony's Caribbean Café tonight. They may still be playing. You wanna go?" Guillermo asks.

"Oh, that sounds like fun," Vanessa replies. "I haven't heard any good, live music in a while. Let's go. I'm excited!"

"I am too! Let the fun continue!"

They continue to drive northbound on East Trade Street coming from the Ritz.

After they pick up the items they need from Wal-Mart, Alex and Gabrielle travel southbound on East Trade Street towards the Ritz, singing, laughing, and having a good time. But traveling eastbound on South Tryon Street are the intoxicated men driving their Ford F-150, still playing their heavy metal music. By now they are even more drunk and obnoxious, throwing beer cans out of the window, speeding through the streets, and shouting obscenities to anyone around.

Alex and Gabrielle are about five blocks from the Ritz, still joyfully singing and dancing, when the men in the truck are rapidly headed towards the intersection of South Tryon Street and East Trade Street. The driver of the truck notices that the traffic light has just turned yellow and says to his friend, "Dude. I'm gonna beat this light."

"Hell yeah, man! Floor it, dude!"

The driver steps on the accelerator and they take off to attempt to beat the light. The speed limit is thirty-five miles per hour, but the truck continues to pick up speed much faster than the limit...forty-five, then fifty, then fifty-five.

Alex and Gabrielle are driving the speed limit and still travel-ing southbound on East Trade Street. The drunk driver's light turns red but he continues to drive through the intersection at the very moment that Alex and Gabrielle are crossing through the intersection. The truck crashes into Alex's vehicle on the passenger side where Gabrielle is seated with such a powerful force that the glass from the windshield and windows shatters everywhere. The car immediately spins around a few times be-fore it eventually comes to a complete stop. The scene is horrific. Both vehicles are damaged form the crash, but Alex's drastically so. Alex and Gabrielle are knocked completely un-conscious—Gabrielle being struck by the door panel, and Alex being struck by Gabrielle. The two men in the truck are totally shaken up. Once they finally regain their bearings, the passenger asks, "What the hell just happened?"

"I dunno but my friggin' head hurts," the driver replies.

He looks across the street and sees the Reed's car and shat-tered glass everywhere.

"Dude. Did we do that?" the driver asks in a state of drunken panic. "What the heck should we do?"

"Nothing. Let's just get the hell outta here fast!"

The driver frantically starts the truck, outs it in reverse, and drives backwards, hitting everything in its path. Both men are frantic and nervous.

"Dude! You can't drive in reverse the whole way. Let's just make a right on Trade and avoid the accident all together."

"Good idea!"

The driver slams on the brakes, shifts into drive, and heads toward the stoplight again in order to flee the scene of the acci-dent, which they caused.

Guillermo and Vanessa are almost at Antony's, still traveling northbound on East Trade Street. The drunk driver is still speeding. He is about to turn the corner onto East Trade but nei-ther he nor his friend sees a car approaching. As he is about to make the turn, his friend yells, "Dude! Watch out!"

The driver slams on the brakes, but a little too late, and proceeds to slam into the driver's side of the vehicle where Guillermo is seated. The impact is so powerful that Guillermo's car flips over twice and ends up on the opposite side of the street. The driver and passenger of the truck are knocked unconscious from hitting their heads on the steering wheel and dashboard. The truck is leaking fluids and smoke is coming out from under the hood. Glass has shattered everywhere and, unfortunately, Guillermo's airbag did not deploy, but Vanessa's did. Neither of them is moving.

After about five minutes from the time of the accidents, a man and a woman driving in a car up East Trade Street come within close proximity of the cars and truck in the middle of the street. They don't get too close to the accident but quickly pull over and call 9-1-1 to request immediate assistance.

Emergency personnel, including the police and fire departments, arrive within minutes. When they get to Alex's car, he is groggy and has no idea where he is, nor does he know what happened. A firefighter communicates to him that he has been in an accident and that he is there to help him. The firefighter notices that although Alex's airbag was deployed, Gabrielle's did not.

"Gabby. Where's Gabby?" Alex mumbles as he regains consciousness.

"She's still in the car, sir. We're working hard to get her out," the paramedic responds. "Are you OK, sir?" The paramedic helps the still somewhat dazed Alex sit on the back of the ambulance.

"I think so. What happened?" Alex asks. "Where's Gabby? Where's Gabby?"

When he looks up, he sees that the glass on the passenger side of the car is completely shattered and the door is damaged to the point that it cannot be opened. Firefighters have to use the Jaws of Life to cut the door open.

"I gotta get my baby outta there!" Alex says as he jumps off the back of the ambulance. The EMT grabs him and tells him he can't go towards the scene of the accident. Once they get Gabrielle out of the car and onto the stretcher, they rush them both to the hospital. Alex is in the back holding Gabrielle's hand, crying and praying that she is not seriously injured.

Guillermo and Vanessa are still in their mangled vehicle. Vanessa regains consciousness and immediately begins to scream and panic. Rescue personnel try to calm her down and get her out of the car safely.

"What happened? Where's my husband? Where is my husband?" Vanessa yells.

An EMT puts a blanket around her and walks her to the back of another ambulance and has her sit in the back. As she sits, she witnesses the rescue team use the Jaws of Life to get Guillermo out of the car. As they tear through the metal of the car, sirens are blaring; lights from the police cars, fire trucks and ambulances are flashing; and medical personnel are running frantically all over the place tending to the victims of the accident. When they finally get Guillermo out of the wreckage, they put him on a stretcher, load both he and Vanessa onto the ambulance, and proceed to the hospital.

Alex is in the back of the ambulance in a daze and can't believe what is happening. As they drive away from the scene, he sees police offices with their guns drawn and dragging the men out of the truck that caused the accidents. After they are handcuffed and face down on the ground, they are placed in the police car and transported to the police station.

Seeing all of this and still being in a daze, Alex is still deaf to the sounds that are going on around him. An EMT is trying to get his attention. Finally, he comes to his senses.

"Sir! It appears that your wife has suffered some substantial injuries and we're transporting her to Novant Medical as fast as we can."

Alex nods his head. He takes out his cell phone and sends a text to family and friends:

Bad news! Gabby and I were in a bad car accident. If you can, meet us at Novant Medical ASAP. I need you all to pray like you've never prayed before. I need you! Alex.

After about ten minutes (which seems like hours to Alex), they arrive at the hospital. The other ambulance, carrying Vanessa and Guillermo in front of them, is quickly unloading the stretcher and rolls towards the emergency room doors. Lead physicians of the hospital meet both stretchers. The EMTs quickly explain the situation and give the vital signs of Gabrielle and Guillermo.

Pointing to the stretcher Gabrielle is on, the ER doctor points to it and says, "Take her to O.R. number one and the other to O.R. number three, NOW!"

Everyone dispatches and both Alex and Vanessa get seated and receive consultation in two separate areas of the ER waiting room. Alex paces back and forth with his cell phone in his hand in case someone calls. In another part of the waiting room, Vanessa, sitting in a chair, rocks back and forth in utter amazement and disbelief of what has happened. After a little while, she gets up and asks one of the nurses if she can use the telephone. She gets to the phone and dials a number.

"Hello. Maria?" Vanessa says. "This is Vanessa. Can you please come the hospital? Guillermo and I were in a bad car accident and it's not looking good."

She pauses as Maria begins to ask questions.

"Everything happened so fast. I...I just don't know. Please hurry. Please tell Carlos and bring Ricky with you. I need my boy with me right now. Please hurry. Thank you. Thank you. Adios!"

Vanessa hangs up the phone and begins to cry and shake uncontrollably. She is comforted and consoled by the nurses at the nurse's station and they get her seated back in the waiting room.

Alex is still pacing the floor with his phone in hand. The doors of the ER open and in come Craig, Nia, the Fosters, the Ellis', the Corruthers', the Maguires, Juni, Keiko, and Jasmine. When Jasmine sees Alex, she breaks away from the rest of the group and runs straight to him.

"What happened, Daddy?" Jasmine asks crying. "Where's Mama?"

Alex answers, "Baby, Mama and I were in a bad car accident tonight. She's in there with the doctors right now and they are doing everything they can to make sure she's OK. We just have to wait."

Alex then hugs Jasmine as tightly as he can as their friends embrace them in support.

After several minutes, Carlos, Maria, and Ricky come through the ER doors and find Vanessa in her chair, still weeping. Ricky slowly comes over to his mother and places his hand on her shoulder. She looks up and smiles.

"Oh, my sweet boy," Vanessa says. "I am so glad to see you."

Vanessa pulls Ricky down to the chair next to her and hugs him tightly.

"Thank you Carlos and Maria for getting here so fast. I'm sorry to bother you," Vanessa says quietly.

"Nonsense!" Maria says. "There is no way you are bothering us."

They all sit down next to Vanessa and begin comforting her.

"The doctors have been in there for a long time and I haven't heard anything yet," Vanessa says. "I'm sure they're doing the best they can to help him."

"Yes, of course they are," Maria says.

After about forty-five minutes, the surgeon calls out, "Family of Gabrielle Reed!"

"I'm Alex Reed. Her husband. How is she, doctor?" Alex asks.

"Sir, would you like to step into one of the conference rooms to talk privately?" the surgeon asks.

"No sir," Alex answers. "We are all family. What you have to say is OK for them to hear as well."

The surgeon proceeds to tell Alex, "Your wife sustained a considerable amount of internal damage. Also, after the preliminary x-rays, it showed that your wife's neck was broken probably from the impact of the crash, a few of her ribs were broken; one punctured her lung and another punctured her heart. She was unresponsive to CPR and any other means we attempted to use. I'm sorry to tell you, Mr. Reed, but your wife has passed away. We tried everything possible to save her. The injuries were just too severe. I'm sorry to deliver such unpleasant news."

Alex shook the surgeon's hand and thanked him and his team for their efforts. He then turns to Jasmine, hugs her, and begins to cry. When he starts, Jasmine starts, and it spreads on from there. Soon, everyone is in tears and in disbelief that their beloved wife, mother, and friend is gone. They all console each another during this time.

Five minutes later, on the other side of the waiting room, another surgeon comes out, "León Family!" he calls out.

"I'm Vanessa León. How's my husband, doctor?" Vanessa asks.

The surgeon answers, "Well, Mrs. León, your husband sustained a considerable amount of internal damage. After looking at the preliminary x-rays, it shows that his neck was broken; probably form the impact of the crash. Also, a few of his ribs were broken. One punctured his lung and one punctured his heart. He was unresponsive to CPR and any other means we attempted to use. I'm sorry to be the bearer of bad news, Mrs. León, but your husband has passed away. We did everything possible to try to save him. The injuries were just too severe. Again, I'm sorry to deliver such unpleasant news."

"No...no...no!" Vanessa screams as she quickly grabs Ricky and cries harder. She continues to scream and shake uncontrollably. Ricky, Maria, and Carlos attempt to comfort her but they are unsuccessful because they are crying and shaken up as well.

In the midst of all the screaming and crying, Alex looks over and notices people hugging and crying, trying to comfort each other. After looking in that direction, he looks away, sheds more tears, and begins to hold Jasmine a little tighter.

Several minutes later, Gabrielle's surgeon returns.

"Excuse me, Mr. Reed," the surgeon says, with a manila envelope in his hand. "These are some items your wife had on her when she came in. I thought you might want them back."

Alex opens up the envelope and in it he finds her cell phone, wedding ring, small clutch purse, and the earrings and necklace Alex gave her earlier that evening.

"Thank you, sir," Alex says, with even more tears in his eyes. "I'm glad you gave these back to me. I can now pass the jewelry down to our daughter." Alex begins to choke up a little.

"It's my pleasure, sir. Again, I am so sorry for your loss." The surgeon turns and walks away.

Just as they are getting themselves together to leave, a police officer enters the ER and inquires about the whereabouts of the Reed Family. The officer approaches Alex.

"Excuse me, folks. Are you all members of the Reed Family?"

"Yes sir we are," says Alex. "How can I help you?"

The officer responds, "My name is Officer Thomas with the Charlotte Police Department and we were going through the wreckage and noticed this case that appears to be undamaged. I'm sure you'd want to keep this and I wanted to get this to you as soon as I could."

Alex opens the case and realizes it is the award Gabrielle received from the Charlotte Business Journal. Alex breaks down in tears again. Jasmine and his friends gather around him once more to offer comforting words and shower him with love.

Several minutes later, another officer comes through the ER doors and stops at the information desk. The person at the desk points in the direction of Vanessa and he goes over to where she is.

"Excuse me, ma'am," the officer says. "Are you with the family of Guillermo León?"

"Yes. I'm his wife," Vanessa says.

"Ma'am, I'm Officer Wright with the Charlotte Police Department. We were going through the wreckage and found this in the back seat of your vehicle. I wanted to bring it to you because I'm sure you would want it."

He hands her the case and she opens it up. It's the award Guillermo received that evening. Vanessa's eyes well up with tears, she slams the case shut, clutches the case close to her chest, and says, "My dearest Guillermo...my dearest Guillermo."

Officer Wright touches her arm. "I'm very sorry for your loss, ma'am."

Vanessa, barely able to speak, looks at the officer and mouths 'Thank you' to him as he walks away.

After speaking with the hospital personnel, both families leave the hospital and return to their homes to make funeral and burial preparations.

Five days later, families and friends gather for the funerals of Gabrielle and Guillermo. Both families decide to have gravesite funerals. The weather conditions are perfect in spite of the circumstances—the day is sunny, skies are blue, and clouds are white and fluffy. Coming into Forest Lawn Cemetery, there are two large caravans of vehicles. The first group, led by a hearse containing the remains of Gabrielle, is in front with at least twenty cars behind it. Her caravan goes in a few hundred feet and veers to the right, heading to the north end of the cemetery.

Not too far behind, the caravan of Guillermo enters the cemetery, also being led by the hearse containing his remains, followed by at least fifteen cars. After the caravan enters the cemetery, they travel a few hundred feet and veer to the left going to the south end of the cemetery.

Once all the vehicles reach the designated spot, pallbearers assist in getting the caskets out of the hearses and place them on the stands that are above the freshly dug grave. Each pastor gives a stirring eulogy, after which the family and friends have the opportunity to give their condolences and words of encouragement. As the people pay their last respects to the deceased, a vocalist sings 'Amazing Grace' and they go back to their vehicles.

Before the caskets are lowered into the ground, Alex and Jasmine place a number of red roses on Gabrielle's casket. As the casket is being lowered, Alex begins to cry again but Jasmine comforts her father and assures him that everything is going to be all right as they embrace each other in a tight hug.

As Vanessa and Ricky see Guillermo's casket being lowered into the ground, they embrace each other with eyes full of tears. Vanessa gets to the point where she can no longer stand, so Ricky helps her to a chair and hugs her tight.

CHAPTER SIX

A Time to Rebuild

Soon after the devastating loss of his darling wife, Alex takes some much-needed time off from work to care for Jasmine and to regain a sense of normalcy in his life, but this is going to be somewhat of a challenge. Now that he is a single parent, there are more things he's responsible for, on top of his other responsibilities: housework, cooking, cleaning, and laundry. Gabrielle has always done these things very well. Now that the tables have turned, he's got to quickly become an expert in these areas. Unfortunately, this is not his biggest challenge. The one thing he's going to need the most help with is keeping Jasmine maintained. Since she was born, Jasmine has always been maintained and groomed by her mother and taught how to dress, how to "act like a lady," and how to keep her hair combed and neat. Alex was never trained in that area so he has his work cut out for him.

Prior to getting Jasmine ready for school or church, Alex watches instructional videos on YouTube to get ideas on how to style Jasmine's hair and make it presentable. No matter how many videos he watches, he just can't get it right. However, Jasmine is a trooper and accepts the style her father attempts to achieve. At times, she instructs him on how to do a particular style, but Alex works through her hair as though he's wearing oven mitts and can never get it quite right.

Not only that, but Alex is not the best cook either. His culinary specialties consist of boxed mac and cheese, Hamburger Helper™, frozen dinners, and hot dogs. He's not a master in the kitchen, so in order for him to increase his repertoire, he spends hours watching the Food Network channel and pulls a lot of recipes from the Internet. As hard as he tries, he can't get it right. If Jasmine gets into the car after school and Alex smells like burnt food (even though he would shower to attempt to get rid of the smoky smell), she would know that his cooking attempt did not go well. It would, however, be an opportunity for them to have a daddy/daughter date night. They would go to a restaurant of choice, talk, laugh, and have a nice meal along with dessert. There would be times where Jasmine would say, "I wish Mama was here."

Alex would grab her hand and respond, "I do too, baby girl. I do too."

They both would shed some tears and after dinner, they would go back home so Jasmine could take a bath and get ready for bed. Once her pajamas are on and she's in the bed, Alex would say prayers with her, kiss her on the forehead, and tell her, "Sweet dreams, baby girl."

"Sweet dreams to you, Daddy", Jasmine would say as Alex would turn off her lamp and tuck her in.

Alex goes into his home office to look at more YouTube videos and Food Network shows. He can't help but look at the picture on his desk of Gabrielle. After looking for a few moments, he reaches for it. Once he has it in his hands, he bursts into tears and holds the picture close to his heart. After several minutes of weeping, Alex turns off his computer and takes the picture into his bedroom and prepares for bed. He places Gabrielle's picture on his nightstand and stares at it until he can't keep his eyes open any longer. "Goodnight, my love," he says to Gabrielle's picture as he drifts off to sleep.

The next morning, which happens to be a Saturday, Alex is resting comfortably, thinking to himself that today is going to be a good lazy day. He turns over, opens his eyes, and sees Jasmine staring at him, smiling.

"Girl! What are you doing?" Alex asks, somewhat startled.

"Good morning Daddy!" Jasmine says. "What are we doing today?"

"I don't know, baby," Alex responds. "I was hoping to be lazy all day. What do you want to do?"

"Welllll..." Jasmine exclaims.

"Oh lord!" Alex says as he rolls his eyes to the back of his head. "Well what, Missy?"

"I think we should go get manicures, pedicures, and go shopping," Jasmine suggests.

"We need to go?" questions Alex.

"Yes sir. We need to go. Men get manicures and pedicures, too."

"If you say so. Let's grab a bowl of cereal, get dressed, and get your hair together. Then we can get out of here."

"How are you going to fix my hair, Daddy?" Jasmine asks.

"I'll do something simple."

"OK then. Let's get moving, buddy!" Jasmine then kisses Alex on the cheek, jumps out of the bed, and gets ready for the day.

Once they're both dressed, Alex now has the task of styling Jasmine's hair. She sits on a barstool awaiting her father.

"Ok Jazzy!" Alex says. "This is where the magic begins."

Jasmine giggles.

"I was thinking of doing two simple ponytails," Alex explains.

So he grabs the comb and brush and begins the styling process. He's quietly talking himself through the process while trying hard to recall the lessons he viewed on YouTube. Unfortunately, he is not that successful. After about twenty minutes of starting and restarting, Alex is finally finished; but the final product is not at all like what he saw on the videos. The ponytails are uneven with hair out of place, having Jasmine looking like a rag doll. Jasmine tries to encourage him as much as she can but he is still frustrated and ends up putting a baseball cap on her head to cover up his work. He figures that they are not going to be out for a long time and will be back home in a little while. No one would notice at all, he thinks to himself.

Alex and Jasmine arrive at Serenity Hair and Nail Salon. This is the place where Gabrielle and Jasmine frequently went. They arrive at the reception desk and are greeted by Felicia, who is very familiar with Jasmine.

"Good morning all!" Felicia says. "What can we do for y'all today?"

"Good morning! My baby girl would like to get a manicure and pedicure today, please," Alex says.

"My daddy is getting one, too!" Jasmine chimes in.

"No, baby girl," Alex says. "You go ahead. I'll just sit by the front door and watch you get pampered."

"But Daddy," Jasmine says in a loud, whiny voice. "You said you were going to get it with me. I know you're not going back on your word and break your little princess' heart by not doing what you said you were going to do."

The more she rambles, the louder she becomes. Alex tries to quiet her down but is unsuccessful. He has to give in.

"Ok...ok...ok!" Alex says. "I'll do it."

"Thank you, Daddy," Jasmine replies in a soft, child-like voice. She then pulls him down to her and kisses his cheek. Felicia is laughing hysterically as she says, "Right this way, please."

Jasmine grabs Alex's hand and they walk towards the large, comfortable massage chairs to begin their pedicures.

Once they are situated, Felicia tells them that Ms. Angie and Ms. Carol will be taking care of them and they thank her. Ms. Angie and

Ms. Carol come to their chairs to begin their treatments. Jasmine is already familiar with this but it takes Alex a few minutes to relax. As he gets further into his pedicure, he begins to relax more and actually begins to enjoy the experience. This time of relaxation is just what he needs. As he closes his eyes and begins to drift off into a deeper state of relaxation, his peace is abruptly interrupted by a somewhat annoying and familiar voice.

"Hey everybody!"

Alex opens his eyes and sees his friend, Nia.

"Hey Auntie Nia!" Jasmine yells and waves to her.

"Hey Jazzy Poo!" Nia replies as she hurries over to Jasmine to give her a hug and a kiss. "Girl, you are getting so big and so beautiful."

"Thank you!" Jasmine responds with a big smile on her face.

"Hey Ms. Nia!" Alex says.

"Well, well, well. What have we here?" Nia says sarcastically. "Is this Mr. Alexander the Great I see getting a pedicure? Mr. 'You will never, ever, in life, see me in a chair getting my feet worked on.'"

Everyone in the salon erupts into laughter—even Alex.

"I must admit; this is very relaxing. I never thought it would be. I think I'm hooked," Alex admits.

Nia looks at Jasmine and notices she has a baseball cap on.

"Uh, excuse me, Mr. Man," Nia says with attitude. "What is this on this baby's head?"

Alex, getting nervous, responds, "Oh it's nothing. She'll be fine."

"That's not what it looks like to me," Nia says as she takes off Jasmine's baseball cap.

"Oh my goodness, Jazzy! Who did your hair like this?" Nia asks.

"My daddy did it!" Jasmine says proudly. "He's been watching YouTube videos trying to learn different styles."

Nia is not happy. She turns her head sharply towards Alex, gives him the evil eye, and proclaims with her teeth tightly gritted together, "When you are finished with your pedicure, Mr. Man, you need to come see me on the other side of this salon. School is about to be in session."

"We have a pretty busy schedule today and quite a bit to get done," Alex says, trying to avoid the situation.

"I don't care what you have to do. Consider your plans cancelled for now. You're going to hang out here for a little while."

"How long will we be here?" Alex asks.

"Until I tell you it's alright to leave."

Nia walks to the back of the salon talking under her breath.

"Auntie Nia doesn't look too happy, Daddy," Jasmine says as she watches Nia walk to the back.

"Yeah, I see that. I wonder what she has up her sleeves," Alex wonders.

"I don't know but we are going to find out real soon."

Several minutes later, Nia comes out with a long table, three mannequin heads with wigs on them, combs, brushes, hair bows, and a host of hair care products.

When Alex is done with his pedicure, Nia calls for him. As he approaches the table, Nia laughs at him. Alex tries to figure out what's so funny and what exactly she has in mind.

With a puzzled look on his face, he asks, "Uh. Nia. What's going on here?"

"This, my dear friend, is Beauty School 101," Nia replies.

"What do you mean?"

"I'll put it to you like this," Nia says. "Today will be the last day you will style Jazzy's hair the way you did today. That is not cute at all."

"I did the best I could," Alex explains. "I thought I was getting on the right track."

"Well, Mister," Nia continues, "I'll give you a gold star for your efforts, but today will be the day you learn from the professionals on how to style a little girl's hair. Are you ready?"

"Do I really have a choice?" Alex asks, with a bit of frustration.

"No you don't. Let's get busy."

Nia explicitly instructs Alex on how to style Jasmine's hair. She patiently takes the time to show him step-by-step to make sure he not only knows how to do basic styles, but also the more intricate styles. Every time Nia shows Alex a style on the mannequin's head, she undoes the style and steps him through it. This activity seems to have caught the attention of other people in the salon. Regardless of the audience, he was focused on getting the styles mastered.

After about two hours, Alex is to the point where he feels comfortable styling hair. Nia is proud of him and the progress he's made in the time they have been together.

"If you have any questions or need my help, please don't hesitate to call me," Nia tells him. "There is no need for Jazzy to ever come out of the house with her hair looking a mess."

"Thanks Nia," Alex says as he gives her a hug. "I think I have it under control now."

Alex thanks everyone while he and Jasmine leave the salon. They continue with a fun day together, shopping and eating.

As time goes on, Alex and Jasmine begin to get into a routine of rebuilding their lives without Gabrielle. Some days are easier than others, but they manage to get through the tough times together. Alex reaches the point where he can finally return to work, and when he does, he excels in everything he puts his hands to. His performance is as though he has not been through a traumatic experience at all. He works just as hard, if not harder, as he always has and the excellence shows. Jasmine is the same way. She is now going about her days as if she never lost her mother. She is still a bright presence at school, church, and everywhere she goes. She, too, continues to excel and make considerable strides in her studies at school. Teachers and friends are amazed at the level in which she continues to exceed. She is performing as if the tragedy has given her an extra boost and has sky-rocketed into greatness.

Holidays and special occasions are extremely difficult and different now. Halloween is different because Gabrielle is not there to force them to dress up and pass out candy to trick-or- treaters. Thanksgiving is different because there is one less place setting to set and one less person at the dinner table to tell what they're thankful for. Christmas is by far the most difficult because every year, Gabrielle would go out to SouthPark Mall and purchase an ornament or angel to be placed on the top of the Christmas tree. Alex is lost again because he's never gone with them and has no idea what the criteria is in choosing. Thankfully, Jasmine knows. She had the pleasure of always going with her mother on those shopping excursions and knows exactly how to pick a good ornament or tree topper.

As Alex and Jasmine arrive at the store where Gabrielle and Jasmine purchase the ornaments, Alex begins to get nervous.

"You know, maybe we should just pick something out real quick or do something different this year."

"No Daddy!" Jasmine declares. "We've got to do this. Plus, Mama and I have always done this. There's no need to worry. I got this."

"OK baby girl," Alex says. "You take your lead."

Jasmine grabs Alex's hand, closes her eyes and takes a deep breath. Once she opens her eyes, she smiles and proceeds to look for the ornament. Alex is watching her every move. He observes the way she looks and acts, and is amazed at how much of her mother's mannerisms and qualities she's developed. After searching a while for the ornament, Jasmine stops, lets out a loud gasp, and runs towards a large display of angels. Alex is behind her, wondering what it is that's gotten her so excited.

Jasmine stops in front of the display and grabs one of the angels off of the display table. She looks at it carefully, in amazement. It's a beautiful angel wearing a pink and green dress, representative of her mother's sorority, Alpha Kappa Alpha. The angel's ensemble is accented with a green belt and green bows, and a pink and green floral hat with bows. But the one thing that leaves both Alex and Jasmine speechless is the undeniable fact that the angel resembles Gabrielle.

"Daddy. Look at this. This is absolutely beautiful!" Jasmine says with a huge smile and her eyes shining. "And it kinda looks a little like Mama."

Alex takes the angel out of her hand and looks at it closely. He examines the angel and is amazed not only at the great detail, but the fact that it does very much resemble Gabrielle. Just before he hands the angel back to Jasmine, he gazes at its face and it seems just for a second that the angel gives him a little smile, and he smiles back.

"Can we get it, Daddy?" Jasmine asks. "I think it would be perfect on our tree. Can we get it, Daddy, PLEEEASE?!!" Jasmine begs.

"Yes, baby girl," Alex answers. "We can get it and I agree with you. This would be perfect for our tree."

"YES!" Jasmine says as she grabs Alex's hand and they both walk to the checkout line to purchase the angel and go back home to start decorating.

Once they get back home and get settled, they begin the task of decorating the house and putting up the Christmas tree. Alex puts on a Christmas music CD and they have a great time laughing and playing around. They have not laughed like this in months and it was a good thing for them to do in spite of the tragedy they have experienced together. This is exactly what they need.

After all the decorations are put up all around the house, including the beautiful tree with all its ornaments, ribbons, bows, and garland, the only thing left to do is to put the angel topper on the tree. Jasmine runs and gets it out of the bag and takes it out of the fancy packaging. She looks at it some more with a smile on her face.

"Are you ready, baby girl?"

"Yes sir. I'm ready," Jasmine replies.

Alex lifts her up so she is able to place the angel on top of the tree. After a few minor adjustments, Alex puts her back on the ground and they both stand back and look at their work. Then they slap high fives as a sign of approval and stand back again to look at the tree for a few more moments.

Later that evening, Alex and Jasmine sit on the couch together and nestle cozily under a soft throw blanket, enjoying the warmth and crackle of the fireplace and the soothing sounds of Christmas music. They sip on steamy, hot cups of hot chocolate with marshmallows. It is the perfect end to a perfect evening. As the night proceeds, Jasmine eventually lays her head on Alex's chest and begins to doze off. He notices her dozing, adjusts the blanket so that it covers her more, kisses her on the top of her head, and puts his arm around her. In the years prior, he had done the same thing with Gabrielle.

Alex cannot take his focus off of the angel on top of the tree. In his mind, even though his "angel" was no longer with him, he believes that this angel on top of the tree will watch over them. Alex continues to sip his hot chocolate and remains on the couch with Jasmine, reflecting and reminiscing about the past and thinking briefly about the future.

Christmas comes and goes and New Year's Day rapidly approaches. All of Alex's friends try to get him out of the house to celebrate but he just doesn't feel up to it. He even asks Jasmine if she wants to celebrate with her friends but she says she would rather stay in with him. His friends are understanding and therefore do not press the issue.

Alex and Jasmine decide to watch the New Year's Eve programs on television. Everything is set. Snacks are on the table and there is a bottle of sparkling grape juice on ice, ready to be opened and poured into two champagne glasses when the clock strikes midnight. They enjoy the performances on television and begin to sing and dance along. They have the best of time together.

At 11:45 p.m., they anxiously await the countdown to the New Year. Jasmine sits next to Alex while eating snacks, but she begins to yawn a lot. She is up way past her normal bedtime but is trying very hard to stay awake so she can bring in the New Year with Alex. After about ten minutes, she is sound asleep. Alex looks over at her and laughs. He thought for sure she would be able to stay up, but he figures she just couldn't hang this time. He makes sure she's covered up on the couch and he turns down the volume on the television as the count-down to the New Year is on the way. Ten, nine, eight, seven, six, five, four, three, two, one...HAPPY NEW YEAR!

On the television, tons of confetti are dropped on the people at Times Square and it looks like a snowstorm. People are hugging, kissing, singing, and celebrating the start of a brand new year. Alex looks over at Jasmine, still sound asleep, kisses her on the cheek and whispers, "Happy New Year, baby girl."

He takes the blanket off of her and carries her to her room. As he is gets her tucked into bed, she wakes up and says, "Is it New Year yet?"

"Yes baby it is," Alex replies. "Happy New Year."

She jumps up out from under the covers, "Did I miss the ball drop? Are we still going to drink the sparkly stuff? Where's the confetti?" Jasmine rambles on.

"Calm down, baby girl," Alex says in a soft and calming voice. "We'll do all of that tomorrow. It's OK."

"You promise, Daddy?" Jasmine asks.

"I promise," Alex says as he tucks her in again, kisses her on the forehead, and turns off her light. He goes into his room and gets in the bed. As he is settling in, he looks over at the picture of Gabrielle on his nightstand and stares at it for a few minutes and whispers, "Happy New Year, my love."

He turns off his lamp and goes to sleep.

For the next several months, Alex and Jasmine begin to get into a good routine in their life as they began to get re-acclimated to the world and back to the normalcy they had prior to the loss of Gabrielle. They take the step to start back getting together with friends and family, just as before. The support and love they've received from family, and especially their friends, has been amazing and overwhelming. Alex and Jasmine really appreciate the support system they have.

CHAPTER SEVEN

Back in the Saddle

Alex is back at work and keeping busy as he always has. At around 10:35 a.m., his phone rings and he answers, "Alex Reed."

"Good morning Mr. Reed! This is Elijah. How are you, my friend?" Elijah asks.

"Hey there, Sarge!" Alex replies. "I'm doing well, sir. How are things with you?"

"All is well, Private. At ease," Elijah says as they both laugh.

"What can I do for you, big brother? What do I owe the pleasure of hearing from you today?" Alex asks.

"Man, I was thinking about you and wanted to check in on you and see how things are going."

"Things are going very well. Thanks for asking, bro," Alex replies.

"Hey, what are your plans for lunch today? Are you tied up?" Elijah asks.

"No sir," Alex replies. "I was actually going to work through lunch but it'll be good to hang out with you; as long as you're buying."

They both laugh.

"It's no problem. Lunch is on me today," Elijah says. "What time is good for you? I got a taste for soul food. What about you?"

"I haven't had some good soul food in a little while. That's perfect," says Alex. "Let's meet at Mert's Heart and Soul on North College at one o'clock. That way, we miss the lunch crowd and can have a good time."

"Sounds like a plan, my man!" Elijah says. "I'll see you then. Over and out!"

"Roger that, big bro. Looking forward to it. See ya at one," Alex says, and he gets back to what he was doing.

Alex arrives at Mert's a few minutes before one and Elijah comes in a few minutes later. They meet with handshakes and hugs and sit to have a delicious meal and great conversation with some laughs. After they eat, they have an opportunity to talk more in depth.

"So, my friend, how have you been?" Elijah asks.

"Man, things have been going well. Things at work are steady and

Jasmine is doing exceptionally well. I can't complain at all. Things are getting back to normal and we've been able to get in a routine and live again," Alex explains.

"That's great news, I'm glad to hear that things are going well. But I've got to ask—how are you?" Elijah asks.

With a puzzled look on his face, Alex responds,

"I just told you. Everyone is doing fine."

Elijah comes back and says, "Yeah, I know you said that, but you didn't answer my question. How are you?" Not Jasmine, not the job, not the football team; how are you doing?"

Alex pauses and begins to understand what Elijah is really getting at.

"I see what you mean, bro," Alex says. He takes a deep breath and looks Elijah square in the eyes. "It's been tough. Doing all the things that Gabby used to do on top of learning how to keep Jasmine maintained, on top of my work responsibilities, it's been a lot to handle, but I have to get it done and keep things moving."

"It's looks as though you've done a great job so far in spite of."

"Thanks sir."

"Let me ask you this," Elijah says. "Have you thought about starting to date again?"

Alex almost spits his water out and grabs his napkin quickly to catch any water.

"Dating?" asked Alex. "That's the last thing on my mind right now. When would I have time to date? I don't even know the rules of dating anymore if I was ready to do it. It's just not going to happen right now and to be quite honest, I don't think I'll ever be ready to get back out there. I miss Gabby too much."

"Trust me, I know what you are dealing with," Elijah explains. "Remember, I was in the same boat when I lost Barbara."

Elijah goes on, "It took me a while to get over the devastation, but I had to come to the realization that no matter how good of a father I was to my girls, there was no way I could teach them to be women. I needed to find someone who would complement not only me, but also the dynamics of my family, and could be a good role model for the girls. I'm thankful that Corrine was that woman and it's been great; even though she gets on my damn nerves every now and then."

They both burst out in laughter.

"I say all that to say this", Elijah interjects. "I have no doubt that you are an outstanding father. I've known you for many years and I can speak personally about your character and your ability to be a responsible parent. The one area you will fall short on every time is being a mother. YouTube can't teach you how to be that mother figure in a young girl's life. Only a woman or another mother can. Give it some thought. Pray about it. I know it's probably not what you want right now, but you have to think about Jasmine too. She adores you but I'm sure she misses her mother. God will give you direction and guidance. Just know that we all are here for you both and want nothing but the very best for you."

"I really appreciate that, big bro," Alex says. "I never thought of it that way but it's difficult to even think about being with someone other than Gabrielle. You know she was the love of my life. I would almost think I was cheating on her if I decided to date again. That would be too much for me."

"Think of it like this," Elijah chimes in. "Do you think Gabby would want to see you unhappy for the rest of your life?"

"No sir," Alex answers.

"Do you think Jazzy will always come to you when she has a 'girly' issue?" Elijah asks.

"Well...no," Alex responds.

"Those are just a couple things to think about. I think it's time for you to get back on the saddle and find someone who's good for and to you. You don't have to marry them right away. Just date and see where it leads. That's just my suggestion. Whatever you decide, I'll still love you, brother," Elijah says.

"I really appreciate that, Sarge, and I know you all have my back," Alex says. "We all have to get together again. We haven't done that in a while. I really miss the crew."

"Well, let's make it happen. Look at some dates and just let us all know."

"I'll do that when I get back to the office. Speaking of the office, I better get back there and finish up so I can get out on time. I really appreciate lunch and the wisdom you shared with me today. I'll give what we talked about some serious thought."

"It was my pleasure. We have to do this more often," Elijah suggests. "Next time, lunch is on you and I want to go somewhere fancy."

They both laugh.

"No problem! You choose the place and I'll pick up the check," Alex says as they get up from the table, shake hands, and then embrace in a hug.

"Love ya, man," Alex says.

"Love you back, Private."

They leave the restaurant and both go back to work to complete the day.

Once Alex gets back to the office, he opens his e-mail and sends out a message to his friends:

Hey All,

I hope this message finds you all well. I wanted to drop in and say that I love and miss you guys and we need to get together REAL soon! If you all are not busy this coming Saturday, let's restart our monthly outings at Petey's at our usual time. I miss hanging out with you all and need to see your smiling faces (and ugly ones too)!!! LOL!!! ☺ Just reply back to this message and let me know. If this is too short of notice, I understand, and we can always go when everyone is free. Looking forward to seeing you all again.

Alex

A few minutes after he sends the message, he begins to receive replies. Fortunately, everyone responds that they can make it and that meeting again will be great. Alex is very happy when he realizes that everyone will be there.

When Saturday evening arrives, and before Alex goes to Petey's, Alex takes Jasmine over to a friend's house before he goes to Petey's. He arrives early, anxiously awaiting his friends' arrival. This is the first time that they all have gotten together in this setting since the death of Gabrielle. After several minutes, they all begin to arrive. It's a very emotional and exciting time for all of them. Everyone's so happy to see Alex again and they pick up where they left off the last time they met. There's a lot of conversation, laughter, and even a little drama between Craig and Nia, but that's always expected when they all get together.

While everyone is finishing dinner, the conversation changes and things get more serious.

"I am so happy to hang out with you guys again," Alex confesses. "I really needed this and I'm glad you all were able to make it."

"Yeah man, it's just like old times," Craig says. "This is something we'd never miss anyway, but glad that it's back on the calendar."

"So tell us, how have you been?" asks Foster. "I can only imagine that things have been kinda rough in spite of."

"All in all, things have been OK," Alex explains. "I still have my moments where I really miss Gabby and it's hard. But there are times I have to keep it together for Jasmine and that works out fine."

"How has Jasmine been adjusting to everything? How has she been doing?" asks Hannah.

"She's been doing a heck of a lot better than me," Alex admits. "Instead of me being a rock for her, I think she's been more of a rock for me, and that's cool. She is so much like her mother it's scary. All in all, she's doing fine in everything- school, church, dance, everything. I couldn't be more proud of her."

"Well, how has it been going with styling her hair?" Nia asks. When she asks, everyone gets a puzzled look on their face. Alex explains to them what happened that day at the salon and how he went through a crash course on how to style a little girl's hair.

"I'm glad you asked, Nia," Alex says. He pulls out his cell phone and shows them pictures of the different styles he did for Jasmine.

"Wow!" Nia reacts to the pictures "I'm impressed. You've been doing a great job, sir."

"Thank you, ma'am!" he replies. "I learned from the best. I never thought in a million years I'd be combing and styling hair. That was the last thing on my mind."

The group laughs while they continue to look at the pictures.

"I'm glad that things are going well for you, brother." Juni says. "But I've got to ask a question and I hope you don't get offended."

"Come on, now," Alex says. "We all have been friends too long. There is nothing you all can't ask me. You all know that. Go ahead and ask."

"Well, I was just thinking, have you given any thought to getting back on the dating scene?" Juni asks.

Keiko nudges him with her elbow and some of the others ask him why he would ask a question like that. Alex looks at Elijah as if he had something to do with Juni asking the question and Elijah looks back and mouths that he didn't say anything to anyone about their previous conversation.

"Guys, I don't have a problem answering the question," Alex answers with a smile. "Someone has already asked me about that and, to be honest, I haven't thought about it at all. I still miss Gabby very much and my focus is on getting my life back and making sure Jasmine is well taken care of."

"I can understand that, but do you think it's time for a little adult company every now and then?" Bradley asks.

"I agree," Alicia chimes in. "It's not like you have to get into a serious relationship too fast; but just have someone to have a good time with. Go to dinner, a movie, ball game, something every now and then just to break out of your normal routine. That's all. Just something to think about."

"Ok. Here's the deal," Corrine pipes up and the group becomes silent. "There is no set time limit for an individual to start back dating after the end of a previous relationship. It's all up to the individual. In your case, Alex, I think now is a good time for you to get back out there, not only for your sake but Jasmine's sake. Here's what I mean: for you, it's been a while since you've dated someone; being married to Gabrielle for the time you have, you've probably forgotten how to date. I know you and her had date nights and went out every now and then, but the difference is that you all were married and you were familiar with each other. Going out on dates as a single person, you are getting to know someone and trying to see if that person is a good fit for you and if are compatible. In this day and age, the rules of dating have changed a bit and what worked before doesn't work today. Not only are you trying to see who's compatible for you, but also you would ultimately want someone around you that will be accepting and compatible with Jasmine. You are a packaged deal now. Not everyone can handle someone with a child or children. One of the most important things you must keep in mind is that no one comes before your child. Many people get into relationships and neglect the child. Don't do that. Keep doing what you're doing. You will know when the time is right when you want to introduce her to whoever you are dating, if it ever gets to that point."

Nia chimes in. "I think Jasmine would be happy to see you dating and possibly settle down with someone special."

"Why would you say that, Nia?" Alex asks.

"Think about this," Nia continues. "Don't get me wrong. You've done an outstanding job at doing all you can for her, including learning how to style her hair. You're a great provider, protector, and awesome father, and she will love you forever for that. But the one thing you can't give her that she will need, if she is not already yearning for it, is a mother figure. That someone that can continue to teach her how to be a lady, someone who she can have 'girl talks' with, someone she can share secrets with. She can't do that with her father. There are some things as a man you will not understand. We can be there for her in any capacity. But for the more intimate things, she needs that mother figure to show her the way. No offense to you at all. It's a girl thing-you just wouldn't understand."

"Wow!" Alex says as he slumps in his seat. He feels as if he's been suddenly downloaded with a lot of critical information to consider. "All of what you are saying is true and I've never thought about it. I was so busy trying to be all that I can for her that I had no idea about any of this. I'll give it some thought and even have a conversation with Jazzy about this. Who knows what she will say."

"It won't hurt to talk with her," says Elijah. "We know you are a wonderful guy that deserves nothing but the very best life has to offer. You deserve happiness, joy, peace, and most of all, love. I don't know when that will happen, but when it does, the world will know, Jasmine will know, we will know, and most of all, you will know. It'll happen in due season. We're confident of that. We are here for you in any capacity. Don't think that you're in this thing by yourself. Whatever we can do for you and Jasmine, you can consider it done."

Everyone's eyes, including Alex's, well up with tears as Elijah speaks.

"Thank you all so very much," Alex says as he wipes his eyes. "I've been blessed by your friendship for many years and you all have never let me down. I know you only want the best for us, so your kind words are appreciated. Trust me, I'm taking all of it to heart and I will seriously give it some thought and also talk with Jasmine to get her take on it. I really don't think it will go over too well; but I will give it a try. What do I have to lose? I love and appreciate you guys."

Everyone stands up to give Alex hugs and kisses, tears streaming from their eyes. After exchanging more pleasantries, they all leave Petey's to go home.

On the car ride back home, Alex has a lot on his mind, mostly what was said at dinner. He knows that there are decisions he eventually needs to make, but he's not sure if he's ready to make them yet. The more he drives and thinks, the more nervous he becomes. He picks up Jasmine from her friend's house, goes home, and they go right to sleep. There's no time for having a conversation with her at this time, but he doesn't know when he will, so he puts it off for another day.

Several weeks go by and Alex and Jasmine maintain their usual routine of work, school, church, and other extracurricular activities. Another weekend approaches and they decide, as they usually do, to stay in and watch movies on television. They decide to look at a show that has been recorded on the DVR. Wearing comfortable clothes, they get cozy on the couch with their popcorn and drinks in hand, and completely ready to have a nice, relaxing evening at home. While watching the movie and enjoying each other's company, a commercial comes on for a dating website, eHarmony.com. They silently watch the commercial in its entirety and when the next commercial comes on, Jasmine looks at Alex and says, "Daddy, can I ask you a question?"

"Yeah, baby girl, what's up?" Alex asks.

"Have you ever thought about going on that website to find a date?"

"No. Not really," Alex responds. "Why do you ask?"

"I think you need to meet someone nice and have a good time," Jasmine declares, as Alex listens attentively. "I think you are a very nice person and I want you to be happy. I know you miss Mama very much and I do too, but I think it's time that you found someone that will make you happy just like Mama did. Plus, I don't want to hang out with you all the time. Whoever she is, we can have girl time."

Jasmine bursts into her signature laugh.

Alex is amazed at what he's just heard Jasmine say. It's not what he expected her to feel or say, and he knows now that he has to really give some serious thought to dating again. They continue to watch the movie until the end.

Afterwards, Alex helps Jasmine get ready for bed. After she puts on her pajamas, she climbs into bed, says her prayers, and lets Alex tuck her in. Just before Alex turns off her lamp, he sits on the side of her bed.

"You know; I don't know about this whole dating thing right now. I don't know if I'm ready, and plus, I'm trying to be the best father and support for you. You are my priority right now."

Jasmine comes out from under the covers, gets on her knees in the bed, grabs Alex's face, and brings it close to hers and says, "Daddy. You are not trying to be a good dad, you are a great dad and you do it very well. You take really good care of me and I love you so much. You need someone else to love you too. So once you get on that website, I'll help you pick someone out."

"OK baby," Alex says in disbelief. "I'll give it some thought and if I do decide to get on there, I'll let you know and we can look together. Is that a plan?"

"That's a great plan," Jasmine says as she gives Alex a kiss and snuggles back under the covers to go to sleep. Alex turns off her light and goes back to his bedroom. He still can't believe that his own daughter is thinking the same as his friends. This is something he never imagined would happen. He thinks about it long and hard until he falls asleep. Nothing else is said about it for the next few days.

One day after Alex picks Jasmine up from school and they head home, they begin their normal after-school conversation.

"How was school today, baby girl?" Alex asks.

"It was good," Jasmine responds. "We had a spelling test today and I got them all right."

"That's wonderful, baby!" Alex says. "You are so smart and always do very well in school. I'm so proud of you."

"Thank you, Daddy," Jasmine says smiling.

"You know what I was thinking we should do today?" Alex asks.

"What?" Jasmine responds giving Alex a puzzled look.

"I think tonight, we should get online and get me a profile on eHarmony so I can find me a date."

"Yes, yes, yes!" Jasmine says as she dances and sings, "Daddy's gonna find a girlfriend...Daddy's gonna find a girlfriend."

"Slow down, missy. We're going to look and see what's out there. I'm not going to rush into anything."

"Don't worry, Daddy, it will be fun and I will help you."

They finally get home and begin their routine: homework, dinner, and chores. Afterwards, they wind down and get to the business at hand of getting Alex set up on the website to find a match. Once they get his profile set up with a picture of himself, then comes the task of looking through a number of women's profiles to see who may be a good match.

"I think for today, I'm just going to just look around and try to get comfortable navigating through this site. We can actually start looking seriously at profiles another day. I'll make sure you are right here with me to help," Alex tells Jasmine.

"OK. This is going to be so much fun!" Jasmine exclaims. "I really hope we find a really nice person for you, Daddy."

"We'll see what happens. Now go ahead and get ready for bed and

I'll be up in a few minutes."

"Yes sir!" Jasmine says as she runs to her room.

Now, Alex is getting really nervous because he hasn't dated anyone since Gabrielle and he is not sure he will succeed at dating again. He begins to have second thoughts, almost regretful that he agreed to go forward with the online dating service. However, some way, somehow, he will need to find a way get over the nerves and face the fact that he is about to enter the wonderful world of dating. He does a few small things around the house before he goes to Jasmine's room to tuck her in and say prayers. When he gets to her room, he finds her already in the bed, under the covers, and sound asleep. He goes over to her, kisses her on the forehead, and softly whispers, "I love you Jasmine."

Alex turns off her lights and goes to bed. After he closes her door, Jasmine's eyes pop open. She wasn't asleep at all. She sits up in her bed and says a prayer:

"Dear God,

Please send a very nice woman to my daddy. He is a very nice man that deserves a nice lady to be with him. Please send someone that is like my mama who is pretty and funny. My daddy would like that very much. I want to like her too. Hopefully, she and I will get along just fine and have a lot of fun and be happy. Thank you very much. Amen."

After she says her prayer, Jasmine gets back under the covers and goes to sleep.

For the next few days, Alex avoids logging into the website but is curious at the same time. The more he thinks about it, the more nervous he gets. While at work, he pulls up his e-mail and drafts a letter to his friends:

Hey Gang,

I hope this message finds you all well. So, in taking into consideration what you all said the other night and consulting with Jasmine, I want you all to know that I have decided to get back on the dating scene. I know this is an "out of the box" experience for me but I'm willing to give it a try. Wish me luck. I'll be sure to keep you all posted on how things go.

Talk with you all soon!!!

Alex

Not soon after he sends the message, he begins to receive encouraging e-mails from his friends. Their words ease the nervousness he has. Now he can move forward without stressing himself out about dating. He makes up in his mind that he will take things day by day.

That following Sunday morning, Alex and Jasmine go to church and enjoy a soul-stirring sermon by Bishop Palmer. After service is over and everyone begins to leave, Bishop Palmer and his wife, Patricia, greet members and guests in the lobby of the church, just as they always do. Alex wants to make sure he and Jasmine have an opportunity to speak to them.

"Bishop Palmer, that was an outstanding sermon," Alex smiles brightly.

Bishop Palmer grabs his hand, shakes it, and then gives him the biggest hug he's ever given him. He also gets a big hug and kiss on the cheek from Patricia.

"Alex, my friend, it's so good to see you," Bishop Palmer says. "How are you doing?"

"All is well, sir. Thank you," Alex replies.

"Look at Jasmine," Bishop Palmer says, giving her a hug. "Look how big and beautiful she is getting."

"Yes she is," Patricia says. "She is looking like a little angel."

"Alex, I'm glad you stopped," Bishop Palmer says. "I've wanted to connect with you for some time but I wanted to give you and Jasmine a little time before I made any efforts to reach out. I did phone you a couple times, but when I didn't hear back, I wanted to respect your space. Do you have a few minutes to talk now in my office?"

"You boys go right ahead," Patricia says. "Jasmine and I will be just fine. Take as much time as you need."

Patricia grabs Jasmine's hand and they go off laughing and talking.

Bishop Palmer and Alex go into the Bishop's study, sit down, and begin to have an in-depth conversation.

"Alex, I know it's been some time since Gabrielle passed away and you all have been in my prayers every day. How have you all been coping? How have you all been, honestly?" Bishop Palmer asks.

"I'll be honest, it's been hard at times," Alex responds. "But with your prayers and the prayers of our family and friends, we've been doing a good job of staying faithful that the pain will continue to lessen and that we will continue to move forward and be there for each other."

"That's good to hear, but how has Jasmine been doing? I'm sure it's not easy for a little girl to cope with the fact that she's lost her mother and friend. How has she managed?" Bishop Palmer asks.

"Actually, she has been stronger than I have," Alex confesses. "She's been my rock and a trooper throughout the entire ordeal. I couldn't be more proud of her. She even says that she's going to help me find someone to date."

"Excuse me?" Bishop Palmer says as he sits taller in his chair.

"You heard correctly. She's going to help me find a date. She says, and I quote, 'You deserve to be happy and be with someone nice,' Alex says.

"Well. That's a first. I don't think in all my years of pastoring I've ever heard of a child wanting their parent to date after the other parent has passed away. But I've got to ask, are you ready for something like that? Do you think you are ready for dating again?" Bishop Palmer asks with a concerned look on his face.

"I've thought about that long and hard because, at first, I said to myself that I was not going to date or even entertain the thought because Gabrielle was my one and all. There was no one that could ever take her place. Ironically, all of my closest friends, and surprisingly even Jasmine, think that it's time to get back on the dating scene. Needless to say, when they first mentioned it, I was at a loss for words," Alex explains.

"This is very interesting," Bishop Palmer declares. "I will say this: only you can determine whether or not you are ready for this task. I caution you to guard your heart and make sure this is something you are certain you're ready for. There are a lot of good people out there, but there are some mean, bad people out there as well. Beware of people that are out to take and not give. Beware of those who are attracted to what you have in your pocket rather than what's in your heart or head. You are an outstanding person who deserves nothing but the very best. It is my prayer that God sends you the person that will be perfect for you and Jasmine. Who knows, she may come along when you least expect it. But if you are ready to dive into dating again and it's OK with Jasmine, I say go for it. Patricia and I will support you in any and every way we can. We want to see you happy."

"Thank you Bishop. Your kind words really mean a lot to me and I really appreciate you all," Alex says. "I'll be sure to keep you posted on how things go. Pray for me Bishop. Pray for me."

"We got you covered, son," Bishop Palmer says, laughing. Both men get up from their seats, embrace in a hug, and walk out together.

"Alex, don't hesitate to call us if you need us. Patricia and I want to be another great resource for you and Jasmine. Even if you have a date and want us to look after Jasmine, we'll be more than happy to do that for you," Bishop Palmer says.

"Thank you very much, sir. I really appreciate that and will keep that in mind."

The two men find Jasmine and Patricia in the church sanctuary at the piano, singing and laughing. Alex and Bishop Palmer decide not to interrupt what's going on, so they stand in the back watching them have a great time together.

"You know what, Alex?" Bishop Palmer asks.

"What's that, sir?"

"In looking at Jasmine interact with Patricia, I think it's a great idea that you are starting to date again. When you do find 'the right one,' you will know it and she will be a great addition to your family. Trust me," Bishop Palmer says.

"That's what I'm hoping for. I'll keep my fingers and toes crossed," says Alex with a chuckle.

"It'll happen. Just wait and see," Bishop Palmer proclaims.

After a few minutes of watching them, they walk towards the piano to get the attention of Jasmine and Patricia. The Palmers offer a few more words of encouragement and they all leave the church. After they leave, Alex and Jasmine grab a bite to eat and head home to relax. Once they finally get home, they go straight to sleep for a good two-hour nap. When they finally wake up, they sit around and watch television. After some time, Jasmine speaks up.

"Dad. When are we going to look for you a date?"

"You know what, baby girl. Let's do that right now," Alex responds.

They both get up from the couch and head to Alex's home office and get on his computer. He pulls up the website, logs in to his profile, and sees that he already has a number of women that have already viewed his profile and expressed some level of interest. They look at pictures and read profiles, but no one has 'caught their eyes,' so to speak. As they continue to search, Jasmine sees a picture of interest.

"Daddy, what about her?" she asks, as she points to the profile.

Alex clicks on a name to read the profile.

Sharon
Single, 36
No children
Boutique owner
Loves picnics, walks in the park, and has an appreciation for art.

Alex and Jasmine take a few minutes to not only read through her profile, but also to look at pictures that she has posted. Alex is pleased with what he sees and takes the required steps to communicate with her. He clicks on the button to send her a private message in hopes she will contact him in return. After a few more minutes of looking at other profiles, he receives a notification from Sharon. He is shocked to get such a quick response. He reads her message and they engage in conversation via the chat feature.

Once Jasmine sees that he is enjoying his time on the computer, she tells Alex that she is going to do some things in her room and gives him a kiss on the cheek. Before she leaves out of the office, she looks back at Alex and notices that he is smiling and laughing. It's been a long time since she's seen him laugh and smile like that. The last time was the night they went to Gabrielle's awards ceremony. She is thrilled to see him slowly, but surely, get back to his normal, happy self. Jasmine goes to her room and remains there until Alex comes up to tuck her in and say their prayers together.

After about an hour, Alex knocks on Jasmine's door and finds her lying in bed reading a book.

"Hey baby," Alex says quietly as he peeks through the door. "What you doing?"

"Oh nothing," Jasmine replies. "Are you done on the computer? Tell me all about it."

"It was OK," Alex says. "Since this was our first time communicating, of course there's a lot more for us to learn about each other, but I think everything went fine. I was still nervous."

"Are you going to go out on a date soon?" Jasmine asks.

"I don't know, baby. We are going to chat on the computer and talk on the phone and see how things go from there," Alex explains.

"That's good, Daddy. I really hope everything works out for you. You deserve it."

"Thank you, sweetheart. Now let's get you into bed. It'll be time for you to get up and get ready for school before you know it."

Alex and Jasmine grasp hands and begin to say their prayers. When they are done, Alex tucks her in and gives her a kiss on the forehead.

"Sweet dreams, Princess," Alex whispers. "I love you."

"Night-night, Daddy. I love you too, very much," Jasmine responds.

Alex turns off her light and closes her door as he goes back to his room to prepare to go to bed. Once he is dressed in his pajamas and ready to turn in for the night, he climbs into bed and looks at the picture of Gabrielle. He stares at it for a long time and begins to feel a little guilty about the possibility of dating again, considering he's not completely over Gabrielle. But he still decides to move forward with dating in hopes of finding someone that he and Jasmine would be comfortable being around. He looks at Gabrielle's picture one more time, turns off his light, and falls asleep.

A little over a week goes by and while Alex is at work one day, he receives a notification on his phone from the dating website. It's a message from Sharon, the woman he was previously chatting with. They exchange a few words and she sends him her phone number to call her when he has an opportunity. He mentions that he is breaking for lunch in a few minutes and he will call her when he is away from the office.

During his lunch break, he goes to his car with his turkey sandwich on wheat bread with Swiss cheese, lettuce, tomato, and mustard; a bag of chips; and a bottle of water. After he takes a few bites, he proceeds to call Sharon. As the phone rings, his hands began to sweat and shake a little. There is even a thought of hanging up the phone and forgetting the whole thing. Just as he is about to hang up, she answers the phone.

"Hello?"

"Good afternoon, ma'am. May I speak with Sharon, please?" Alex asks.

"This is Sharon. Who may I ask is calling?"

"This is Alex. We've been communicating online and I wanted to give you a call."

"Well, hello Alex. It's good to finally talk with you," Sharon says. "How is your day going today?"

They begin to engage in conversation while laughing and getting to know each other better. However, Alex is very careful not to give too much information by keeping the conversation as generic as possible. That's how the conversation proceeds and they both are okay with that. In a forty-five-minute span of time, they learn quite a bit about each other and like what they hear.

"WOW!" Alex says. "Funny how time flies when you're having fun. I can't believe it's almost time for me to get back to the office. I hope that I didn't bore you all this time."

Sharon laughs.

"No, not at all. I thoroughly enjoyed the conversation. Hopefully we can do it again soon."

"I'm sure I can make that happen," Alex replies. "Better yet, I have an idea."

"Oh yeah, what's that?" Sharon asks.

"Since you are a fan of art, I'd like to take you to a museum. I know that's something you like, right?"

"It is something I love," Sharon responds with excitement. "I've been wanting to go to the Mint Museum Uptown for quite some time now. I've heard it is really nice."

"Well, check your schedule and see what Saturday you have available and it's a date."

"I will do that and let you know as soon as possible. It was really great talking with you."

"It was great talking with you as well," Alex replies. "Have a great rest of the day and I'll chat with you soon."

"I'm looking forward to it. Goodbye," Sharon says as she hangs up the phone.

"Bye bye," Alex says as he hangs up.

He looks at his watch and realizes his lunchtime is almost over so he hurries to finish his lunch and get back to the office to complete the day. After he gets back to his desk, he receives a text message from Sharon:

Hey Alex. Great talking with you today. I'm free next Saturday if you want to get together then. Just let me know. ☺Sharon

Alex replies:

Hey Sharon! Good talking with you as well. Next Saturday is perfect. Since this is our first outing together, would you like for me to pick you up or will you meet me there? I want to be respectful.

Sharon replies:

You can pick me up. I don't think you're a stalker! LOL! I'll text you my address by next Friday. See ya!

Alex replies:

LOL! Sounds good. Have a good one!!!

Alex proceeds with the rest of the day and once work is done, he leaves to pick Jasmine up from school. While driving, the anticipation of going on a date grows by the second. Nothing can wipe away the smile that he has on his face. He pulls up to the pick-up area at Jasmine's school and sees her standing in a group, waving at him. He drives up to where she is, gets out, opens her door to the back seat so she can get in, and closes the door. Once he gets back into the driver's seat, he tells her to buckle up and they head home.

"How was your day today, Princess?" Alex asks Jasmine.

"I had a really good day, Daddy," Jasmine answers. "We had a math and social studies test today and I got 100% on both."

"That's awesome, baby girl!" Alex says. "It doesn't surprise me that you're so smart. Keep up the good work."

"How was your day, Daddy?" Jasmine asks.

"Well, my day was pretty good. I was on the phone a lot, had a few meetings, and also got a date."

"Huh?" Jasmine says. "Date? What kind of date?"

Alex laughs.

"Remember when we were looking at those pictures on that website a little while ago?"

"Yeah..."

"And you said that I should contact her?" Alex proceeds.

"Yeah..." Jasmine says again as she sits forward in her seat with a huge smile on her face.

"Well, we talked on the phone today and we are going on a date next Saturday."

"Yippee!" Jasmine screams. "Where are you going? Will I get to meet her?"

"Well, you probably won't get a chance to meet anyone I date unless I really like her," Alex answers Jasmine. "I don't want to get in the habit of bringing a lot of women around you and there is no guarantee they will be around a long time. Plus, I want to make sure she will be a good person for us to be around."

"I see what you're saying, Daddy," Jasmine says. "You just don't want to make it seem like you're a ho."

Alex is startled at what Jasmine just said.

"What did you just say, little lady?" Alex asks. And in the same tone as before, Jasmine says, "I understand why you don't want to bring a lot of women around. You don't want to seem like a ho."

"Baby girl, where did you hear that from? Alex asks. "That's not a good thing to say."

"Auntie Nia said that a while ago," Jasmine explains. "She told me that if you ever started to date, to make sure you don't act like a ho and bring a bunch of women around me."

She can see from looking into Alex's glare through the rear view mirror that he is not happy.

"Daddy. Did I say something wrong?" Jasmine asks.

"You're fine, baby," Alex says. "Just make sure you don't say that word again. It's not very nice."

"Which word, Daddy? Ho?" Jasmine asks.

"Yes, that one! Wait until I have a little conversation with Ms. Nia about this," Alex says as he shakes his head, yet laughs under his breath.

"Well, I'm glad you're going on a date. I hope you have a good time. Where are you going?" Jasmine asks.

"We are going to a museum and maybe get a bite to eat," Alex explains. "If it's a bad date, I'll be home really early, but I think it will go fine. What do you think?"

"Well, I think it will go fine too. Hopefully she is very nice so you can go on more dates with her and maybe one day I could meet her...only if she is the one."

"Only time will tell, baby. Only time will tell," Alex says.

When they get home, Jasmine starts her homework and Alex changes clothes to begin to prepare dinner and have a nice, relaxing evening with his little princess. As the evening progresses, they talk and laugh. Alex makes sure Jasmine's homework is complete and then they watch a little television before they prepare for bed. Once Alex and Jasmine say their prayers and Jasmine is tucked in, Alex hears his text notification on his cell phone. As Jasmine settles in and closes her eyes, Alex tips out and goes into his room to see who texted him. It was Sharon.

Hey Alex! Sorry to bother you so late. Just wanted to say hello and goodnight. Didn't know if you were still up or not. If you are, text me. If not, I'll catch you tomorrow. ☺Sharon

Alex replies:
Hey there Sharon! I'm still up. Will call you in a few if that's OK.

Sharon replies:
K

Alex's heart begins to beat fast and he has to calm down to keep his hands from shaking so much. Once he regains his composure, he restarts the conversation with Sharon that lasts for hours. They share with each other back and forth, but still keep the conversation somewhat generic until their first meeting. As they are wrapping up the conversation, Alex says,

"Well, I'd better let you get some sleep. I'm sure you have a busy day tomorrow."

"I do, but I'll be OK. You get some sleep and we'll talk later. Goodnight."

"Goodnight, sleep well," Alex says.

Alex then lies in the bed for a little bit before turning off his light and going to bed.

onds later the door opens and there stands Sharon—a beautiful 5'5" beauty with short black hair, smooth, caramel-colored skin, and a smile bright enough to light up a night sky. She is beautifully dressed in an orange sleeveless maxi dress with beige sandals. When she takes her first look at Alex, she smiles from ear to ear. He is handsomely dressed in black slacks, a black Polo shirt, newly shined black shoes, and a gray blazer. For a few seconds, they stand there looking and smiling at each other in amazement.

"Please forgive me for staring but I'm just mesmerized by your beauty. You must be Sharon," Alex says as he extends his hand out to shake her hand.

"And you must be Alex," Sharon says as she shakes his hand. "Pleasure to finally meet you in person."

"The pleasure is all mine. Well, your carriage awaits you. Shall we depart?" Alex asks as he holds out his arm for her to hold onto.

He walks her to the car, opens her door, and makes sure she is secure in her seat before he closes it. Alex then gets in the car and he drives to the museum. During the ride, they enjoy good conversation with each other and a lot of laughter. Alex can't stop thinking to himself how beautiful Sharon is and that he is actually out on a date. He's still a little nervous, but determined not to let her notice.

They arrive at the museum and they go in and walk through the various galleries, looking at the vast number of pieces on display. Sharon seems to be an expert when it comes to art because she is very familiar with the artists and can point out facts about the paintings and sculptures that an uninformed person wouldn't see. Alex is captivated.

"Wow!" Alex says. "I'm impressed that you know so much about art. That's fascinating. I've always liked art but it seems you have a deep appreciation for it. Where did you learn so much about it?"

"I was an art major in college and have always loved it even at a young age. It's something that has always kept my attention and out of a lot of trouble."

They both laugh as they continue walking along into the museum's gallery for the collection of modern and contemporary Native arts.

"Well I know all about that," Alex says as he puts his hands into his pockets. "I was involved in sports and that definitely kept me out of lot of trouble. But, I think I got into more trouble in sports than outside of sports. That's just the type of kid I was," Alex says as they both chuckle.

CHAPTER EIGHT

Ready...Set...Date

The day has come for Alex to go out on his first date since the untimely death of his darling wife, Gabrielle. He has already communicated with Sharon and gotten her address with plans to leave home a little early to ensure he is on time when picking her up. Before the date, he drops Jasmine off at Nia's house. Before walking out the door, he instructs Nia to not corrupt his daughter by teaching her bad words. Although he's serious, he and Nia laugh and he then tells Jasmine he will see her later.

Alex gets in his car and puts Sharon's address in the GPS on his cell phone. Siri gives him step-by-step directions; however, the more he drives, he begins to notice that the directions are taking him away from where he thinks he needs to go. The further he gets into this journey, the more lost he becomes. He gets to a point where nothing around him seems familiar and he pulls into a grocery store parking lot and calls Sharon.

"Hey Sharon! This is Alex. How are you?"

"I'm fine Alex. How are you?" Sharon asks.

"I'd be a whole lot better if I knew how to get to your place," Alex says. "My GPS seems to have taken me way off course and I think I'm lost."

"Yeah, I should have told you that, for some reason, GPS takes people out of the way. I hate that. Where are you now?"

"I pulled into the Publix parking lot on Providence. How far is that from you?" Alex asked.

"Oh my goodness," Sharon replies. "It took you in a totally different direction. The good thing is that you're not too far off. I can guide you in."

"Thanks. I would appreciate that very much," Alex says.

Sharon stays on the phone with Alex and gives him detailed directions to her house (which happens to be just a few exits up from where he pulled off to call her). Once he gets to the house, he pulls into the driveway, walks to the front door, and rings the doorbell. A few sec-

"Hey. Are you hungry?" Alex asks. "There is a nice little restaurant in the front of the gallery. I heard it was nice."

"Sure. I'm not going to turn down a meal from a good-looking man such as yourself," Sharon says, as she takes his arm and they walk to the restaurant. Of course, Alex smiles from ear to ear.

In the restaurant, they get seated and are greeted by their waiter. They order something to drink and have small talk while looking at the menu. After they order, they begin to have a more in-depth conversation.

"So tell me more about yourself, Alex," Sharon says.

"Well, I'm a pretty simple guy. There's really not too much to say about myself. I'm a native of Charlotte and really love this city. I attended Harvard Law School to become an attorney. I've been in practice for over fifteen years now and I love what I do."

"Attorney, huh?" Sharon says. "I bet you have a lot of female clients call on you all the time."

Alex laughs.

"No, not at all. I mainly deal with the upper management and legal departments of corporations. I rarely deal with clients one on one."

"That's nice, but from your picture on the site and looking at you now, I could have sworn you were a salesman or banker," Sharon says.

"What do you mean?" Alex asks.

"Well, most lawyers I've met over time have the flashy cars and big bank accounts, Sharon replied. "Don't get me wrong, you are a very handsome man but, to me, you don't fit the lawyer look."

Her comments catch Alex off guard and he tries hard not to let it show on his face. As they continue to talk, the waiter returns with their dinner.

"Well, enough about me, tell me some more about you, Sharon," Alex says.

"I was born and raised in Columbia, South Carolina, and moved to the Charlotte area after high school. I am a lover of art and fashion and wanted to pursue a career in that field so I attended the Art Institute of Charlotte and majored in Fashion Marketing and took art classes at Central Piedmont Community College just for fun. That's how I gained my appreciation for art. Now I'm the owner of my own boutique here in Uptown and things are going very well for me," Sharon says.

"That's awesome," Alex continues. "It must be a good feeling to be your own boss."

"It is," Sharon boasts. "I can do whatever I want whenever I want to do it and nobody can stop me. That's the attitude I have."

Suddenly, just as well as the conversation had gotten off to a good start, it takes a turn for the worst. Sharon begins to dominate the conversation and puts the entire focus on her. She doesn't let Alex get a word in at any time.

"I love the finer things in life. I guess you can say I have very expensive taste," Sharon says. "I am very particular about the clothes I buy, the jewelry I wear, and even the makeup I put on. I don't like anything cheap..."

The more she rambles on and on about herself, the more uninterested Alex becomes. Sharon's arrogance is really making an appearance, and it is definitely not one of her attractive features.

"Do you see the jewelry I'm wearing?" Sharon asks Alex. "This was a special order from Tiffany's flagship store on Fifth Avenue in New York. I dated a guy once that worked there and I got in good with the manager because I get a lot from there and they know what I like. Some of this I bought myself while a lot have been gifts. Everyone that knows me knows that if they are going to buy me a gift, it needs to cost no less than $250. That's just how I roll. My expectations are very high and most people, men included, can't handle that. I want to come and go as I please and take trips and vacation around the world. That's why I don't have any children. By the way, do you have any children?"

Oh, this has definitely gone downhill, Alex thinks to himself before answering. "As a matter of fact I do," Alex proudly responds. "Her name is Jasmine and she is eight years old."

"Hmmm...that's interesting," Sharon says. "Answer this for me: if we were together and we were going on a vacation, where would she stay while we were gone?"

Uncontrollably, Alex's face begins to frown because he is totally turned off with her line of questioning.

"Well, first of all, if we were together, we would have a discussion regarding where we were going and if it is kid-friendly; hopefully you would be comfortable enough and she would be comfortable enough with you that we could all go together and have a great time. Would that be a problem?" Alex asks.

"It's a problem if I wanted just us to go somewhere," Sharon replies. "I like to be spontaneous and do things on the spare of a moment and not have to worry about getting babysitters and all of that. That's why I refuse to have any children. They would cramp my style. Don't get me wrong. I'm sure your daughter is cute and adorable and all that, but I'm sure there would be times that we want to do something without her being around..."

The more she talks the more Alex clenches his teeth. Yet, he tries his very best to keep his composure without blowing up.

"Yes, there are times when getting a babysitter is necessary, but when a child or children are involved, you have to also take them into consideration and plan events, trips, vacations, WHATEVER, that will include them as well. Why should they be left out? There is no way that I'm going to kick my child to the curb for ANYONE. That's one thing I refuse to compromise on. If the person I am with can't accept and understand that, then she is not supposed to be in our lives in the first place," Alex says with a straight face.

"Hmmmm, well, I see you're very passionate about that."

"Yes ma'am, I am," Alex declares. "I don't mess around when it comes to that."

"Mmmm hmmm," Sharon says as she slowly shakes her head up and down and does not say another word.

Alex looks at his watch.

"I know it's getting late and I'm sure you have a busy day tomorrow at the boutique. I promise not to keep you out too late."

"Yes. I am expecting some clients early tomorrow afternoon and will be open to the public as well. Busy will be an understatement. There is a lot of money to be made and I want to be the one to make it. What do you have planned for tomorrow?" asks Sharon.

"Jasmine and I have a busy day with church, errands to run, and, of course, get a nice Sunday nap in," Alex replies.

"Church? Oh, I don't do the church thing," Sharon exclaims. Alex gives her a look that she is not expecting. "I haven't been to church in years and don't see a reason to go. I've been doing very well without church and don't see how it could benefit me now. I've got everything I need and more. If it's working for you, I'm glad it is. It's just not my thing."

Alex is completely silent at this point. Speechless. Sharon looks at him and notices that he is becoming detached, almost annoyed or upset. Unfortunately, she doesn't care and proceeds to display her arrogance even more. Alex does not get a chance to participate in the conversation much, not that he wants to at this point. After enduring several more minutes of torture, Alex feels relieved when the waiter comes back around to check on them.

"Can I get either of you anything else?" the waiter asks. "Will you be having dessert today?"

"No, thank you. I'll have the check now, please," Alex says, with emphasis on the word please, as he takes out his credit card and gives it to the waiter.

"I'll be right back with your receipt," the waiter says as he takes away the plates from the table.

After a few minutes of silence and foot tapping, the waiter comes back with the receipt and Alex's credit card. Alex signs it, leaves a nice tip, and they get up from the table and head for the car. Even though he is furious and can't wait for this date to end, he's still a gentleman and opens her door and treats her like a man should treat a lady. The car ride is a quiet one. No one wants to say anything and the only thing that can be heard are the other cars on the road. After several minutes of driving, he pulls up to Sharon's driveway, gets out, opens her door and walks her to her front door. As she opens her front door, Alex reaches out his hand to shake hers and says,

"You have a wonderful rest of the evening. I wish you well in your boutique and in all you aspire to do. Take care."

"Thank you, Alex," Sharon says, shaking his hand. "Thanks for taking me to the museum and to dinner. I really appreciate it."

"No problem. Bye," Alex says as he walks quickly back to his car and drives off. He comes out of her driveway and stops at the end of the street and sends a text to Nia:

Hey Nia! I'm headed your way to get Jazzy. Date was horrible. Details later. See ya in a few. Alex

When he arrives at Nia's house, Jasmine jumps into his arms and gives him a kiss on the cheek.

"How was your date, Daddy?" Jasmine asks.

"Yeah," Nia chimes in afterwards. "What happened?"

"Well, she is a very beautiful woman who owns a boutique and runs a very successful business. The problem is that she's self-centered and arrogant. She is looking for a Sugar Daddy and that's not me. She made it a point to mention that all of her jewelry was special made by 'Tiffany & Company' and she doesn't wear anything cheap. But the thing that really turned me off was the fact that she does not have a desire to be around children or want anything to do with them," Alex explains. "She is too absorbed with self and I can't deal with that. She even had the nerve to tell me that if we were together and were going on a trip, I'd need to find a babysitter for Jasmine. Oh, and she doesn't like going to church. She feels that she doesn't need God and she has everything she needs."

Nia stood there amazed.

"I can't believe her. I really hate that things didn't go well but I am glad that she showed her true colors early so you would not have to find out about her craziness later on after you've invested a lot of time and energy into her. Keep your head up. Something great will happen. I know it will," Nia says.

"We will see what happens," Alex says. "Hopefully the next time will be better."

Alex thanks Nia for letting Jasmine hang with her and Jasmine gives her a hug and a kiss as they leave out. Alex gets Jasmine in the car and they go home. All the way home, Alex talks with Jasmine about what she did at Nia's house. She talks about all the fun they had and the snacks they ate and mentions a little about their girl talk. She assures him they didn't talk about anything bad, that it was all great conversation. He laughs a little and shakes his head because he's sure Nia said some off the wall things to her. Once they get home, Alex tells Jasmine to get her pajamas on and get ready for bed. When she is dressed for bed, Alex comes to her room and they talk more.

"Daddy, I'm sorry that your date wasn't good," Jasmine says to Alex.

"That's OK, baby girl. Maybe the next one will be better."

"It will," Jasmine continues. "I know it will. So when are we going to look at the website again? Can we do it tomorrow?"

"I guess we can," Alex answers. "Hopefully, I will have better luck."

"Can I help you look again, Daddy?" Jasmine asks.

"Absolutely," Alex replies. "You know I can't do this without you. I always want to get your input."

"Yea!" Jasmine says as she jumps up and gives Alex a hug and a kiss on his cheek. Then she gets under the covers. As always, they say their prayers and Alex turns off her light. He goes to his room and prepares for bed.

The next morning, Alex and Jasmine get up and have a wonderful time at church. After service, they grab a bite to eat and head back home so they can get back on the dating website and look for another date for Alex. Once they're home and have changed clothes, Jasmine immediately heads to Alex's office and turns on his computer. He finds her waiting for him to get logged on so they can begin the search. Alex sits down, gets logged on, and they both go through a number of profiles and pictures. They search for what seems like hours and can't seem to agree or see anyone that interests them. But as they continue to scroll through, Jasmine spots someone.

"Daddy! Stop!" she says. "What about her?" she asks, as she points to a picture.

Alex looks at the picture and her name—Monique. Based on her image, his interest is peaked so he clicks on her profile. She's forty-three, divorced, and has two children. She is a bank manager who enjoys walks in the park, cooking, reading, and listening to music. He continues to read more, and begins to like what he sees.

"Do you think I should contact her?" Alex asks.

"I think you should," Jasmine confidently says, nodding her head. "She's pretty and she may be nice. I think you should give her a chance."

"OK. If you think so, I will contact her. With your approval."

Alex composes a message to Monique and then he clicks the send button with a little reluctance. After only a few minutes, he receives a response from her and they begin chatting back and forth. Once Jasmine realizes that the chat may continue for some time, she kisses Alex on the cheek and goes into the living room to watch television.

Alex stays on the computer for almost an hour and when he is done, he feels good about the communication with Monique. He walks into the living room to tell Jasmine all about it. Instead, he finds her taking a nap on the sofa with the television still on. He stands over her and looks at how peaceful she is sleeping, thankful that she fully supports his moving forward. He sits on the other end of the couch and peacefully drifts off to sleep.

After about two hours, Jasmine is up from her nap, standing over Alex looking at him while he's lying down. He is not asleep; he just has his eyes closed; yet he can feel that someone is looking at him. He opens one eye and sees Jasmine staring at him.

"Little lady, what are you doing?" Alex mumbles.

"Oh, nothing," Jasmine answers. "Just waiting on you to wake up.

What did you and that lady talk about?"

"That lady's name is Monique and we just talked. Nothing major. I'd rather talk to her in person to try to get to know her better," Alex says. "We will probably chat a few more times before we go out on a date."

"Can I meet her too?" Jasmine asks with a pleading look in her eyes.

"I don't think so, baby girl," Alex explains. "The person I want you to meet is the one I know will be around for a long time, and right now, that person has not shown up yet. You'll meet someone in due time. I'll make sure of that."

"OK. I'd like that very much," Jasmine says with a smile on her face.

They joyfully hang out the rest of the day watching television, laughing, dancing, and acting silly. These are the moments that continue to help them get over the pain of losing Gabrielle. They take advantage of every opportunity to bring laughter and happiness into their lives.

Later that night, when Jasmine is in the bed and Alex is in his room, he lies there in deep thought and begins to question whether or not he should be dating.

How can I ever love the way that I love Gabrielle? Can anyone possibly be as good a mom to Jazzy as Gabrielle? It's probably a waste of time to get back in the dating game. At this day and time, it's hard to know people for who they really are. What are the odds that I will meet someone worthwhile on a dating website? But then Alex remembers what his pastor advised him, as well as the words of his friends on their recent trip to Petey's. Maybe finding love again is possible, and will make life more fulfilling then being alone. What if Gabrielle is looking down on us, giving us a blessing to move forward?

He goes back and forth in his mind for quite some time. But mostly thinking about Jasmine, he ultimately makes the decision to give love another chance. So he goes to sleep that night with a mind made up and all ready to tackle to upcoming workweek.

A few days later, Alex receives a notification from the dating website app on his cell phone. It's Monique. They exchange a few pleasantries and eventually agree on a time where they can meet in person. After their conversation, Alex can feel nervousness creeping up again. He doesn't like the emotional roller coaster involved in trying to meet the right person, getting his hopes up seems to be very risky. He doesn't want to have an experience like he had on his previous date. He and Monique schedule a time to get together for this upcoming Saturday evening to go to a movie and possibly grab a little something to eat.

Once Alex gets off work and picks Jasmine up from school, he tells her about the date.

"Remember that lady I was chatting with the other day?" Alex asks.

"Yes sir. Monique, right?"

"That's right. Well, she and I are going on a date this Saturday."

"That's awesome, Daddy!" Jasmine shouts. "What are you all going to do?"

"We are going to the movies and maybe grab something to eat afterwards," Alex responds.

"That sounds like fun. I'm sure you'll have a good time."

"I sure hope so," Alex continues. "This dating stuff is getting worrisome."

"You will be fine," Jasmine reassures Alex. "Like I told you before, the perfect person is out there. She'll come."

"I sure hope you're right," Alex says.

"Just wait and see Daddy, she'll show up when you least expect it."

"OK."

"Can I go over to Auntie Nia's or Auntie Corrine's house while you're at the movies?" Jasmine asks.

"I'll contact them and see if they are available. I'll let you know."

"OK," Jasmine says, as she goes to her room to start on her homework.

Alex takes out his phone and composes a group text to Nia and Corrine asking about their availability for the upcoming weekend:

Hey Ladies! I hope all is well. Quick question. Are any of you ladies available this weekend for a couple of hours? I have a date Saturday and was wondering if either one of you could let Jazzy hang with you until after my date. Please let me know. Thanks! Alex

After a few minutes, Alex gets a reply.

Nia: *I'm available. I'd love for us to hang out.*

Corrine: *I'm available as well. Hey Nia. Let's make it a girl's night. We can get the other ladies involved and we could have a good time. Let me know.*

Nia: *That's perfect! I'll call the other ladies and we can make it happen. Alex, I'll pick Jazzy up from your place. We'll take good care of her.* ☺

Alex: *Oh Lord! Should I be concerned?!!?!? LOL!*

Nia: *Whatever dude! You just worry about your date and we'll take care of Jazzy.*

Alex: *LOL! OK. Thanks ladies!!!*

Right before bed, Alex lets Jasmine know that she will be hanging out with all the ladies while he goes out with Monique, which makes her very excited. Because of her excitement, it doesn't take her long to fall asleep after she says her prayers with Alex. He turns off her light and heads to bed.

For the rest of the week, things seem to be going great between Alex and Monique. They talk and exchange texts and e-mails consistently, enjoying every minute. From their communications, she doesn't seem to have any similarity to Sharon (at least he hopes not). They confirm their date for Saturday evening and even plan out what movie they want to see and where they can go afterwards. Alex is having a good feeling about this. Could this be the one? Only time will tell.

CHAPTER NINE

A Second Try

Saturday evening arrives and Alex begins preparing for his outing with Monique. Jasmine is acting as his fashion coordinator and making sure he looks nice for the date. She helps him pick out clothes and shoes and even selects the cologne he should wear. Since it's a casual evening for going to the movies, Alex is dressed in a nice pair of jeans, a brown shirt, and some brown moccasin loafers.

"Daddy, you look very nice today," Jasmine declares.

"Thank you, baby girl," Alex responds, giving Jasmine a quick kiss on the cheek. "I couldn't have done it without you. Thank you very much for all your help."

"I'm happy to help. I want to make sure you look your best."

"And you have done a great job at it, too. I really appreciate that," Alex replies.

"It's my pleasure. Maybe since I'm doing such a good job, you can increase my allowance," Jasmine says, only half-jokingly, with her signature giggle and smile.

Alex laughs.

"I'll take that into consideration. We'll see."

While they are putting the final touches on Alex's attire for the evening, the doorbell rings. Jasmine runs to the door and looks out the side window. Nia, Corrine, Keiko, and Hannah are waiting at the door. Jasmine lets them in and they all shower her with hugs and kisses. When they walk in, they eye Alex and decide to tease him.

"Well, well, well!" says Nia. "Look what we have here, ladies. A strapping, well-dressed, and good-smelling young man here in our midst. He must be from another planet because you can't find that around here."

Everyone bursts into laughter, including Alex.

"Hey big brother!" Nia says, as she gives him a hug.

"Hey crazy Nia. Ladies, how are you all doing tonight?" Alex asks.

"We're fine. Are you ready to paint the town red?" Keiko asks.

"I don't know about painting the town, but hopefully at least have a nice time," Alex replies.

"So who is the lucky lady? What's her name?" Corrine asks.

"Her name is Monique and she is a divorcee with two children. She's a manager at a bank," Alex replies.

"When are we going to meet her? Do we need to meet you all at the movies so we can check her out?" Alicia asks.

"No, No, NO!" Alex says. "I don't need you all to come up there embarrassing me. I'll tell you like I told Jasmine: I will not bring anyone around her unless I know without a shadow of a doubt she is the one for me and meets Jasmine's seal of approval. I'm sure you all will give your input as well."

"You doggone right!" Nia says as they all erupt into laughter.

"You ladies have a great time tonight and please stay out of trouble, please. Be a good role model for my daughter," Alex says with a straight face.

"Like I told you before, we got her. You don't have to worry about a thing," Nia says. "She's in the best of hands with her aunties."

"OK. You all have fun," Alex says. "I'll text you when the date is over and I'm en route to picking Jasmine up."

"You just go ahead and enjoy yourself," Nia says. "Jasmine can actually stay at either one of our houses tonight. We can have her ready for church in the morning."

"Can I Daddy? Can I Daddy? Please? Can I?" Jasmine pleads.

"If it's OK with your aunties, that's fine with me," Alex answers.

"Yes!" Jasmine says as she runs to her room to grab clothes for church the next morning.

"I really hope you have a great time, Alex," Corrine says. "I'm very proud of you for taking these steps in dating."

Thanks Corrine. It's kinda scary but I think I'm up for the challenge. Plus, Jasmine is really adamant about me getting back out there. It's amazing how supportive she has been through this process."

"She just wants to see her daddy happy," Hannah says. "You're a great guy Alex, and you deserve to be happy."

"Thank you very much, Hannah," Alex says.

"Yeah. As long as you're happy, Jazzy is happy. When Jazzy is happy, you're happy. And when you all are happy, we all are happy," Keiko adds.

"I really appreciate the kind words ladies. I really do," Alex interjects. "But you all better get out of here so I can get going."

They all laugh and Alex calls for Jasmine to hurry along so they all can leave. Once she comes out of her room with her bag packed, she gives Alex a hug and kiss and wishes him well on his date. When they leave, he gets into his car, puts Monique's address in his GPS and drives to her house. Once he gets there, he walks up to the door and rings the doorbell. After a few minutes of waiting, he hears a number of footsteps coming towards the door. The footsteps stop and suddenly the door opens, revealing two little boys in the doorway.

"Hello. May I help you?" asked the older of the two boys.

"Yes sir, you may. I'm here to see Monique. Is she home?" Alex politely asks the boy.

"Who are you?" asked the older boy.

"My name is Alex. What's your name?"

"I'm Aiden and this is my little brother, Evan."

Alex reaches out his hand and shakes both of their hands.

"Pleasure to meet you guys. Could you call your mother to the door, please?" Alex asks.

"MOM!" Evan yells without moving. "Alex is at the door for you."

"I'll be right there," Monique yells back.

After a few more minutes of Alex standing in the doorway and having small talk with Aiden and Evan, Monique comes to the door and seems to be out of breath.

"Hi Alex. I'm Monique. It's a pleasure to meet you. I see you have already met my boys."

"Pleasure to meet you as well and yes, your boys and I have met and we have been having a nice conversation," Alex says. "So are we ready to go?" Alex asks.

"Well, we have a bit of a problem," Monique says.

"What's that?" Alex asks.

"My babysitter bailed on me at the last minute and I can't find anyone this late in the evening," Monique explains.

"It's no problem. I understand," Alex says. "If we need to reschedule, that's fine. Just let me know what day and time is good for you."

"Well, I was thinking that we could all go out together. Let's take the boys to Chuck E. Cheese's or something so they can run around while we talk," Monique suggests.

Alex tries his best to not let a negative expression show on his face, but he is not happy and turned off by the fact that she is basically changing their date plans without taking his thoughts into consideration. He is totally thrown off guard. Regardless of how he feels, he still wants to give this date a chance.

"OK. If you don't have a problem with me being around the boys so early on, then let's go have some fun."

"Great," Monique exclaims. "Alright boys, go get your tokens. We're going to Chuck E. Cheese's."

The boys cheer and both slap Alex a high five as they run to their room to get their leftover tokens. After that, they all get in Alex's car, fasten their seat belts, and proceed to go have some fun. As they approach Chuck E. Cheese's, Alex notices that the parking lot is full and there is even a small line outside the building.

"Wow. It looks like everyone in Charlotte is out tonight. Would you like to go somewhere else?" Alex asks with a glimmer of hope that she may change her mind.

"No," Monique replies. "The line is not that long and it's probably not that crowded in there anyway."

"OK," Alex says as he grits his teeth, trying his best not to say something mean. He pulls into a parking spot and they all file out of the car. Aiden and Evan are jumping all over the place, running across the parking lot without looking at oncoming traffic, Monique is yelling at them to watch out and threatens to spank them if they didn't stop running. They eventually get to the end of the short line and have to wait several minutes to get in. Once they get through the door, they see that the place is packed, loud, and kids are running around everywhere. It's mass hysteria. Fortunately, they are able to find a table to sit while the boys run around and play games. Alex and Monique can barely hear each other speak and they have to resort to yelling in order to be heard. As they talk, the conversation begins to be interrupted by the boys coming to ask for money to buy more tokens. When the boys approach Monique for money, she looks at Alex and expects for him to give them money. So he reaches into his pocket and gives each boy five dollars and off they run to get more tokens. In addition to providing money for games, Alex ends up paying for pizza and drinks. After the food is brought to the table, Alex searches through the multitude of children in the play area for Aiden and Evan. Once he finds them, he tells them that it's time to eat and they run off to the table. The boys immediately tear into the pizza without saying grace. Not only are they eating like savages, they start a mini food fight at the table, throwing sausage and pepperoni at each other and trying to toss pieces into their mouths. They are not always successful, so a lot of food eventually ends up on the floor. To make matters worse, they also spill their drinks. Monique is slow to help control them or to even clean up the mess. Alex frantically gets napkins to clean up the mess but Monique is slow to help. At this point, it's obvious that Alex is becoming more and more frustrated. Monique tells the boys to play a little while longer so she and Alex can talk.

"I take it you have a problem with my boys," Monique says with an attitude.

"What are you talking about?" Alex asks as he cleans soda spills off the table.

"Ever since we left my house, it seems like you've had an attitude since my boys are with us. Do you have a problem with a woman with children?"

"No I don't. I have a daughter of my own. Your boys are not the issue. The issue I have is that I can't get to know you better if I can barely hear you in this place. We're in a place that's not private at all and I can't talk to you without yelling. This is not my ideal first date. I really wouldn't have been upset if we had decided to reschedule our date. I totally understand. Things happen. I get that. But I had specific plans for us this evening and coming to Chuck E. Cheese's was not part of those plans.

"Well Mister. I'll tell you what. Since coming to Chuck E. Cheese's is beneath you and you have issues with my boys, I think it's best that we wrap this evening up and you can take us home since we are such an inconvenience," Monique says, as she gets up from the table and goes to get her sons.

"We are going to the restroom and when we come back, we'll be ready to leave," Monique says, as she takes her sons by the hands and leads them to the restrooms. Alex looks around the area where they were eating and it looks like a tornado came through. Alex is embarrassed. He motioned for a worker to come to the table.

"Ma'am, I am very sorry about the mess. If you need me to help you clean this up, I will," Alex politely says.

"It's no problem, sir. This is mild compared to what is normally left to clean."

"I still feel really bad, so please take this," Alex says as he hands her a twenty-dollar bill. "It's the least I can do to convey how sorry I am for the mess."

"Thank you, sir. You really don't have to do this."

"Please. I insist," Alex says. "Thank you for your help."

"It was my pleasure. You all have a great evening."

Alex cannot believe how Monique made it seem like he had a problem with her children. That was furthest from the truth. He just wanted to have a nice evening getting to know her. When she gets back with the boys, she walks past Alex and goes right to the car. Once everyone is loaded in and seat belts are fastened, they go back to Monique's house. As they pull up in the driveway, the younger son, Evan, says,

"Mr. Alex?"

"Yes sir?"

"Will you be our new daddy?"

"Evan!" Monique yells. "Don't ask him that. We may not be seeing him anymore."

"Aww man!" Aiden says. "He's a lot cooler than the other guy from last week."

"I hope you guys had a good time," Alex says, to try to change the conversation. "It sure looked like you did."

"Yes, we did. Thank you," says Aiden.

"You're welcome," Alex responds.

Everyone gets out of the car and the boys run to the front door. When Alex and Monique get to the front door, Monique opens it and the boys give Alex a high five and run inside. Before Monique goes into the house, she unleashes some last words for Alex.

"This will be the last time you ever see me. Since you seem to have a problem with me and my children, I think it's best if we don't try to take this any further. You seem like a good guy but I don't think you are my type or will be a good fit for my boys. Good night." With that, she walks into the house and slams the door.

Alex is still perplexed and doesn't even know what he did wrong. All he can do is shake his head, get back in his car, and drive home. As he is driving home, he calls Nia to see how Jasmine is doing. She doesn't answer so he leaves a message. A few minutes later he receives a text from Nia:

The girls are having a great time. Leave us alone turkey. Enjoy your date. LOL!

Alex laughs and continues home. Once he gets there, he gets out of his clothes and changes into his pajamas. He sits on the couch and seriously thinks about not going on another date because the last two have been total disasters. He decides not to make a definite decision until he consults with Jasmine. As he sits on the couch channel surfing, he eventually falls asleep.

Alex doesn't wake up until the next morning. The sound of the alarm on his phone is what eventually wakes him up. He gets showered and ready for church so he can meet Jasmine there.

He is finally reunited with Jasmine after the church service and they share hugs and kisses.

"Thank you, ladies for looking after my princess last night. I really appreciate it," Alex says to Nia and Corrine.

"It's was no problem at all," Nia says. "We are going to do this more often, especially when you go out on your dates."

"I don't know if that will ever happen again," Alex admits. "This one was a total disaster. I'll have to tell you about that one later."

"That doesn't sound good at all," Corrine says. "It's almost time for our monthly get together anyway. Maybe you can give us all the details then. I'll send out a date later this week."

"Sounds good. I'll be looking forward to it," says Alex.

"Thank you aunties for a great evening. I had a lot of fun," Jasmine tells Nia and Corrine as she gives them hugs.

"You all enjoy the rest of your day. Talk to you soon," Alex says as they walk to his car. Alex is not his talkative self and Jasmine is also particularly quiet. Alex figures she is probably tired from the exciting evening she had with the girls the previous night. Alex is quiet because he's still perplexed about the outcome of the date with Monique. Once they get home, they grab a quick bite to eat and relax on the couch until it's time for them to go to bed.

Jasmine doesn't ask about how Alex's date went, but she does talk with him about what she did that evening and how much fun she had. When they are both ready for bed, Alex and Jasmine say their prayers together and he tucks her in for the night. Alex goes to his room and for some reason, he is not able to go to sleep. He tosses and turns; yet nothing helps. A lot is on his mind. He begins to seriously consider not going on any more dates. The two painful experiences he's had are really making him rethink going down that road again. While in deep thought, he suddenly hears a knock at his bedroom door.

"Daddy, can I come in?" Jasmine asks, sounding as if she'd been crying.

"Come on, baby girl," Alex says.

Jasmine climbs into bed with Alex and says, "I can't sleep. May I stay in here with you?"

"Sure you can, sweetheart," Alex says as he makes room for her in the bed. He puts covers over her and she puts her head on his chest and her arms around his body and begins to weep.

"What's wrong, baby?" Alex asks.

"Nothing," Jasmine says. "I just really miss Mama."

She begins to cry harder, which makes Alex cry along with her.

"I miss her too, baby. I miss her too."

They eventually cry themselves to sleep.

For the next few weeks, Alex doesn't look at the dating website, nor does he get any notifications from anyone. Dating is the last thing on his mind. But then one day, all of a sudden, he gets a notification on his cell phone from the website. He's puzzled because he is usually the one that initiates the first contact. This is different. Someone has contacted him. He clicks on her profile to read and he notices that he also has a private message from her. Her profile reads:

Brooklyn, Single, 38, Dental Assistant, no children, plays the violin and piano, loves music including old school R&B, attends church and enjoys sports, cooking and having quiet evenings at home.

Everything about this woman, including her beautiful looks, sparks an interest in Alex, but he is not sure if he should respond since he's decided to give up on dating. After pondering for a while, he decides to respond. The two of them engage in some brief conversation via the chat feature. They agree to chat later when the both get off work. Although Alex has some reservations, he decides to go ahead and communicate with her further. Later that evening, he and Jasmine are at his computer and he decides to show her the newest person he has chosen to communicate with.

"She is very pretty, Daddy," Jasmine states. "What do you think?"

"I agree. She is very pretty and she seems to have qualities that those other women didn't have," Alex points out. "If we decide to go out, hopefully I will find out quickly what she is really like."

"I'm sure you will," Jasmine responds. "When are you going on a date with her?"

"I'm not sure. We may talk about it when we chat a little later."

"OK. Have fun. I'm going to my room to read my book. I'll see you in a little while," Jasmine says as she gives Alex a kiss on the cheek.

"Thank you, sweetie. Happy reading!" Alex says.

Once Jasmine leaves the room, he pulls up Brooklyn's profile and types a message to her. A few minutes later, she replies. They chat back and forth for quite a while. In one of the messages, Brooklyn sends her phone number and asks Alex to call her. He writes down the number and he calls.

"Hello," says a voice on the other end of the phone.

"Hello. May I please speak with Brooklyn, please?" Alex asks.

"This is Brooklyn. Who am I speaking with?" she replies jokingly.

"This is Alex. You wanted me to give you a call."

"Who?" Brooklyn asks.

"It's Alex from eHarmony. You sent me your number to give you a call," Alex says.

"I'm sorry. You must have the wrong number," Brooklyn says attempting to keep herself from laughing.

"I apologize, ma'am. I must have dialed the wrong number. Have a great evening," Alex says, surprised at himself for getting the number wrong.

"Alex! Don't hang up. I was just joking," Brooklyn says as she bursts into laughter.

"Oh. I see you are a jokester. What have I gotten myself into?" Alex says, also bursting into laughter. "How are you doing today Ms. Brooklyn?"

"I am doing well, Mr. Alex. Thank you very much for calling."

"Thank you for allowing me to call and even making me believe I had the wrong number. Do you do this to all the guys that call you?"

"Actually, no. I normally don't do that, but from looking at your profile picture, you seemed like you have a good sense of humor."

"Really now? You can tell that just by looking at a picture?" Alex asks.

"Yes I can," Brooklyn responds. "You do have a good sense of humor don't you?"

"Yes I do."

"I rest my case."

After they exchange pleasantries, they engage in a long conversation, getting to know one another. They laugh, joke, and have a good time. To Alex, this is by far the best phone conversation he's had. They have so much fun talking that they lose track of time.

"I'd better get off the phone and tuck my daughter into bed." Alex says when he notices how late it is.

"Aww! That's sweet. How old is she?"

"Jasmine is eight years old."

"That's a beautiful name and I bet she is a beautiful girl. Be sure to kiss her good night," Brooklyn says.

"I do that every night. You have a good night as well," Alex continues. It was great talking to you. I hope we do it again soon."

"We will. Let's chat again tomorrow when you have time," Brooklyn suggests.

"I'd like that a lot. Good night."

"Good night, sir," Brooklyn says before she hangs up the phone.

Alex feels really good about this phone call but he doesn't get his hopes up too high. For the moment, he is happy just with what he has experienced. Alex goes into Jasmine's room and sees that she is sound asleep. He walks over to her bed and kisses her forehead. She slowly opens her eyes.

"Hi Daddy," Jasmine says, barely awake.

"Hey baby girl. Go back to sleep. I was just checking on you and wanted to kiss you good night."

"Ok, but we didn't say our prayers," Jasmine says, attempting to sit up in the bed."

"Shhhhh. You go back to sleep. I'll say them for us. You get you some sleep," Alex whispers.

"Ok. Good night, Daddy. I love you."

Jasmine drifts back to sleep.

"I love you, too, Princess," Alex gives her another kiss on the forehead, covers her up, and goes to his room. After he gets his pajamas on, he says a prayer and goes to sleep.

For the next several weeks, Alex and Jasmine go about their normal routine as usual. From time to time, Alex and Brooklyn talk or exchange text messages quite often and the more they talk, the more they find out how much they have in common and how much they are attracted to one another. Each conversation gets easier and Alex gradually gets comfortable letting her get to know more about him. During one of their conversations, Alex gets the nerve to boldly ask her out on a date.

"Brooklyn," Alex says. "I was wondering; if you aren't busy this weekend, would you like to catch a movie and grab a bite to eat afterwards? If you are busy, I totally understand.

"Are you kidding?" Brooklyn replies. "I'd love to go to the movies. I haven't gone in a long time. What would you like to see?"

"I think I'll surprise you. From what I can tell, we like some of the same things, so I think you will like what I choose."

"Great! I love surprises," Brooklyn says. "I'm sure I won't be disappointed."

"I don't think you will be. I'll make sure of that. I'll check out some times and let you know. Just let me know what will work for you."

"Any time will work for me. I'm really looking forward to this date," Brooklyn says.

"So am I," Alex replies. "Send me your address and I'll pick you up. I'll be sure to let you know the time of the movie later today and we can go from there."

"I'll send it to you when we get off the phone," Brooklyn says. "You had better get back to what you were doing. Don't let me hold you up. I'm sure we will be chatting later."

"Absolutely," Alex responds, happily. "Have a good rest of the day and I'll chat with you later. Bye bye."

"Bye now."

Alex can't help but to smile from ear to ear. He feels as though Brooklyn is different from the other women he's communicated with and hopes that good things will continue to happen. He finishes his work for the day and heads out to pick up Jasmine from school. Once she gets in the car and is buckled in, they drive off and Alex asks her about her day.

"How was school today, baby girl?" Alex asks.

"It was OK. It was kinda boring today for some reason."

"I'm sorry to hear about that. Maybe what I'm about to tell you will pick you up a little."

"Oh yeah. What's that?" Jasmine asks with sudden excitement in her voice.

"Well, do you remember that lady on the computer that contacted me a few weeks ago?"

"I think I do. Her name is Brooklyn, right?" Jasmine asks.

"That's right," Alex exclaims. "Well, we are going out on a date this weekend."

"That's great, Daddy!" Jasmine exclaims. "What are you all going to do?"

"We're going to catch a movie and maybe grab a bite to eat. Nothing big," Alex declares. "I just hope this one works out. I don't want a repeat of the other dates."

"I think this one will work out and I'm sure you'll have a great time," Jasmine assures Alex.

"I'll keep my fingers and toes crossed," Alex says. "Hey- let's do something different today."

"Like what, Daddy?"

"You and I have not gone out for a daddy-daughter dinner date in a while. I think today will be a perfect opportunity."

"That sounds like fun, I would like that a lot!"

"We'll go to your favorite place. Is that fine with you?"

"Yes sir! That would be awesome," Jasmine exclaims.

They make a slight detour and head towards Jasmine's favorite restaurant. Once they get there and get seated, they begin to talk, laugh, and have a great time together. They also enjoy a great meal.

"Jasmine. I have to ask you a serious question," Alex says.

"OK. You can ask me whatever you like," Jasmine responds.

"OK. My question is, does it bother you that I've been going out on dates? How do you really feel about that?"

Without any hesitation, she answers very maturely,

"I don't have a problem with you going out on dates at all. I want you to be happy and that's all that matters. You do such a great job being my dad that you need some time with other grownups. Even though I'll always miss Mommy, I want you to have fun, be happy, and find a nice lady. You deserve it."

It takes everything within Alex not to shed a tear. As amazed as he is at what Jasmine tells him, he is happier that she doesn't disapprove of his dating; he is actually relieved.

"Thank you, baby girl. I really appreciate your honesty," Alex says, admiring her insight. It's at moments like this that he reflects on the influence of Gabrielle upon Jasmine's life. "If at any point, you don't want me to, I won't do it anymore. I have to take your feelings into consideration as well. I want you to be happy too."

"Daddy, as long as you are happy, I'm happy."

"Thank you, sweetheart. That really means a lot to me."

They finish their meals and share a strawberry sundae. After eating, they head home. Once they get there, Jasmine goes straight to the kitchen table and starts on her homework. Alex gets on his computer and looks up movie times for the upcoming weekend. He sees a couple times that may work so he sends Brooklyn a text to see what she thinks.

Alex: *Hey you! I have some times for you to consider. What about 6:45 or 7:30? Just let me know.*

Brooklyn: *7:30 is perfect!* ☺ *My address is 6108 Bircher Ave.*

Alex: *It's a date. I'll pick you up around 7. Enjoy the rest of your evening. Chat later!*

Brooklyn: *u 2!*

Alex shuts down his computer and goes into the kitchen to check on Jasmine. Once she is finished and her work is checked, she takes a bath, gets her pajamas on, and gets in the bed. She and Alex say their prayers and he tucks her in as usual.

"Since I will be going on a date this Saturday, you know you can spend the night with your Aunt Nia," Alex informs Jasmine.

"Yes!" Jasmine says. "That's going to be fun!"

"I'm sure it will be. Good night, baby girl. I love you."

"Good night, and I love you more," Jasmine says as Alex gives her a kiss on the forehead and a warm, tight hug. When he gets to his bedroom, Alex grabs his cell phone to send a text message to Nia:

Alex: *Hey Nia! Sorry for the late text. I have another date this Saturday. Could Jazzy hang out with you again? Let me know. Thx.*

Nia: *Hey Alex! No prob. Just let me know what time to pick her up and I'll be there.*

Alex: *Thanks. You can get her about 6.*

Nia: *Gotcha. See ya then. Nite nite.*

Alex: *LOL! Good nite.*

When he's done texting, he gets dressed for bed, lies down, and falls asleep almost instantly.

CHAPTER TEN

Third Time's A Charm…Right?!?!?!

Once Saturday afternoon arrives, Alex begins getting ready for his date with Brooklyn while Jasmine gets some of her things together to spend the evening with Nia. As Jasmine packs clothes, Alex can't seem to keep it together—dropping things and running into walls. He begins talking to himself to try to calm his nerves.

As he finally calms down, the doorbell rings. It's Nia, Corrine, Kieko, Hannah, and Alicia at the door ready to hang out with Jasmine again. They all come inside the house singing "Ladies Night" by Kool and the Gang. Jasmine runs out of her room and hugs all of the ladies and starts to sing with them. Alex just stands there shaking his head and laughing.

"I see you ladies are ready for another fun-filled evening, huh?" Alex laughs.

"Yes we are, and we are going to have so much fun," Nia says. "Hey Jazzy! Are you ready to party? Let's roll out!"

After they say their good byes and exchange hugs and kisses, they all leave out singing their song once more. Before Jasmine leaves out, Alex gives her a hug and kiss.

"Have fun, baby girl. Make sure they all stay out of trouble," Alex jokingly says to Jasmine.

"I will Daddy. Have fun on your date. Can't wait to hear about it."

Jasmine runs out of the house to catch up with the other ladies. They all wish him well on his date, get in the car, and drive off to have another fun-filled girl's night out. After they drive off, Alex calls Brooklyn to let her know that he is on his way to pick her up. She tells him that she is ready and very excited about their date.

He gets into his car, enters her address in his GPS, and follows the instructions to her house. As Alex is driving, he begins to get an uneasy feeling; however, he just attributes it to his nerves. But for some reason, he can't seem to shake it so he deals with it the best he can. When he finally arrives at her house, he gets out of the car, walks to the front door, and rings the doorbell.

When the door opens, Brooklyn stands there with a big, beautiful smile and says, "You must be Alex. I'm Brooklyn. Please come in."

"Thank you and yes, I am Alex. Pleasure to meet you Brooklyn," he says as he reaches out his hand to shake hers.

"I'm a hugger, so give me a hug," Brooklyn says as she approaches him and gives him a nice, warm hug.

With that being said, Alex gets a smile on his face that's big enough to be seen miles away. He hugs her then steps back to look at her. She is casually dressed and very beautiful.   She's wearing a nice pair of jeans, a gray shirt, some beautiful silver jewelry, and black shoes. She has a very nice short haircut that accentuates her facial structure and attire. Alex is very pleased at what he sees but prays to himself this will not be another date from hell.

"Well, if you are ready, we should get going. The movie starts at seven thirty" Alex says.

"I am ready but no need to rush. The movie theater is only ten minutes from here. We'll get there in plenty of time," Brooklyn says confidently.

When they leave the house, Brooklyn closes her front door and she and Alex walk to his car. He opens her door and she responds with a look of amazement.

"Wow. You actually open doors for women?" Brooklyn asks.

"Yes I do. I always have and always will," Alex replies. Brooklyn smiles as Alex closes her door.

"So, are you going to tell me what we are going to see?" Brooklyn asks during the drive.

"Nope," says Alex. "It's a surprise. I want to see if my instincts are correct."

"OK Mr. Instincts. We'll see," Brooklyn laughs.

On the way there, they enjoy engaging conversation, which calms Alex's nerves just a bit.

They arrive at the theater, find a great parking spot, and walk to the ticket window. When Alex tells the booth attendant that he needs two tickets for the movie Fast & Furious 6, Brooklyn gasps and grabs a hold to Alex's arm.

"Oh my goodness," she whispers. "I've wanted to see this movie and I just haven't had a chance to see it. I guess your instincts were correct Mr. Alex. That scored you a few more brownie points."

"So you mean to tell me that we have not been on our date for an hour yet and you've already got me on the brownie point system? Dang. I must be special."

They both laugh.

"Yes you are. You just need to make sure you don't get any points taken away for bad behavior."

"I'll make sure I stay on my best behavior then," Alex says, as they walk to the concession stand to get snacks.

They make their way into the theater to find seats, and thankfully they're early enough to have lots of options to choose from. Once they choose their seats, they make more small talk and laugh a little until the start of the previews. As the previews are playing, Brooklyn leans over and tells Alex,

"I hope you don't do a lot of talking during movies. If you do, I'll make you sit somewhere else."

"You don't have to worry about that," Alex responds. "I was about to tell you the same thing."

They both laugh and spend the rest of the time snacking and watching the movie.

After the movie is over, and they stand up to exit, Brooklyn hooks her arm with Alex's and they walk to the lobby of the theater.

"Are you hungry?" Alex asks Brooklyn.

"I am," she admits. "Do you have a taste for anything in particular?"

"No. Not really. Is there anything you have a taste for?"

"Strangely enough, I have a taste for some breakfast food," Brooklyn says.

"That sounds like a winner to me. I think we passed an IHOP on the way here didn't we?"

"We did, but I know of a place that's much better and it's not too far from here. It's a nice little place called Park Place Diner. They sell breakfast all day and it is very good."

"Well that sounds like the place we're headed to," Alex says, as they walk to the car and drive to the restaurant. When they get there and get seated, they begin to converse more and laugh more. So far, the evening is going well and Alex is earnestly having fun but still has that uneasy feeling he had earlier. Since the date is going good and they are having fun, he tries to ignore it.

The meals they order are very good, even to the point that they began to share their food with each other. They are having so much fun that the manager of the restaurant comes to their table to let them know it is time for the restaurant to close. Alex looks at his watch and is amazed at the time-it is after 1:00 a.m. They have completely lost track of time. Alex apologizes, pays the check, leaves a tip, and they both quickly go get in the car.

"I can't believe we closed that place down. I guess we were having too much fun, huh?" Alex says.

"Yes we were. This was a great evening. Thank you very much," Brooklyn says as she looks into Alex's eyes.

"It was my pleasure. It was a lot of fun. Too bad it's too late. I know you have to get home because it's way past your bedtime," Alex says laughing.

"You're absolutely correct," Brooklyn replies. "Usually I am in bed by ten, so this is way past my bedtime. It's going to be hard to get up to go to church but I have to get up. I hate missing church for any reason."

"I'm the same way," Alex replies. "I hate missing church as well. I make it a point to be there every week unless I have the flu or something."

"Wow! That's great to hear. Usually guys take advantage of every excuse not to go to church. To me, most of them miss out on so much and that's a shame."

"Well, I'm not one of those guys. My daughter and I love going to church and we have a good time. If you don't mind me asking, what church do you attend?"

"I'm a member of Northside Baptist," Brooklyn says.

"I've heard of your church. Your pastor is awesome. I've heard him before."

"Thanks. He's my uncle and I make sure he stays on top of his game. Where do you attend church?"

"I'm a member of New Grace Church," Alex replies.

"Bishop Palmer is your pastor, right?" Brooklyn asks.

"Yes, he is."

"I've met him and his wife a couple times. They are a lovely and powerful couple."

"They are very precious people and we love them dearly," Alex says.

"Yes they are. You mentioned you have a daughter. How old is she?"

"Jasmine is eight and she is my heart," Alex replies.

"I'm sure she is, "Brooklyn says. "Maybe one day when you're ready, you'll show me a picture of her. I bet she is a cutie."

"She is and I will one day. I gotta make sure you're going to be around a while," Alex says laughing.

"Ha ha, Mr. Man. You're very funny," Brooklyn says while laughing. "If being with you is this much fun and you're a nice guy, I can see myself being around for a while, if that's what you want."

"I like the sound of that," Alex admits. "Let's just take things one day at a time. So far, I like what I'm seeing."

"Uhhh, Alex. Do you know you've passed my house about five times already?" Brooklyn asks.

"I know," Alex replies. "I didn't want the date to end but I know I've got to get you home."

"Awww! That's sweet. Hopefully we will go out again soon."

"You can count on that. I'm looking forward to it," Alex says.

"Me too," Brooklyn says with a big smile.

Alex pulls up in Brooklyn's driveway and helps her out of the car. They walk up to her front door.

"Well, Ms. Brooklyn, you have finally made it home."

"Yes I have. Thank you again for a wonderful evening. I thoroughly enjoyed myself."

"I had an awesome time myself," Alex states.

"Drive safely and text me when you get home," Brooklyn says as she gives Alex a hug and a kiss on the cheek.

"Thank you, and I will. Good night!"

"Good night," Brooklyn says as she closes her door.

For the first time in a long time, Alex is on cloud nine and he's so happy that he survived the date with no problems. He can't help but to smile the entire drive home. Maybe things are beginning to turn around for him. It is possible that Brooklyn could possibly be a great match for him. He doesn't want to get his hopes up too much, he wants to go out with her more and see what she's really like. In the meantime, he's enjoying the moment. When he finally gets home, he takes off his clothes and puts on his pajamas. Once he is in bed, he texts Brooklyn to let her know he made it home safely.

Alex: *Hey Brooklyn! Just wanted to let you know that I've made it home ok. Thanks for a lovely evening. Hopefully we can do it again soon. Sweet dreams! Alex*

Brooklyn: *Hey Alex! Glad you made it home. I had a wonderful time too. Let's get together soon. We'll chat later. Good night!*

Alex turns off his light and goes to sleep.

The next morning, Alex gets up and prepares to go to church and to see Jasmine. After a soul-stirring sermon by Bishop Palmer, Alex meets up with Jasmine, Nia, and Corrine after service.

"Hey Daddy!" Jasmine yells as she runs into Alex's arms and gives him a big hug.

"Hey baby girl! How was your evening?" Alex asks.

"It was great," Jasmine says. "We girls had a lot of fun. When are we going to do it again?"

"I'm sure it will be real soon, Jazzy," Nia says. "We did have a great time. So how was your date, Mr. Reed?"

"Actually..." Alex starts. "It went very well and we will go out another time."

"That's great, Alex!" Corrine says. "Details. We want details."

"I can't give you details now. Maybe when we have the get together we were supposed to have some time ago, I'll fill everyone in on it," Alex says sarcastically.

"Well, that's all my fault," Corrine confesses. "I got so tied up at work that I completely forgot and apparently everyone else did too. Now that things have calmed down, I'll send something out this week to see if everyone is available."

"Ok. We'll hold you to it," Alex says.

"Yeah, plus, we need to get together. It's long overdue," Nia adds.

"Yes it is. I miss all of you guys and it'll be good to reconnect," Alex says. "We'll make it happen."

"Can I come too, Daddy?" Jasmine asks.

"Usually, we don't have little munchkins like you around, but we may have to make an exception this time," Nia says.

"Yes!" Jasmine exclaims with excitement.

"Thank you again for letting Jasmine hang with you ladies. I really appreciate it," Alex says.

"Thank you for letting her hang with us. We always have so much fun and can't wait to do it again," Corrine says.

"Thank you Auntie Nia. Thank you Auntie Corrine," Jasmine says as she gives both of them a hug and kiss.

They all say their goodbyes and go their separate ways. Alex and Jasmine get into the car and drive off. They talk about what they would like for dinner and Jasmine suggests that they get something out, bring it home, and stay in for the rest of the evening. Alex agrees and does just that. He's glad Jasmine suggested going home because he is so tired from the previous night's festivities with Brooklyn, that he prefers to have a nice, quiet evening at home.

After getting home and changing clothes, Alex and Jasmine sit at the dinner table, enjoy their meal, and have a good conversation.

"So, how was your date, Daddy?" Jasmine asks.

"It went very well. I was pleasantly surprised that everything went as well as it did."

"Do you like her?" Jasmine asks, as she sits forward in her chair with a huge smile on her face.

"She seems very nice and so far I like what I see," Alex explains. "I still have to get to know her better, hang out with her, and talk with her some more. I'm just taking it one day at a time."

"Will I get a chance to meet her?" Jasmine asks.

"Not right now, baby girl. Like I've told you before, I'm not going to bring a lot of people around you if they are not going to be around for a long period of time. I'd rather wait for that special person to come along that I know, without a shadow of a doubt, would be around for a very long time."

"I know you said that," Jasmine declares. "I was just trying to see if you were going to change your mind."

"No ma'am," Alex says with a chuckle. "I am not going to change my mind. However, if Brooklyn is the one, I'll be sure to let you meet her and you'll have a chance to get to know her as well. We will just have to wait and see."

"Ok. I tried," Jasmine states.

"Yes you did. Good try though."

They laugh, talk, and continue eating their dinner. Eventually they do their routine of getting dressed for bed, saying prayers, getting Jasmine tucked in, and Alex going into his room and falling fast asleep.

For the next month and a half, in addition to going about their normal daily routines, Alex and Brooklyn begin to talk more and, go out more. In fact, they start to develop feelings for one another. Whenever they go out, they hold hands and even share a kiss every now and then. Things are beginning to heat up and even though Alex is beginning to let his guard down and let Brooklyn into his world more, he still, from time to time, has that uneasy feeling. As much as he tries to shake that feeling, he is not able to; but he still somehow manages to suppress it and enjoy all the time he is afforded with Brooklyn.

One afternoon while Alex is at work, he gets a text message from Brooklyn that catches him by surprise:

Brooklyn: *Hey you! I hope your day is going well. Do you think you can find a babysitter for Thursday evening about 7-ish? I know we were planning to go out Saturday but I wanted to do something different. Let me cook dinner for you and let's stay in and make it a movie night at my place. How does that sound? Also, I have a little something for you too. Let me know. Kisses. Brooke*

Alex reads the text and he is beyond excited, wondering what the surprise is. All kinds of thoughts are going through his mind but he doesn't want to stress himself out trying to figure out what it is. So he replies to her text message:

Alex: *Hey there! All is well. Hope you're having a good day as well. I don't think I'll have a problem getting a babysitter, I just hope you can cook! LOL! Just kidding. I'll be happy to come over. I'll get back with you ASAP. Alex*

Brooklyn: *K*

Alex then promptly sends a text message to Nia and Corrine to see if they will be available to look after Jasmine while he dines with Brooklyn.

Alex: *Hey Ladies. Hope your day is well. Got a huge favor to ask. Are any of you available Thursday evening to hang with Jasmine for a few hours? Brooklyn and I are having dinner at her place. Please let me know when you can. Thx. Alex*

A few minutes later, he gets replies from Nia and Corrine:

Corrine: *Hey Brother! Sorry but Elijah and I have to attend a Par-*

ent/Teacher conference.

Nia: *Hey Alex! I don't have anything going on. She can hang out with me. What time do you want me to pick her up?*

Alex: *Thanks Corrine. No problem. I know this is last minute but this was a pleasant surprise that was sprung on me today. Nia- you don't have to pick her up. You all can hang out at the house and do whatever you like.*

Nia: *No prob. I'll be there. What time?*

Alex: *You can come around 6:30. Is that OK?*

Nia: *Yep. Perfect. See ya then.*

Alex: *Thanks. You're a lifesaver.*

Nia: *Anything for you and my Neicey Poo.*

Alex then sends a message back to Brooklyn:

Alex: *Hey there. Me again. I secured a babysitter and I'll be seeing you Thursday evening at 7:30-ish. Looking forward to it. Is there anything you need me to bring?*

Brooklyn: *No. You just make sure you bring your handsome self to my house and don't be late. LOL!*

Alex: *Yes ma'am. See you then!*

Alex goes on with the rest of his day with all smiles. Ever since he's met Brooklyn, he's been so much happier and to him, life has gotten so much better in spite of his devastating loss and regardless of the horrible dates he's been on in the past. The time he's spent with Brooklyn has been enjoyable and he's always excited to be in her presence.

After work, Alex picks up Jasmine from school, gets her settled in her seat, and they drive home.

"Jasmine, I have something I need to tell you."

"Ok. What is it Daddy?"

"Well, Brooklyn asked me out on a date this Thursday evening and I wanted to go. Are you OK with that?" Alex asks.

"Yes sir!" Jasmine says with excitement. "Where are you going?"

"She invited me over to her house for dinner."

"That sounds like fun. I'm sure you are going to have a good time," Jasmine says.

"Guess who is going to come over to the house to hang out with you?" Alex asks.

"Who?"

"Your Auntie Nia," Alex answers.

"Yes!" Jasmine screams. "We're going to have sooooo much fun!"

"I'm sure you will. So, you don't have a problem with me going out on dates with Brooklyn?" Alex asks again.

"Daddy. I keep telling you that I don't have a problem with it," Jasmine sighs. "For the last time, I want you to be happy and find a very nice woman to be with. Maybe Brooklyn is the one."

"Only time will tell, baby girl," Alex says. "Only time will tell."

They continue towards home and go about their routine once they get there. When it is time for bed, Alex and Jasmine say their prayers, Jasmine gets tucked in, and Alex goes to his room. He does not fall asleep as fast as on previous nights. This night, he can't sleep. He thinks it could be a combination of excitement, nerves, and possibly some uncertainty about his relationship with Brooklyn. No matter what it is, he's still very happy that he's able to spend time with a beautiful woman who has great potential. After at least an hour of tossing and turning, Alex finally falls asleep and gets a good night's rest.

Thursday evening arrives and at 6:30 p.m. sharp, the doorbell rings. Jasmine goes to the door.

"Who is it?" Jasmine asks.

"It's Auntie Nia."

Jasmine opens the door and Nia comes in with a handful of movies and a grocery bag full of snacks. They act as though they have not seen each other in years. They greet each other with hugs and kisses. Then Alex greets her with a hug.

"Nia, I really appreciate you hanging out with Jasmine on such short notice. I owe you big time," he says.

"It's no problem at all. I wasn't doing anything anyway so it worked out perfect. I'm sure I'll need a favor from you one day," Nia declares.

"Well just know that I'll be there for you, whatever it is."

"I know you will. I'm not worried."

"You have free reign of the house. Help yourself to anything you need. You are at home. If you need me for anything, just call or text me," Alex says, with a bit of concern in his voice.

"You just worry about having a good time. I got this over here," Nia assures Alex.

"I know you do. I'm not worried."

"Have a good time tonight, Daddy," Jasmine says as she jumps in his arms and gives him a hug and kiss on his cheek.

"Thank you, baby girl. I will," Alex says. "I'll see you all later. Jasmine, you are not going to stay up all night. Make sure you get to bed at a decent time. I'll check in on you when I come back."

"Yes sir!" Jasmine gives Alex a sergeant's salute.

"Don't worry. I'll make sure she is all-together. Now get out of here and enjoy your date," Nia tells Alex.

"Ok. I'm leaving. I'm leaving."

He gets in his car and sends Brooklyn a text to let her know he is on his way. She is anxiously awaiting his arrival.

When Alex finally arrives at Brooklyn's house, he walks to the door and rings her doorbell. The door opens almost instantly. Alex immediately notices that the lights are dimmed and soft jazz music is playing in the background. But what really catches his attention is how she is dressed—in an all-black dress and black heels.

"Welcome back, Alex. Please come in," Brooklyn says in a flirty voice.

As Alex comes through the door, she greets him with a hug and a small kiss on the lips.

"Thank you very much for the warm welcome. You have a lovely home," Alex says.

"Thank you. Come in and have a seat. Dinner is almost ready. Are you hungry?"

"Yes I am. What may I ask is on the menu for tonight?"

"I'm glad you asked, sir," Brooklyn says in a funny voice. "Tonight we will start out with a Caesar salad with homemade Caesar dressing garnished with homemade croutons. The main course is a grilled Porterhouse steak; cooked medium well and topped with butter and mushrooms, roasted red potatoes, grilled asparagus, and toasted sourdough bread. For dessert, we will have strawberry shortcake with fresh strawberries and whipped cream. Lastly, the selected beverage for the evening, which is paired perfectly with the steak, will be...red Kool-Aid."

Both Alex and Brooklyn burst into laughter.

"That sounds absolutely amazing, especially the red Kool-Aid. That sounds like it came straight from the vineyards of France. I hope it's a good year," Alex says sarcastically.

"No, really, we're going to have a great Cabernet Sauvignon with the meal. Is that OK?"

"That is perfect," Alex replies.

"Great. Let's head to the dining room. Right this way," Brooklyn says as she takes Alex's hand and leads him to the dining room. Once they get there, he sees how eloquently the table is set and candles are lit everywhere. Needless to say, Brooklyn knew exactly how to set the mood for a romantic dinner. Alex and Brooklyn sit down and Alex pours them both a glass of wine. After he is finished pouring, Brooklyn asks Alex to bless the food before they eat. After he says the blessing, they begin to eat their salads and engage in conversation while gazing into each other's eyes and smiling like never before. Once they are done with their salads, Brooklyn collects the dishes and takes them into the kitchen so she can bring out the main course.

"Is there anything I can help you with?" Alex asks.

"No sir. You make yourself comfortable. I'll be back there in just a second."

A few minutes later, Brooklyn comes out with a dish that looks as though it should be on the cover of a food magazine. The plate is immaculate. Alex can't wait to dive into it. Once Brooklyn sits down, they both proceed to eat.

"MMMMMM...Oh my goodness," Alex says with his head tilted back and his eyes rolled to the back of his head. "This is by far one of the best steaks I've had in a very long time. This meal is absolutely delicious. I must admit, you are an excellent cook and I'm thoroughly impressed."

"Why thank you very much," Brooklyn says blushing. "I'm glad you are enjoying it."

"Oh I am, very much," Alex says as he continues to eat.

They spend more time talking, laughing, and enjoying each other's company. As they finish up the main course, Brooklyn collects the plates again and takes them into the kitchen.

"Do you have room for dessert?" Brooklyn asks from the kitchen.

"I believe I have room for a little more," Alex replies.

"Good. I'll have dessert out in a few minutes," Brooklyn says as she puts the finishing touches on dessert. After a few more minutes, she comes out with the strawberry shortcake and they began to eat. During this course, Alex doesn't do too much talking. Most of the sounds that come from his mouth are moans or, "MMM...MMM...MMM!" Brooklyn is amused, yet flattered because she knows he enjoyed every bite of the entire meal.

When they are finished with dessert, she collects the dishes and puts them in the kitchen.

"Alex. Why don't you go ahead and make yourself comfortable in the living room on the couch and I'll be there shortly," Brooklyn says to Alex.

He goes into the living room, sits on the couch, and relaxes as he listens to the music that Brooklyn has playing. She comes out of the kitchen with something else—a bowl of strawberries and some whipped cream. She places it on the coffee table and sits next to Alex.

"That was an outstanding meal you prepared, Brooklyn. Thank you very much."

"It was my pleasure. I'm glad you enjoyed it."

"You better be careful, a guy like me could get used to something like this."

"I sure hope so because a girl like me could get used to doing it," Brooklyn replies.

"Here, have a strawberry," she says as she takes a strawberry, dips it in the whipped cream, and feeds it to Alex. Alex returns the favor by taking a strawberry, dipping it into the whipped cream, and feeding it to Brooklyn. She takes the strawberry into her mouth and licks a little of the whipped cream off of Alex's finger. Alex's heart begins to race.

As they finish the strawberry escapade, Alex and Brooklyn gaze into each other's eyes, grab one another's hand, and begin to slowly approach for kiss. It begins as an innocent peck on the lips, but transitions into a hot and heavy passionate kiss. Alex is totally caught off guard but he is not going to stop. The kiss becomes more passionate, but all of a sudden, Brooklyn pulls away. Alex becomes puzzled. Then, out of nowhere, Brooklyn straddles Alex on the couch, grabs him by the collar of his shirt, and says, "Alex, we are going to gooch tonight."

"Gooch? What does that mean?" Alex asks with a puzzled look on his face.

"It means we are making love tonight and I'm not taking no for an answer."

Just as Alex is about to speak, she puts her hand over his mouth, forcing him not to say anything and says, "Shhhhh. Just sit back, relax, and enjoy."

She gets up from her straddle and stands directly in front of Alex and begins to unbutton her dress. After it is unbuttoned, she stands there with nothing but black panties and a matching black bra. She then reaches behind her back and unhooks her bra to exposes her breasts. Alex's eyes almost jump out of the sockets.

She straddles him again and they continue with the passionate kisses. This time, Alex's hands are caressing her breasts and wandering all over her body. Brooklyn is slowly unbuttoning his shirt and things are really starting to heat up. Alex's shirt is almost completely unbuttoned and as he is about to unbuckle his belt, they hear some keys rattle at the front door. After a few seconds, the door opens and a man's deep voice resounds through the house.

"Brooklyn! Baby, I'm home."

"Oh my goodness! This can't be happening," Brooklyn says.

"What's going on?" Alex asks.

"What the hell is going on in here? Who the hell is this and where are your damn clothes?" the man yells.

Brooklyn covers up herself and jumps off of Alex and stands by the coffee table. Alex looks up and sees a very muscular, bald-headed man; about six foot four inches tall, and with rage in his eyes.

"Brooklyn. Who is this man?" Alex asks as he gets up from the couch and buckles his belt.

"This idiot is my husband. We've been separated for six months and preparing for divorce. I took the keys from him when he left. He must have had another set made," Brooklyn responds with frustration in her voice.

"Husband? You're still married? I thought you were single," Alex shouts.

"Nah, fool!" The man says. "She is happily married and you need to get the hell out of my house before I throw your ass out."

"Sir, with all due respect, I didn't know she was married. I'm not here to cause any problems. I'll gladly leave," Alex says in a calm voice.

Just as Alex is buttoning his shirt and preparing to leave, the man charges Alex, grabs him by his shirt, picks him up and throws him against the wall. Alex hits the wall and falls. He doesn't want to fight this man so he tries to get out of the house as quickly as he can. Somehow the man catches up to him, grabs him from behind and throws him on the couch, which falls over. By this time, Alex is furious. The man runs over to Alex and the two begin to fight, slamming each other into walls and rolling around on the floor. Alex finds a way to break loose from the man, not wanting to fight anymore or cause more damage to the house, but the man is insistent upon fighting some more. He rushes towards Alex and with one quick punch, Alex hits the man in the face and he's stopped dead in his tracks. Alex punches him in his groin area, picks him up and body slams him on the coffee table and completely breaks it. The man is in a daze, barely moving. Alex then looks at Brooklyn in disgust.

"How could you do this to me? How could you lead me on like this and play with my emotions? What were you trying to gain?" Alex asks. "You know what? Every ounce of trust I have in women is completely gone thanks to you. Do me a huge favor. Lose my number. Don't ever call me, text me, forget you ever knew me. I'm even deleting my account off of that stupid ass website. Thanks for shattering my hopes of being happy again. Thank you very much."

"Alex, baby, I'm sorry," Brooklyn says, crying.

"Yes, Brooklyn, you are sorry. Very sorry. Screw you."

Alex leaves the house, gets in his car, and drives home. He is so angry that he speeds all the way home with no concern of getting a ticket, which is totally out of character for him. He now knows what that uneasy feeling was he experienced when he first met Brooklyn. He was feeling all along that something was not right about her but he ignored it every time. He didn't have to worry about that anymore because in his mind, he will never date again.

When he finally gets home, he comes in, slams his keys on the table and says to Nia, "I know it's late and if you want to stay here the night, it's fine. You are welcome to stay in the guest bedroom."

Nia sees that Alex is very upset and she asks, "How was the date?"

Alex looks at her with his bloodshot red eyes and says,

"I'm done. DONE! I will live happily by myself and take care of my daughter.

"What happened, Alex?" Nia asks.

"I don't want to even talk about it. Good night."

Alex goes into his office, turns on his computer, logs into the dating website, and deletes his profile. Next, without any hesitation, he pulls out his phone and deletes the phone numbers for Sharon, Monique, and definitely Brooklyn. After that, he looks in on Jasmine and finds her sound asleep. Seeing her peaceful face gives him reassurance that he just did the right thing by removing himself from any connection with the dating website and the women he unfortunately encountered.

He then goes to his room, gets dressed for bed, and lies down. As he stares at the ceiling, he glances over his right shoulder and sees that picture of Gabrielle he always looks at each night before he goes to bed. As he looks at her picture, he begins to cry—something he hasn't done in quite a while. He cries for what seems like hours. He just keeps looking at the picture and tearfully apologizing.

"I'm sorry Gabby, for betraying you. I was a fool to think that anyone could ever take your place or be a good mother to our child. I was wrong and I am so sorry Gabby. I'm so sorry."   After quite a bit of time crying, Alex eventually falls asleep and doesn't wake until the next morning; when he does, he is not his normal self—he is quiet and not nearly as upbeat as he normally is. Jasmine tries her best to cheer him up but it does no good; even the car ride to school is a quiet one. Once they arrive at the school, Jasmine unbuckles her seatbelt, climbs into the front seat, kisses Alex on the cheek, and says, "Have a wonderful day, Daddy. I love you."

"I love you too baby girl. You have a wonderful day as well."

Once he gets to work, Alex finds it hard to stay focused and is very antisocial. He closes his door to his office and only comes out unless he absolutely has to. While trying to work, he receives an email from Nia:

Hey All,

I hope you all are doing fine. It's that time again for us to break bread and do some catching up. Let's meet at Petey's this Saturday at the usual time. Don't worry about trying to get babysitters. Bring the kiddos and we can have a separate table for them to do whatever they do. See you all Saturday evening!!! I love and miss y'all!!

Nia

Alex reads it and decides that he really doesn't want to go. But he then remembers that he was the one saying that they all needed to get together soon, so he feels obligated to go.   He replies to the e-mail confirming that he and Jasmine will be there, although deep in his heart, he really does not want to go. With much struggle, Alex manages to get through his workday. He does find pleasure at the end of the day when it's time to leave and go pick up Jasmine from school. When she gets in the car, she immediately asks Alex if he's all right.

"Daddy, are you OK? You have not been your usual self."

"I'm sorry, baby. I had a really bad night last night and I've been upset ever since. I apologize."

"It's fine, Daddy," Jasmine tells him. "I just want to make sure you are OK. Why didn't you have a good evening?"

"Let's just say that she was not what she said she was," Alex explains, avoiding the gory details.

"Are we going to look on the website for another date?" Jasmine asks eagerly.

"No ma'am," Alex says decisively. "I'm never getting on that site again. I really don't think that dating is for me right now. I have to put my focus on taking good care of you and making sure you have everything you need. Finding someone to date is no longer on my priority list."

Jasmine completely understands everything Alex is saying and she doesn't say anything else about it.

"Hey! Guess what?" Alex says.

"What?" Jasmine asks.

"This Saturday, you and I are going to hang out with all your aunts and uncles and their children. We haven't seen them all in a long time and it will be good to have fun with them."

"Yay!" Jasmine proclaims with excitement.

They continue to converse as they proceed home to eat dinner, do homework, and relax.

Later that evening, after they've gone through their nightly routine and Jasmine is tucked in, Alex finds it easier to fall asleep because he is still tired from the night before. The next morning, things are back to normal and Alex is himself again, having been fully rested.

When Saturday evening arrives, Alex and Jasmine are the first to arrive at Petey's and they anxiously await the others' arrival. By now, Alex is looking forward to the fellowship. After a few more minutes of waiting, everyone else starts to trickle in, excited to see each other. They exchange kisses, hugs, and high fives and have a great time talking and laughing like they have done in the past. The addition of the children brings another element of joy; seeing how they have grown over the years amazes everyone. The evening is becoming more perfect as time goes on. The adults sit at their table and the children at another table nearby, having a blast. As they all order drinks and meals, the adults engage in their deep conversation and the topic of the evening happens to be Alex.

"Ok Alex!" Craig yells. "The last time we were together, you mentioned that you were going to get back in the dating game. How has that been going?

"I'll put it to you all like this: I am completely out of the dating scene and will never, ever go on another date again as long as I live," Alex says with conviction. The rest of the friends are stunned at what Alex says and they begin to ask questions.

"Whoa, wait a minute. What's been going on, man?" Elijah asks.

"This experience has been nothing but a nightmare," Alex confesses. "Nothing went right on any of my dates and I think it's best that I don't go that route anymore."

"What happened that was so bad?" Alicia asks.

Alex tells the stories of all the dates he's been on. The group is speechless and their mouths drop in utter amazement at what Alex has gone through.

"Now you see why I can safely say that I am DONE with dating. I have a great career and a beautiful smart daughter to care for. Dating is not top priority," Alex declares.

"I can't believe that's happened to you, brother," Foster interjects. "That's messed up."

"Yeah. Good things are supposed to happen to good people like you," Juni adds.

"I thought the same thing too, Juni, but it just didn't work out that way," Alex replies.

"Maybe if you just give it some more time, things will turn out better. What do you think?" Hannah asks.

"Or maybe it's just that the right woman has not come to you yet. You have to be a little patient when it comes to things like that," Keiko says. "You know how it was with Juni and me."

"Yeah, I know," Alex says. "But when you are developing feelings for someone and you think they are too and you find out they were telling a lie the entire time... that's unacceptable and I'm not going to go through that again. I'm done."

"I really hate to hear that, man," Bradley says. "We all were hoping that you were having a great time and that you found someone that you really liked. I honestly believe there is still hope. You just have to believe it too, bro."

Alex looks Bradley in the eyes, "I'd really like to think that, Brad, but I'm not as optimistic as you. Besides, Gabby has always been the love of my life and I honestly don't think anyone could ever take her place. It would take a miracle for that to happen."

"If you want my advice, just let it happen naturally. If it's going to be, it will be," Corrine declares. "I truly believe that the woman for you is still out there and God is preparing her to be a perfect fit for you and Jasmine. Will you two be perfect? Of course not, but you will be perfect for each other. She will compliment you in more ways that you can imagine and vice versa. Your relationship with her is going to be a living testimony that only you all can give. There's a message in your story that the world needs to hear and you all will be the ideal people to deliver that message. How that's going happen, I don't know, but it's going to happen."

"I believe that, too," Elijah chimes in. "I can speak for all of us and say that you are an amazing man. I've told you this before as well. You and Jazzy deserve nothing but the very best and the very best is on the way. I wish I could tell you when and who it is, but I know the type of guy you are and whoever she is will exceed your expectations. Mark my words. We'll all be back here and you'll be telling us all about it. Just prepare yourself for it."

"I really do appreciate all of you guys' love and support over the years and even during this trying time in our lives. Words cannot express how much love is in my heart for you all. There is nothing I would not do for any of you and if I didn't have it, I would go to the ends of the earth to get it for you. That's how much you all mean to us. Your words of encouragement really do help me and I know they are honest and true. I love you guys beyond comprehension. I don't know what I would do without you."

There is not a dry eye at the table. Everyone gets up and begins hugging each other, showing Alex more love and support.

"All right, enough with all this mushy stuff," Craig says while wiping his eyes. "Alex, let's go hit up a strip club. It's on me today."

Everyone bursts into laughter.

"Shut up, idiot," Nia says. "You really know how to mess up a great moment. You would probably mess up a wet dream, you loser."

"Loser! Oh, I got your loser," Craig retaliates. "You're just mad because they kicked your old ass out of the strip club because you were too old and sagging."

"Forget you, Craig. You walking man whore," Nia says as she throws a napkin at him. As always, they get into a shouting match and have to be calmed down by the other friends. To Alex, this feels like old times, minus Gabby. He enjoys being around everyone again regardless of Craig and Nia fighting. It is almost always expected to happen. If it doesn't, everyone will just assume that either or both of them are not feeling well.

After dinner and dessert, they all say their goodbyes and go their separate ways until next time. Alex and Jasmine get into the car and drive home.

"Daddy. What were Uncle Craig and Auntie Nia arguing about?" Jasmine asks.

Alex laughs and says, "They do that all the time. I think that's their way of saying that they really like each other. They crack us up all the time."

"Don't you think it's easier just to say 'I like you?'" Jasmine asks.

"Different people do different things and that may be their way of expressing that. It's weird, but that could be their way," Alex explains.

"Oh," Jasmine says as she continues to look out of the window as Alex heads home.

Once they get home, they get their clothes together for church in the morning. Jasmine takes her bath and puts on her pjs, Alex gets cleaned up, and they both have a little time to talk before going to bed. After they talk, laugh, and say prayers, Jasmine gets tucked in. Alex then goes into his room and lies in bed, but he stays up a little while thinking about all that was said at dinner. Even though he has made up his mind that he is not going to date anymore, he has taken their words to heart and appreciates their faith and encouragement. After a little while, he drifts off to sleep. The next morning, he wakes up refreshed and ready for a great time at church.

Several weeks have gone by and Alex and Jasmine have been happy with their usual routine. One morning, Alex is sitting at his desk after a conference call, thinking about what he can do to celebrate Jasmine's birthday, which is coming up in two weeks. He racks his brain and can't come up with anything creative. So he makes a phone call to Nia and Corrine. (They are his proposed party planners.) All three are on a conference call hashing out the details of what they think Jasmine would like at her party. As they work out the details, they come to the conclusion that they will host a surprise party at the clubhouse in their subdivision. There are some minor details that Alex is uncertain about and he wants to talk with Jasmine to see what information he can get from her without giving the surprise away. He tells the ladies he will talk with her later in the evening and he will let them know so they can get what they need to make this party special for Jasmine.

Later that day, when Alex picks up Jasmine from school, he starts with small talk, but begins to ask Jasmine questions.

"Jazzy, I need your help on something."

"OK, Daddy. How can I help?" Jasmine asks.

"Well, one of my coworkers has a daughter about your age or a little bit older and she is planning a birthday party for her. She was asking me all kinds of questions about what should she do, what the decorations should look like, what kind of food she should have and all of that. I was absolutely clueless. She wanted me to ask you. So, if someone were to throw you a birthday party, what would you like to see or have at your party? From decorations to food to entertainment, what would make you happy? Be very specific."

Jasmine pauses for a minute, thinking about what she would like at a party. As she is thinking, Alex gets his phone ready to record everything she has to say. After a few minutes of silence, she begins to let Alex know her ideas.

"Well, if it was my party, I would want the decorations and balloons to be pink and green just like Momma's sorority colors so it could be kinda like a tribute to her since she is not with us. I would also like some pearls to be part of decorations too. Momma liked pearls. I would also like it to be a princess party. I used to like it when you called me your little princess and having a princess party would be fun and I would dress up in a princess dress and wear a tiara. That would be fun. For the food, maybe some little fancy sandwiches, chicken wings, sparkly grape juice, and of course ice cream and cake. I think something like that would be fun."

"Ok-is that all? Is there anything else you would have for the party?" Alex asks. He wants to make sure she has everything she desires.

"No, I think that's it," Jasmine replies. "That little girl would have a very nice party if she has that stuff, I'm sure she will be very happy."

"I'm sure she would too," Alex responds as he gently touches the off button for the recorder, so as not to be too obvious.

They proceed home and get dinner prepared. After Jasmine gets her homework completed, they take some time to relax and talk before going to bed. When Jasmine goes to take her bath, Alex takes advantage of the perfect opportunity to send the recording via e-mail to Nia and Corrine so they can get started with getting the items together for Jasmine's party.

Thank you ladies so much for helping me pull this party off. I want to make this the best birthday she's ever had. I will meet up with one of you to give you my card so you can purchase what you need to make it happen. I will reserve the clubhouse in the morning but if there is anything else you need me to do or get, please let me know. Love Y'all!!
Alex

After he sends the e-mail, he goes to check on Jasmine. She has already finished with her bath and has her pajamas on, waiting for Alex to come into her room. After they say their prayers and Jasmine is tucked in, Alex goes to his bedroom and drafts a guest list for the party. He makes a mental note that invitations need to go out and a cake needs to be ordered before the end of the week and he does not want to procrastinate. That's why he has called upon the expertise of Nia and Corrine, because he knows they are more than able to plan the best party a girl like Jasmine could ever have. He's thankful that her birthday falls on a Saturday this year.

Alex puts a lot of thought about what gifts he can get for Jasmine. Not only was he able to narrow it down to two major things she's been talking about for months, but he has a brilliant idea of something that will make her party extra special; so special, he is not going to tell Nia or Corrine about it. It will be a complete surprise to everyone.

A few days before Jasmine's birthday, as Alex and Jasmine are watching television together after school, Alex interrupts what they are watching to speak to Jasmine.

"Jazzy, I almost forgot to tell you. I gave your ideas and suggestions about the birthday party to my friend at work, who loved it, and she has invited you to come."

"Really? When is it?" Jasmine asks with a big smile on her face.

"It's actually this Saturday, which ironically is your birthday too. I didn't know if you wanted to do anything special or go anywhere for your birthday."

"Hmmm, there is nothing I really wanted to do for my birthday but maybe go out to dinner. But we can go to the party. I'm sure it will be a lot of fun. Let's go!" Jasmine says.

"Great! We will go then. We don't have to stay long and can leave whenever you're ready. But there is one other thing that needs to happen," Alex mentions.

"What's that Daddy?" she asks.

"She wanted all the girls to dress like princesses."

"I think I'm going to like this party already. I can't wait to go. When are we going to pick out a princess dress?"

"We can go tomorrow after school."

"Yes! This is going to be so much fun!" Jasmine says as she jumps up and down on the floor. Alex can't help but to smile seeing her excitement about a party that's actually for her, yet he keeps his composure.

Once it's bedtime for Jasmine, it's hard for her to sleep knowing that tomorrow she is going shopping for a princess dress. (She definitely has her mother's shopping knack.) Once she finally dozes off, Alex turns in for the night as well and prepares his mind for the upcoming activities.

After school the next day, Alex keeps his word and takes Jasmine to shop for a princess dress for her party. They go to a bridal shop and tell the owner what they are looking for. They look through a number of dresses and nothing catches their eyes. Just when they are about to give up, Jasmine sees one she likes. It's a pearl white dress with a pink ribbon on the front.

"Daddy, this is the dress I want. Can we get it, please?" Jasmine pleads.

"Yes baby. If you're sure you like it, we can get it."

"Yes!"

Jasmine tries the dress on at the suggestion of the shop owner and it turns out to be a perfect fit. Alex buys the dress with the pleasure of seeing her so happy and he then takes her to another store to buy shoes to match. Once their shopping spree is complete, they go back home to unwind before turning in for the evening.

Once again, it's hard for Jasmine to get to sleep. She can't stop looking at the beautiful dress that's hanging up in her room. During the shopping trip, she secretly wished that her mom was alive to have gone with her and Alex. It would have been a perfect day. Now, as she lies in bed, she wishes that her mom could see her in the dress tomorrow. Eventually, her thoughts drift off to a peaceful sleep, with a precious vivid dream of her mom.

The next morning, Jasmine wakes up to a delicious aroma coming out of the kitchen. Bacon, eggs, and blueberry pancakes are on the menu. She hastens to the kitchen to fill her belly.

"Happy birthday, princess!" Alex delightfully yells. He gives her a kiss and spins her around, both with big smiles on their faces.

"Thank you Daddy! Is this all for me?" she asks.

"Yes it is!" Alex exclaims. "It's a meal fit for a princess. Please have a seat, Your Highness."

Alex pulls out Jasmine's chair and helps her in her seat. He takes out a napkin and places it on her lap. He pours some milk in a glass and then places it in front of her along with a plate with bacon, eggs, and blueberry pancakes.

"This is very nice, Daddy. It's great having all of my favorite foods for breakfast and on my birthday. This is so cool."

They say a blessing over the food and they begin to eat. Jasmine enjoys every bite of the delicious food. Alex is happy seeing her eat with such joy.

"Daddy, what time is the party and when can I put on my dress?"

"The party is at one o'clock so we have plenty of time."

"Are we going to take a gift or get a card for the girl?" Jasmine asks.

Alex is caught off guard with that question so he has to think of something to say fast.

"No. We don't have to get one. She just wants kids to come and have a good time and not have to worry about getting cards. Some of the kids may not be able to get cards because they don't have enough money, she doesn't want anyone to feel bad because they are not able to bring anything."

"Oh. I understand. That was very nice of her. Well, I can't wait to have fun."

"Great! Go ahead and get cleaned up and we can do whatever you want before the party. It's your birthday and I want this to be a great day for my little princess."

"I don't want to do anything in particular but go to the party, so is it OK if we stay around the house until then?" Jasmine asks.

"Sure, baby! That's no problem. Like I said, today is your day and we can do whatever you like."

"Thank you, Daddy. You're the best!" Jasmine says as she gives him a hug and a kiss on the cheek. Then she darts off to the bathroom to get washed up.

While Jasmine is in the bathroom, Alex texts Nia and Corrine to see how everything is coming along and they reply that everything is set up and the clubhouse looks amazing. They send him pictures and Alex is amazed at décor. It shows that a lot of work has gone into getting the place just her to see it.

At 12:30, Jasmine is fully dressed in her new dress and shoes, ready for the princess party.

"Wow! You look beautiful, baby girl! You look like a true princess," Alex says.

"Thank you, Daddy. I feel like a princess, too," Jasmine beams.

"Let me take your picture," Alex suggests as he takes out his phone and takes several photos of Jasmine posing. Then Jasmine suggests that they have a little fun taking a few selfies-some fun and some serious.

"OK, Princess, it's time to go to the party, are you ready to go?"

"Yes sir, I am," Jasmine proclaims. "Shall we go now?"

"Yes we shall," Alex says, as they hook arms, walk out of the house, and get into the car.

They drive off to the clubhouse, which is only a few minutes from where they live. Once they get there, Jasmine notices that a lot of cars are parked.

"Wow! There really are a lot of people here. She must be a good friend to a lot of people!" Jasmine says.

"Yes, baby! And I'm sure she is loved by all who are here.

"That's so cool," Jasmine says.

Alex parks the car, opens Jasmine's door, and helps her get out of the car. They lock arms again and walk towards the front of the club-house. They observe one man dressed in what looks like some type of military uniform with a sword, and behind him, along the walkway leading to the door, are more men with swords standing across from one another and two men at the door.

"Good afternoon sir and ma'am. Who do we have visiting with us today?" one of the men asks.

"I am Alex Reed and this is Her Majesty, Princess Jasmine Reed."

"Very well," the guard says, then does an about face and yells to the men behind him, "Her Majesty Jasmine Reed is here! Present arms."

Once he gives that command, the men standing across from one another, quickly raise their swords over their heads at the same time and make what looks like a bridge leading to the front of the door. They walk up the walkway and when they get to the door, the remaining soldiers open both doors at the same time and all of a sudden, they hear a loud, "SURPRISE!" Jasmine is scared for a brief moment then notices a lot of familiar faces and soon realizes that the party is for her.

"Oh my goodness!" Jasmine yells. "Daddy, this party isn't for another little girl is it?"

"No, Princess, this is all for you. Happy Birthday!" Alex says.

All of the guests clap their hands and cheer for Jasmine. Alex hooks her arm again and leads her to a table where she sees a throne. Alex assists her to her seat on the throne and then he places a tiara on her head and whispers in her ear, "Now, you really look like a princess."

Jasmine is still in awe of what's taking place. As she looks around the clubhouse, she sees everything she mentioned to Alex-the pink and green balloons, the pearls on all the tables, the small sandwiches, chicken wings, sparkling grape juice, and of course, the beautifully decorated cake. Then she looks out at all of her family and friends from school. She is elated to have all of these people come out to celebrate her birthday. She fights back tears as she watches all of her guests, wishing her mom could witness this special moment. People are playing games, dancing, laughing, eating, and having a great time.

After everyone eats, it's time to cut the cake and sing "Happy Birthday." Alex lights the candles on the cake, and directs everyone to sing to Jasmine.

"OK, Princess, make a wish," Alex instructs Jasmine.

She thinks about it for a minute, closes her eyes tightly, and mumbles her wish under her breath. When she opens her eyes, she takes a deep breath, and blows out all the candles at once. Everyone adoringly claps and them quickly lines up to get cake and ice cream. Once everyone has finished dessert, Jasmine sits back on her throne and begins to open her many presents. She receives a lot of gifts, gift cards, and money. She takes the time to thank everyone that's given her a gift.

After Jasmine has opened her last gift, Alex motions to everyone to be silent so that he can make a special announcement.

"I wanted to thank you all for coming out to celebrate my princess's birthday with her. There is no way I could have done this by myself, so there are a number of people I have to thank for doing such an awesome job at pulling everything you see here together. First, a big thank you to Jasmine's uncle, Elijah Corruthers, and the soldiers for the wonderful military salute Jasmine received. That was amazing and it's something we all, especially Jasmine, will never forget. Next, thanks to all of you for taking time out of your busy schedule to make this day special for my baby girl. Words cannot express how much we love you guys and appreciate your kindness. Lastly, a special thank you to the dynamic duo of Aunties Nia and Corrine for the decorations and everything you see in this place. All I had to do was let them know what I wanted and they exceeded my expectations and made it happen. I love you ladies for helping a brother out. Before we get back to the party, there is one last thing I would like to say. Nia and Corrine don't know about what I'm about to do. I wanted this to be extra special and I hope I can get through this without crying, so here I go."

Alex then turns the focus to Jasmine.

"Princess Jasmine, I love you more than words can say. You have been my rock when times were hard and I appreciate you so much. Even though this is a happy day because it's your birthday, it's also sad because this is the first birthday that your mom is not here. She may not be here physically, but she is here in spirit and in another way. I want to give you this special gift and hope that it brings you a lifetime of joy."

Alex hands Jasmine, who has tears in her eyes, a beautifully wrapped box. She unwraps it and opens it up. Her mouth drops open and tears begin to flow from her eyes. It's a string of Gabrielle's favorite pearls. Everyone in the clubhouse begins to cry.

"Daddy. Were these my mama's pearls?" Jasmine asks.

"Yes, baby. I'm sure she would want you to have them. This was her favorite pair and always said that she couldn't wait to give them to you when you got old enough. I figured today would be the perfect day to pass them on to you."

Alex takes the pearls and places them around her neck. "I love them Daddy!" Jasmine says, and hugs Alex around his neck. There is not a dry eye in the place.

"OK everybody. Let's keep this party going," Alex says as he motions to the DJ to continue with the music. Everyone continues to dance and have a great time until the party is over.

When all of Jasmine's gifts are loaded into the car, Alex takes the time again to thank Elijah, Nia, and Corrine for all of their efforts. Nia and Corrine can't stop crying, showering him and Jasmine with hugs and kisses before they take off.

When Alex and Jasmine return home, she goes straight to her room to take off her dress, but decides to leave on her pearls. She carefully tucks the strand into the inside of her pajama top, nestled closely to her skin.

She and Alex stay up and talk about how great the party was and how much fun she had. They talk for hours, laughing and crying. After a while, Alex decides to go and get all of Jasmine's gifts out of the car, making several trips back and forth. After he's done, he goes back to Jasmine's room to check on her, and she is already in bed looking at the ceiling.

"I'm glad you had a great time today, Princess,"

"I did. This was the best birthday EVER. Thank you, Daddy."

"You are very welcome. You deserved it. You're a great daughter," Alex tells Jasmine.

"And you are a great father."

"Thank you very much."

"Daddy, do you wanna know what I wished for before I blew out my candles?" Jasmine asks out of the blue.

"You don't have to, but you can if you want to."

"I'll tell you. I wished that God would send you a very nice lady to love us the way Mama did and so you could be very happy. I know you miss Mama just like I do, but you have to be happy again. Mama would want you to be happy," Jasmine declares.

Alex fights back tears because he never thought he would ever hear his daughter say what she just said. It's as if she is giving Alex the permission to find another wife.

"We'll see what happens, baby. Get some rest and I'll see you in the morning."

Alex says prayers with Jasmine, kisses her on the forehead, tucks her in, turns off her light, and leaves her room. Once he leaves and goes to his bedroom, Jasmine sits up in her bed and says another prayer, hands folded tightly together:

"Dear God. Thank you for a wonderful day. Thank you for all the nice gifts I received today. Please God, send my Daddy a very nice lady that is just like my Mama. She has to be pretty, smart, a lot of fun, and will love my Daddy just like Mama did. Most of all, I just want to see him happy again. Please do this for me. Thank you. Amen."

Jasmine gets back under the covers and drifts off to sleep.

Alex gets in bed and begins to think some more about the events of the day and how wonderful it was to surprise Jasmine. He is so thankful for everyone who showed up or helped out with the party planning. The more he dwells on the day, the drowsier he becomes until he finally falls asleep. Both of them are able to get a good night's sleep and rise up cheerfully the next morning for church.

CHAPTER ELEVEN

A Heart Change

The holiday season has come around again without Gabby's presence, and Alex and Jasmine are not as enthusiastic about it as they normally are. It just hasn't been the same since Gabby passed away, no matter how much effort they put into enjoying it. The table setting is not the same anymore during Thanksgiving. The smells of turkey, dressing, greens, sweet potatoes, macaroni and cheese, and an assortment of cakes and pies no longer fill the house. Alex and Jasmine no longer sneak into the kitchen to sneak samples of the delicious food; and Alex no longer gets the opportunity to walk up behind Gabrielle while she is cooking, wrap his arms around her from behind, and kiss her on her neck or cheek. Both Alex and Jasmine realize that those days are long gone and now, somehow, they now have to make new traditions.

Christmas is also a difficult holiday. Even though they still decorate the house and trim the tree, it's not the same anymore. The traditions of the past are just not what they used to be without Gabrielle. The only thing that has remained the same is Jasmine placing the angel on top of the tree. Instead of getting a new one every year like Gabrielle did, Jasmine determines that they will use the one she picked out last year, which reminds her of her mother.

Just as the Christmas holiday is approaching, Jasmine is preparing to get out of school for the two-week break and Alex is wrapping up some things at the office when he gets a call. He answers his phone.

"Alex Reed," Alex answers his phone.

"What's up Alex? This is Craig. How are you?" Craig says.

"Hey, Craig!" Alex replies. "All is well. What's up with you?"

"I'm doing great. Quick question-are you going to be busy this Friday evening? Please say no," Craig pleads.

Alex pauses, then looks at his calendar, and says, "Actually, no. I don't have anything going on. Why, what's up?"

"Cool. I wanted to know if you would go with me to my company's Christmas party. It's usually a lot of fun with free food, drinks, and a sea of beautiful women. You just may get lucky."

"Craig, you know I'm not interested in trying to find any women right now. That's not my focus. Plus, I'm sure you won't have any problems having your way with some or all of those women. Thanks, but no thanks," Alex declares.

"Aww come on, man. Help a brotha' out. At least come as my guest and try to have some fun. There will be enough people there for you to mix and mingle with and you might even gain some new clients. More importantly, I'm trying to get your big-headed self out of the house for a change," Craig says laughing.

"For once, you do have a point," Alex says, laughing. "OK. I'll go with you, but don't expect me to go there looking for someone, and don't try to set anything up for me."

"I just want you to have a good time, man. That's all," Craig says. "Meet me at the Bank of America Corporate Center at eight o'clock, sharp. Don't be late and dress to impress."

"Dang bro! I have to drive myself too? That's messed up," Alex jokes.

"No offense, bro," Craig responds. "I may get lucky and may need to take a young lady home; you know; in the event she has had way too much to drink. Friends don't let friends drive drunk. Whoever she is, she'll be in good hands."

"Fine. I'll meet you there Friday evening. Get off my phone and do some work. I'll talk with you later," Alex says.

"Later dude!" Craig says as they both hang up the phone.

Alex then places a call to Nia to see if she will be able to look after Jasmine this Friday night.

"Hey Nia! This is Alex. How are you doing today?"

"I'm great, Alex. How are you?" Nia asks. "When and what time would you like for me to come over and hang out with Jazzy?"

Alex is caught off guard and is silent for a few seconds before he bursts into laughter.

"How did you know I was going to ask about that?"

"I felt it in my bones that you were going to call. It's no problem though. What day and time should I be there?" Nia asks.

"This Friday evening and could you be at the house at seven o'clock?"

"I'll be there with bells on," Nia replies. "It's always fun hanging out with her."

"I really appreciate it. Are you sure you don't have anything planned already? I don't want to interrupt anything."

"No sir!" Nia replies. "I have nothing planned at all. Even if I did, I'd do anything to hang out with my girl. I'll be there at seven on Friday. Where are you going? You got a hot date?"

"No," Alex replies with a chuckle. "I'm going to a Christmas office party with your buddy, Craig."

"Craig?" she says. "You're going out with that idiot?" I'm surprised at you! You better watch your back and stay away from the crazy women he deals with. Better yet, you may want to take some mace. You never know who may come out of the woodworks on you all," Nia exclaims with seriousness and disgust in her voice.

Alex responds in laughter.

"Well, the good thing is that I'm not going to try to find a date. He just wants me to get out of the house and hang out with him. We'll see how it goes."

"Just make sure you don't get mixed up in his foolishness," Nia suggests. "You're a good guy and I don't want that rotten apple to ruin your good reputation."

"No need to worry about that. I'll be very incognito," Alex says. "I'll do a little networking and a lot of people watching. If I'm not having a good time, I'll go home. It's that simple."

"Sounds like you already have a plan. Good for you," Nia replies.

"Thank you so much for agreeing to come by. I'll be sure to let Jazzy know so she will be expecting you," Alex says.

"You are very welcome. I've got to get on a conference call in a few minutes so I will chat with you later. Have a great rest of the day," Nia says.

"Thanks. You do the same," Alex responds as they both hang up the phone. As soon as he finishes out the rest of his day at work, he leaves to pick Jasmine up from school. Once they arrive home, they change clothes, Jasmine works on homework, and Alex prepares their dinner. As they eat, Alex decides to let Jasmine in on the surprise.

"Baby girl!" Alex says. "I have a little surprise for you."

"Really, Daddy! Where is it?" Jasmine asks with excitement.

"It's not anything in particular but I think it's something you will like."

"Well, what is it?" Jasmine asks again.

"Well, this Friday evening, Uncle Craig has asked me to go to this party with him and since it's a grown-up party and unfortunately, you can't go, I asked your Auntie Nia to come over and hang out with you," Alex shares.

"Yes, yes, yes!" Jasmine says as she jumps up and down on the dining room floor. "We are going to have some fun!"

Alex grins from ear to ear watching Jasmine express her joy.

"I'm sure you will. I wasn't going to go because Craig said that I could possibly find a nice lady there and I didn't want to go just for that."

"You never know, Daddy. The person that you've been waiting for could be there too. It is possible you know," Jasmine declares.

"You're right baby, anything is possible," Alex says, nodding his head. "But I won't get my hopes up. I'll go and try to have a good time."

"I'm sure you will, especially with Uncle Craig around. He is funny."

"Yeah, more like crazy, but he is a funny guy," Alex states, as they both laugh and continue with dinner.

After dinner they talk and get their clothes and things ready for the next day. Jasmine takes a bath, puts on her pajamas, and gets in the bed. She and Alex say their prayers together and he tucks her in for the night. He goes to his bedroom, turns off the light, and quickly goes to sleep.

On Saturday evening, Alex begins getting ready to meet Craig for the Christmas party in Uptown. While he is putting on the last of what he's going to wear, the doorbell rings.

"I'll get it Daddy!" Jasmine yells.

A few seconds later, he hears a bunch of screaming and laughing. He runs to the living room and finds Jasmine and Nia acting like a group of girls at a boy band concert. He can't do anything but shake his head, walk away, and finish getting dressed in his bedroom. Once he is dressed, he comes back out to speak to Nia.

"You all sounded like Freddy Kruger is coming in to slice you all up. I hope the neighbors didn't hear you and call the police," Alex jokes.

"Oh, quit being an old fuddy-duddy, Alex," Nia says. "Me and my girl are just having fun. That's all."

"I can see that. You two always manage to have too much fun," Alex says laughing. "Since it's a Friday night, and we don't have too much going on, Jasmine can stay up a little later tonight and you are welcome to stay if you like, Nia. You know where everything is."

"Oh, I came with my bag packed. I'm one step ahead of you, brother," Nia says, while doing a dance. "Now don't you have somewhere to be? We need you to go so we can have fun."

"Ok...ok...I'm leaving," Alex calls out. "Baby girl, have fun, and please keep Auntie Nia out of trouble. Call me if you need me."

"We'll be fine, Daddy," Jasmine says. "Have a great time." She gives Alex a hug and kiss on the cheek and goes back to where Nia is standing.

"I'll be sure to tell your buddy, Craig, you said hello," Alex says to Nia.

"Please don't," Nia says with an angry face. "You need to ask that dog if he got his shots yet."

Alex bursts into laughter and says, "You all are a mess. I really think both of you are in love with each other and don't want to admit it."

"Whatever. Please leave," Nia says as she pushes Alex out the door.

"Have fun! See you all later!" Alex says as he gets into his car and drives to the party.

When Alex arrives at the Bank of America Corporate Center, he parks his car and goes inside to the top floor. Once the elevator doors open, he sees a host of people so he begins looking for Craig. As Alex looks around, Craig spots him and walks over.

"Hey man!" Craig says. "I'm glad you made it and didn't stand me up."

"I wasn't going to miss this for the world. If I did, I'm sure you would have not let me live it down," Alex responds.

"You are absolutely correct. I wouldn't have. Come on in and let me introduce you to some people."

Craig takes Alex around and introduces him to his friends and colleagues. During his conversations, Alex is able to talk business with a lot of people, as well as exchange business cards. Meanwhile, others are beginning to get intoxicated- including Craig. After making introductions, Craig is on a mission to see what woman or groups of women he can take advantage of.

"Dude! Do you see all these beautiful women in here?" Craig says. "You mean to tell me you don't want to go home with one or two of them?"

"I told you I was not coming here for that," Alex reminds Craig. "I know that's what you want to do, so go right ahead. I'll grab me a drink and hang out at one of the back tables. If I get too bored, I'll find you and let you know I'm leaving."

"Awww, man!" Craig says. "I thought you were the dude. I think you are beginning to turn into a dud. OK, grab you a drink and I'll catch up with you in a little bit. I think I see a few women I'd like to wake up to in the morning. See ya later, alligator."

"See ya, bro. Be careful," Alex says, shaking his head and laughing. He gets a glass of wine and finds an empty bar-height table that he can stand at and do some people watching, which he does for quite some time. Just when he thinks that it's time to leave, Alex notices two women walk through the entrance to the party. Both women are very attractive, but one of them catches his eye right away. He finds himself staring at her, amazed at her natural beauty. He has to snap himself out of it and look away in case she notices him looking at her. But he feels pulled towards her presence, finding himself looking at this woman over and over again, admiring her beauty from a distance.

As the woman walks along with her friend throughout the party, mingling and meeting people, he notices that she doesn't seem to be interested in being there—her body language and facial expressions show it. He feels the urge to go up to them and talk to her but he is afraid to, so he continues to stand at the table with his drink and just watch, casting aside his decision to leave the party. The urge to talk to her takes him by surprise, as he has adamantly vowed to completely be done with the dating game.

After some time, he notices that his interest is sitting alone, with a number of men constantly approaching her to no avail. When he witnesses how she blows all of them off, turning guys away left and right, the thought of him going over to her to introduce himself quickly leaves his mind, so he stays right where he is to continue being a safe observer. He looks at her again and receives eye contact. They both look away. After a few seconds, they look at each other again, give a little smile, and look away again. In shyness, they both continue to sneak a peak at the other without letting eye contact linger. Alex finally gets the nerve to go over and talk to her. He figures that if she were to shoot him down like she did the other guys, he would definitely go straight home. He girds his loins, puts one foot in front of the other, and walks over to her to start a conversation.

"Hello ma'am. How are you this evening?" Alex asks.

"Hello sir. I am doing fine. How are you?" she responds.

"I'm doing well as well—I mean, I'm doing fine," Alex replies, as his heart beats fast and his hands begin to sweat.   She giggles.

"Are you having a good time?" he asks.

"It's OK. My friend dragged me out of the house and forced me to come. I really could have stayed at home," she says.

"That sounds like me. My friend told me the exact same thing. I know I'm a bit of a homebody, but I'm not into seeing a bunch of folks get loud and drunk. That's just not my cup of tea."

"I agree."

"Please excuse my manners. My name is Alex, Alex Reed," Alex says, as he reaches out his hand to shake hers.

She gently extends her hand to Alex.

"No problem. My name is Vanessa León. It's a pleasure to meet you."

"The pleasure is all mine," Alex responds, still shaking her hand while they both look into each other's eyes.

"Would you like something to drink?" Alex asks Vanessa.

"Sure. I'd love to have a glass of Moscato if they have it. I'm not much of a drinker so that's probably all I would be able to handle."

Alex laughs.

"I understand. I've had this same glass for over an hour and you see I'm not done with it yet."

They both laugh.

"I'll be right back," Alex says as he turns and goes to the bar to get Vanessa a drink. As he walks, he thinks to himself how beautiful she is and hopes he does not trip and spill that drink on her, so he's trying his best to maintain his composure. After he gets her drink and heads back to where she is, he notices her friend talking with her, and she seems a bit aggravated.

"Here you are, Ma'am. One Moscato just for you," Alex says as he hands Vanessa her drink.

"Thank you, sir. Alex, this is my friend Maria. Maria, this is Alex."

"Pleasure to meet you, Maria," Alex says.

"Pleasure to meet you, Alex. Please excuse us for one quick second. I'm sorry."

"No problem. Would you like for me to step away and give you your privacy?" Alex asks.

"No. You are fine. It'll only take a minute," Maria replies.

Alex couldn't help but to hear that Maria has to leave and it will be difficult for her to take Vanessa back home because she lives on the other side of town. Maria apologizes for having to leave so early and offered to pay for a cab for Vanessa to get home.

"I'm sorry for butting in, but I couldn't help but to overhear, if you are looking for a way home, I'll be more than happy to take you. I don't mind. I know we just met and I'll be happy to give you my cell number and a number to my friend, Craig, who is here. He can vouch for me. I'm a really nice guy," Alex declares.

Maria looks at Vanessa.

Vanessa smiles.

"I don't have a problem with it. I'll be fine."

Maria looks at Alex and Vanessa again and she smiles and says, "Ok. Please call me the minute you get home to let me know you made it safely."

"I will. Be careful," Vanessa says as they embrace in a hug.

"I will. It was nice to meet you Alex."

"It was nice to meet you as well," Alex says. "I'll be sure to get her home safe and sound."

"Thank you," Maria says, and then she walks out of the party.

Alex and Vanessa sit on the couch together and began to talk. The more they talk, the louder the party seems to get and it becomes more difficult to hear.

"Would you like to go for a walk?" Alex asks Vanessa. "I know that's a weird request, but it's very hard to hear. We could go some-where else so we wouldn't have to yell at each other."

"Actually, I'd like that very much."

They finish their drinks and get ready to take their walk when Craig walks up to them.

"Hey man! You having a good time?" Craig loudly asks. It's obvious he has had one too many to drink, but he is still able to function.

"I'm having a great time now," Alex responds. "Craig, this is Vanessa. Vanessa, this is my good friend Craig."

"Nice to meet you, Craig," Vanessa says.

"It's nice to meet you too, Ms. Vanessa. Damn Alex," Craig says loudly, without taking his eyes off Vanessa. "She's fine! Oops. Did I say that out loud? My bad. Blame it on the alcohol."

Alex shoots him a look that says I can't believe you just said that. Vanessa bursts into laughter.

Craig continues, "Man, I'm having a great time and I may be getting out of here pretty soon. I found a cutie I might be going home with. I'm sure glad you drove. I'll chat with you later, bro. It was very nice meeting you, Veronica."

"Vanessa!" Alex exclaims.

"That's what I said," Craig responds. "Don't do nothing I wouldn't do. I'm outta here. See ya."

Vanessa is laughing so hard she is in tears as they walk out of the party.

"I am so sorry you had to experience that. He's a cool guy but is a complete idiot at times," Alex explains.

"It's OK. No need to apologize," Vanessa responds. "I bet he's the life of the party."

"Yes indeed he is. He always has us laughing. I just wish he would settle down instead of jumping from one woman to the next. Maybe one day. I haven't lost hope for my guy," Alex says.

"Maybe one day the love bug will hit him," Vanessa suggests.

"I sure hope so," Alex says as he walks next to Vanessa. "Let's keep walking."

As they walk, they engage in small talk and enjoy each other's company. They stop and look out of a huge window overlooking Uptown.

"Wow!" Vanessa says. "This is a beautiful view."

"It sure is. In all my years in Charlotte, I've never seen this view from here. This is absolutely amazing."

"Really? Are you a native of Charlotte?" Vanessa asks.

"Yes ma'am. I am. Born and raised here. I've been to a lot of places here, but never been to this area to see this."

"This sure beats being on the inside with all of that noise and the heavy drinkers," Vanessa expresses.

"You got that right," Alex agrees. "I know we just met and since we both really don't want to be here; would you like to grab a cup of coffee or a bite to eat? I'd really like to get to know you better if that's alright with you."

With a big smile on her face, Vanessa says, "I'd like that very much. I'm not very hungry but coffee sounds fine."

"Great. There's a coffee shop not too far from here. That'll be a good place to go."

Alex and Vanessa take the elevator to the parking garage and walk to his car while continuing to converse and get to know one another. Alex opens the passenger door for her and helps her in. She seems surprised, yet impressed, that Alex is such a gentleman. As they drive to the coffee shop, they do not stop talking. Nor do they stop when they get there, go in, and place their order for coffee and pastry. They discover that they have a lot in common. Alex is amazed at not only how beautiful Vanessa is, but also how intelligent she is. The more they talk, the more he likes her. There is something different about her that attracts him to her, but he can't put his finger on it. Regardless of what it is, he wants to keep it suppressed so as not to get too ahead of himself; keeping in mind the horrible experiences he's had trying to date. He wants to make sure he is not getting set up for yet another failure.

As they continue to enjoy their coffee, Alex decides to ask Vanessa some more questions that will give him a true sense of her character.

"If you don't mind me asking, what do you do, Vanessa?" he asks.

"I don't mind at all," Vanessa responds. "I'm an English professor at Johnson C. Smith, I've been there for twenty years, and I absolutely love what I do. I have a great group of students to whom I enjoy mentoring and empowering, especially the young women. I have a heart for women and I want to do all I can to be a positive influence in their lives."

"That's awesome," Alex says. "I can feel your passion and I sense you love what you do. It's more than just a job for you; it's your ministry to those young ladies. From what I can gather about you, you'll have an effect on a multitude of women. Just keep doing what you are doing," Alex says.

"Thank you, Mr. Reed. What about you? What do you do? If you don't mind me asking."

"I don't mind at all," Alex answers. "I am a corporate attorney and senior partner at Goldberg, Oswald, and Danielson. I've been there for fifteen years and I love what I do as well. I, too, have a heart for people, but mainly young boys. I'm a coach for a Pop Warner football team and I get a chance to pour into them about being respectful, responsible, and hard work. It's sad that some of my boys don't have fathers in the home so the other coaches and I are the only positive males they interact with. That's why I take out so much time with them. I want to be a positive reflection of what a man really is and not what they see on TV. So far, they are all doing well and I'm thankful for that," Alex explains.

"That's wonderful Alex. Young boys need positive role models like you around. There's more to life than being a professional athlete with a fancy car and house. They need to know that if they work hard, they can have all of those things. But having influences like you who are attorneys, doctors, engineers; that's where you can make the biggest impact and you seem to be doing it. I applaud you for that."

"Thank you, Vanessa. I try my best to reach as many of them as possible."

"Well, you keep doing what you're doing," Vanessa says with a smile. "So I take it that you are a sports fan."

"Yes indeed I am," Alex eagerly responds. "I've always loved sports. What about you?"

"I am as well. I've been around it for so long because my dad and brothers were either involved in it or watching it. I just developed an appreciation for it."

"That's awesome. I see we have something in common already and this is only the first date," Alex states with a wide grin, hiding his own astonishment that those words just came out of his mouth.

They both giggle. Alex is thankful she has a sense of humor, at least from what he can see right now.

"What else do you like to do?" Alex asks.

"Well, my friend thinks I'm an exercise freak," Vanessa admits.

"Really?" Alex says. "I love to exercise as well. What's your favorite workout?"

"I do several," Vanessa answers. "I like Zumba® and yoga, and at times I do a treadmill workout. Do you exercise?"

"As a matter of fact I do," Alex responds. "I've done P90X®, Insanity®, and treadmill work as well. I try my best to stay consistent with it and get in the best shape I can. Sometimes I'm on track and at times I'm not. I just have to get back on when I fall off."

Alex looks at his watch and is shocked at the time.

"We have been having so much fun that we have lost all track of time," Alex says. "It's getting late and I'd better get you home. I'm sure your friend, Maria, probably thinks I've kidnapped you."

They both laugh.

"No, I doubt it," Vanessa states. "I'll touch base with her when I get home."

"OK. If you say so. Come on, I'll get you home," Alex tells her.

He pays the check, leaves a tip, and they walk to the car. Again, Alex opens her door and helps her in. He drives off to Vanessa's house. Once they arrive, he pulls into the driveway, gets out to open her door and help her out, and walks her to the front door.

"I see chivalry is not dead. I like that," Vanessa says as they get to her front door.

"My mother and grandmother always taught me to treat women with respect and I've been doing it all my life," Alex admits. "So for me, chivalry is not dead."

"Impressive, Mr. Reed. Impressive," Vanessa says with a smile. "I really had a nice time tonight and I'm actually glad Maria dragged me out of the house to come to that party. You really made the evening much better. Thank you."

"You are welcome," Alex replies. "I had a wonderful time as well. I'll be sure to thank my friend, Craig, for making me come too. Trust me, I had my mind made up that I didn't want to go, but I'm really glad I gave in."

They both stand there looking at each other with a smile.

"Vanessa, if I'm not being too forward, would it be possible that I can call you sometime?" Alex bravely asks, officially breaking his promise to be done with dating. "I really enjoyed your company and I'd like to get to know you better, if that's alright with you."

"I would like that very much," Vanessa answers. They both take out their cell phones to share each other's contact information.

"Have a great rest of the evening and make sure you call Maria," Alex says with a laugh.

"I will do that right away, sir," Vanessa says. "Thank you again for tonight. I'll be talking with you soon."

"Yes ma'am you will," Alex says, as they walk towards each other and embrace in a hug that lasts for about a minute before they separate.

"Drive safely and text or call me when you get home," Vanessa says to Alex.

"I will. Good night."

"Good night," Vanessa waves to him as he drives out of her driveway and down the street.

On the way home, Alex can't stop smiling and doesn't believe how much fun he had with Vanessa. His heart is racing, but he is trying not to get his hopes up again. Even though this is the first time he's met Vanessa, he feels that she is somehow not like the other women he's dated. He decides that he will take this one day at a time and see how things progress. Once he gets home, he finds Nia on the couch watching television. When he comes through the door, Nia notices that he is glowing with a smile, and of course decides to mess with him.

"So, you go out and you come back glowing and smiling. What happened tonight, mister? I want all the juicy details," Nia says.

"Where is Jasmine?" Alex asks, trying to avoid Nia's questions.

"She's asleep in her room. Tell me what happened," Nia states more forcefully.

"Let me go check on her and I'll be right back," Alex pronounces as he runs to Jasmine's room.

"You better hurry up, turkey. I'll be here waiting."

Alex goes to Jasmine's room and finds her sound asleep. He kisses her on the forehead and leaves her room going back to the living room where Nia is—right there waiting for him on the couch.

"Well, I'm listening. What happened tonight?" Nia asks with her arms crossed.

"I'll say this," Alex explains. "I don't want to jinx anything, but I had a great time tonight with a very nice and attractive woman. That's all I'm going to say. If things happen to progress in the future, I will make sure you all know."

"I understand," Nia says. "I just want happiness to find and overtake you. You're a great guy who deserves a great girl. We will see what happens."

"Yes we will," Alex says. "I really appreciate you for staying with Jasmine. I'll be cooking breakfast in the morning if you want to eat with us."

"You? Cook for me? I don't think so," Nia shakes her head. "You sleep in and I'll fix breakfast. You probably still can't cook. You're not going to get me sick. Go to bed, lover boy. Have a good night."

Alex laughs. "Thanks. Good night."

Alex goes to his room, changes into his pajamas, lies in the bed, and gets his phone out to text Vanessa.

Hey Vanessa! This is Alex. Just wanted to let you know that I made it home. Thanks again for a wonderful evening. Rest well and I'll chat with you soon. Good night!

Vanessa replies back immediately:

Hey Alex! Glad you made it home ok. Maria says hello and thank you. LOL! The evening was great. Looking forward to talking/hanging out again. Good night.

Alex does not fall asleep right away. He's still on cloud nine from his impromptu date with Vanessa. The time spent with her just keeps playing over and over in his mind; which is very unusual because this didn't happen before when he dated the women he connected with through the dating website—even Monique. It's a great feeling. The more he thinks about her, the happier he becomes.

Eventually, he falls asleep and doesn't wake up until the next morning when he's aroused to the smells of bacon, sausage, fried potatoes, and pancakes. He jumps out of bed, washes himself up, and goes into the kitchen to find Nia and Jasmine in the kitchen cooking breakfast.

"Good morning ladies!" Alex says.

"Good morning Daddy!" Jasmine says as she runs and jumps into Alex's arms.

"Hey baby girl! You're helping Auntie Nia cook this morning?" Alex asks.

"Yes sir," Jasmine replies.

"Well, it looks and smells delicious," Alex tells Jasmine. "Good morning, Nia. You didn't have to cook breakfast. I really appreciate it."

"Good morning. It's no problem," Nia says. "I wanted a good, hot breakfast and since I was here, I made sure you all had one too. Let's sit down and eat. The food is ready.

They all sit at the table, bless the food, and begin eating.

"Daddy, how was the party you went to?" Jasmine asks. Nia looks at Alex waiting for him to speak.

"It was good, baby. Better than I expected," Alex replies.

"Mmmm hmmm!" Nia exclaims. Alex looks at her and motions her to not say anything about the time he spent with Vanessa. He doesn't want to get her excited about it only to possibly run the risk of breaking her heart if things don't progress with Vanessa.

"I met a lot of nice people and your Uncle Craig was the life of the party as always," Alex continues.

Nia giggles.

"I'm glad you had a nice time, Daddy," Jasmine says. "If you ever go out again, can Auntie Nia come back over? We always have a fun time."

"I don't mind," Alex answers. "As long as she is not busy and doesn't have any other plans, that's fine with me; but you have to ask her."

"You know I don't mind, Jazzy," Nia responds. "I'll come anytime you want."

"Yes!" Jasmine shouts.

"This breakfast is really good, Nia. Cooking like this will get you a husband in no time," Alex declares.

"Trust me, I know."

Everyone bursts into laughter.

"I'm not in a rush to get into a relationship though," Nia says. "My time will come. Don't you worry."

"I know it will. Someone will notice you and be exactly what you need. Then you will be a match made in heaven," Alex says.

"Yours will be too. It's coming. Mark my words. It's coming," Nia states in a serious tone.

Alex remains quiet and everyone continues eating breakfast. After they finish eating, they all remain seated around the table, stuffed and sleepy.

"Nia, thank you again for breakfast. It was very delicious," Alex sighs.

"It's no problem, big brother. It was my pleasure. Plus, I just saved myself ten dollars by not going to IHOP."

"Yes you did," Alex says, laughing.

"Well I'd better get going. I've got some errands to run. Do you mind if I take Jazzy with me?" Nia asks.

"I don't mind at all."

"Do you want to hang out with your Aunt Nia for a while?" Alex asks Jazzy.

"Yes!" Jasmine yells as she jumps up from the table to get ready.

"Nia, I really appreciate what you and the others do for Jasmine. She really enjoys being around good positive women and she really needs that. She has been a trooper since Gabby died but I know she still needs that female interaction that I can't give her. Words cannot express how much you all mean to us," Alex says.

"No need to thank us, Alex," Nia says. "We're all one big happy family and that's what we do. I'm sure if either one of us was in the same situation, you all would be there for us, so we don't have a problem with it."

"I know," Alex continues, "but I still wanted to express my gratitude. I never want to take anyone's kindness for granted," Alex continues.

"We know. You're alright with us," Nia says, as she gives him a hug. Jasmine comes from her bedroom dressed and ready to go.

"You ladies have a great time. More than likely, I'll just hang out around the house and get some things done," Alex says.

"Alrighty!" Jasmine states. "We'll see you later, alligator."

"After while, crocodile," Alex retorts. "Thanks again, Nia."

"Don't mention it," Nia calls out.

Jasmine and Nia leave out and Alex goes back into the kitchen to clean up. As he rinses off dishes and puts them in the dishwasher, he gets a text notification on his cell phone. He looks at it and sees that it's a message from Vanessa. Now he can't stop smiling.

Vanessa: *Good morning Alex! I hope you slept well last night. I hope this doesn't sound weird but I thought a lot about you last night. I'm sorry if this "spooks you out" but I wanted to let you know.*

Alex: *Good morning! Good to hear from you. I'm not spooked out at all. I thought about you as well. Weird huh?!?!? LOL! How are you?*

Vanessa: *I'm doing fine. Needing to go out and run some errands. You?*

Alex: *Just loaded the dishwasher and going to do a few things around the house. Nothing much. Enjoy some peace and quiet.*

Vanessa: *That sounds like fun. Maybe one day I could join you.*

Alex: *That would be perfect. I was going to suggest that. Maybe we can go out again soon and continue getting to know each other better.*

Vanessa: *I'd like that very much. When?*

Alex: *You check your schedule and let me know. I'm ready when you are.*

Vanessa: *I will do that and get back with you. Enjoy your day!*

Alex: *You do the same.* ☺

Alex's head is in the clouds now. It was a pleasant surprise to get a message from Vanessa. His excitement level has skyrocketed now that he knows she wants to go out with him again and he can barely contain himself; but he does. He still doesn't want to get overly excited just in case he has another experience like he's had before. Nonetheless, he is still elated that he's come in contact with someone that has his interest.

A few days later, they get together again to enjoy each other's company and conversation. During this time, they learn more about each other and begin to talk more about their personal lives.

"We've been communicating for quite some time now and I've never asked, do you have any children?" Alex asks Vanessa. "If I am getting too personal, please let me know."

"It's no problem," Vanessa says, blushing as she smiles. "I was hoping we would get to this point. I have a son. His name is Enrique and he's fourteen years old. What about you? Do you have any children?"

"I do," Alex says. "I have a daughter, Jasmine, and she turned nine years old a little bit ago. She's a little firecracker and so much fun."

"I bet she has you wrapped around her finger too," Vanessa says.

"Yeah. That pretty much sums it up," Alex says, laughing. "She's a really good kid and she's not spoiled rotten. She is not what some would call a typical only child. As a matter of fact, I'm an only child."

"Oh, really," Vanessa says, with surprise in her voice. "I would have never guessed that."

"How so?" Alex questions.

"In most cases, only children have been known to be selfish and spoiled, and would go crazy if they didn't get their way all the time. You don't find that too often in children or people that have grown up with siblings. Looking at you and the way you carry yourself, I assumed you were surrounded by brothers and sisters," Vanessa explains.

"Nope. I was an only child," Alex goes on to say, "My mother passed away when I was sixteen and I was devastated. My dad was not around but I'm thankful my grandparents were there to take really good care of me and help me get to where I am today. I don't know what I would have done or where I could have ended up if it were not for them."

"Wow! That's an amazing story. I appreciate you sharing that with me. I would have never imagined you had so much going on in your young life and turned out to be the very nice, handsome, and respectable man that you are. Your mom and grandparents did an outstanding job."

"Thank you very much," Alex replies. "I try to be the best I can be and set a good example for my daughter. My folks instilled in me an awesome work ethic and tried to live by that every single day; from my personal life, my work life, when I coach my football team, and at church, I give my all and work very hard to make sure I stay on top of my game and make an impact."

"Wait a minute, wait a minute," Vanessa interrupts. "I see a lot more things are coming out now. Are you hiding things from me?"

"What do you mean?" Alex says smiling.

"You just mentioned you attended church and coached a football team," Vanessa answered. "Where did all of this come from? You are the modern day renaissance man, aren't you?"

"I wouldn't say that," Alex says, laughing and blushing. "I just love to do different things and have fun at the same time."

"That's good to know. I guess I can tell you that my son is a football player as well and he's pretty good too."

"That's awesome. What position does he play?" Alex asks.

"I think he's a wide receiver," Vanessa answers, laughing.

"He's going to be a great man," Alex says.

"How so?" Vanessa asks.

"Because that's the position I played when I was in school," Alex replies, as they both erupt into laughter. "Maybe one day, in due time, we'll get a chance to meet and I can show him some pointers or maybe he can show me some since I haven't played in years."

"I'm sure in due time that would be possible," Vanessa says.

"That's good to know. OK, enough about me, what do you want to tell me about you, ma'am?" Alex asks.

"I really don't know what to say," Vanessa says blushing again. "I was born and raised in Dallas, Texas. I have two brothers and two sisters. I am the middle child."

"I bet you were a handful, huh?" Alex says, jokingly.

"I was, but in a good way," Vanessa explains. "I got into trouble a lot when I didn't go to bed on time because I was always reading something. When everyone else was outside playing, I was sitting under a tree, on the porch, or hiding in a closet with a flashlight reading. It's something I've always loved to do."

"Jasmine is the same way. She loves to read and, at times, it's hard to get the book out of her hands. There have even been times where she's fallen asleep with a book in her hands. It's the cutest thing," Alex says. "I don't get on her about it, though. I let her enjoy herself."

They both smile at each other bashfully.

"So tell me more about your family life," Alex requests.

"Well, my family has a strange dynamic in that I come from an interracial family. My father is Latino and my mother is African-American. Even though Texas is a very diverse state, there weren't too many people that were in favor of our family unit. Going to school and getting teased and talked about was not fun at all. I'm thankful for my parents because they always instilled in us to love who we were and not be ashamed of it. I saw how they loved each other through thick and thin and I wanted to mirror that in my life. My parents and siblings are still in Texas and are doing well."

"Sounds like you had a very interesting life," Alex interjects. "I don't want to assume but I'm curious, do you speak Spanish as well?"

"As a matter of fact, I do," Vanessa replies. "What gave it away? My accent?"

They both burst into laughter.

"My father made sure we all knew Spanish. Even my mother," Vanessa continues. "He engrossed us in the language and the culture and we all grew to appreciate it."

"Jasmine has somewhat taught herself Spanish," Alex offers. "She's been fascinated with the language and has some computer software that she's been using to help her learn. She's pretty good at it surprisingly."

"That's great!" Vanessa says. "Maybe I'll get a chance to hear her one day. It's always good for kids to learn a language at a young age. So much more can be retained and by the time they reach a certain age, they will be experts. My son is that way, but he does not speak it that often. He's more interested in sports and girls."

"That's usually how boys are," Alex says with a laugh. He looks at his watch and is shocked at the time.

"Here we go again," Alex says. "We're having so much fun; we've completely lost track of time. We have to do more of this. I really hate to go, but I know you have responsibilities and can't stay out all day."

"I've been having a great time as well. Hopefully, time will free us up so we can do more of this," Vanessa says. "I'd like that very much."

"I'd like that as well and look forward to it," Alex replies as he walks Vanessa to her car. As they walk, their hands meet, so Alex gently grasps Vanessa's hand to which she delightfully accepts. They look at each other and smile. When they get to Vanessa's car, Alex opens her car door and before she gets in, they hug one another, which transitions to a delicate kiss on the lips. The unintentional kiss catches them both off guard, but they are pleased it happened.

"Have a good rest of the day, Vanessa," Alex says.

"I will, and you do the same," Vanessa replies. "Will I hear from you later?"

"Of course you will. I promise."

After they go their separate directions, they spend the remainder of the day reminiscing about each other and the kiss they shared. Alex regards that moment as special, and it felt good.

As the days and weeks go by, Christmas is on the horizon and people are flooding the shopping malls and retail stores to start their shopping. Alex has already finished his shopping, although most of it was done online and gifts have already been delivered and wrapped. Jasmine doesn't even have a clue as to what she is getting.

While at work one day, Alex debates in his mind about whether or not to get Vanessa a Christmas gift. Even though they've been communicating a lot, gone out on several dates, and are developing feelings for one another, he doesn't want to seem like he is rushing into things; but on the other hand, he doesn't want to seem insensitive or not in the spirit of giving. He sits at his desk for a few minutes pondering about what he can get for her. He decides to call her and hopes that she is available to talk.

"Hello. This is Dr. León," Vanessa answers.

"Hello Dr. León," Alex states. "This is Alex Reed. How are you doing today?"

They both laugh.

"I'm doing well Mr. Reed. How are you?" Vanessa asks.

"I'm doing very well, thank you. I know you're probably busy but I have a quick question for you."

"I'm just preparing for my next class but I have time. What's up?"

"I know we've talked about a lot of things since we've met, but I've got to ask you this. When you think about all the things you like to do, what would you say is the one thing you like to do the most or what's the one thing you would like to do that you haven't done in a while?"

Alex asks.

"Hmmm..." Vanessa says and she gets quiet for about a minute. "Well, there are a lot of things I like to do, but the one thing I have not done in a while that I would love to pick back up is writing. A few years ago, I used to write and journal a lot but lately, I haven't been able to do anything relating to that. I really would like to get back to doing that. Why do you ask?"

"I was just curious," Alex explains, "It's just another element about you that I'd like to know about you."

"That's awfully sweet of you," Vanessa responds. "I'll make sure you learn all that you need to know about me."

"And I'll be sure to do the same. Don't let me hold you up. I know you are trying to prepare for class. Have a great rest of the day and I'll talk with you later."

"Sounds good. Good bye," Vanessa says.

"Bye-bye!" Alex says as he hangs up the phone.

Immediately after he hangs up the phone, he gets online and searches for a potential gift for Vanessa. He searches three websites and is not impressed with anything. As he sits and thinks some more, he has an idea and searches on another site. As he looks around, he sees exactly what he would like to get for Vanessa. He calls the store to ask if they have the items in stock and is delighted when he finds out that they have what he wants. He places them on hold so that he can go pick them up after work. After he hangs up, he feels really happy that he found a gift for Vanessa and he hopes she will like it.

After work, and before he picks Jasmine up from school, he goes to pick up the gift and gets a blank card to write a special note. Afterwards, he hurries to Jasmine's school to pick her up so they can go home and complete their day together. Throughout the evening, he and Vanessa exchange text messages to each other and all they can do is smile.

Jasmine sees Alex smiling while he's texting and she asks, "Daddy, what's making you smile so hard?"

"Oh, nothing," Alex replies, still smiling.

Jasmine doesn't buy it and she has a look on her face that shows it.

"Oh yes it is. What are you keeping from me?" Jasmine asks.

"Come have a seat, baby girl and let's talk," Alex looks up at Jasmine and motions for her to move close.

Alex and Jasmine sit on the couch and he turns to her and says,

"OK. The reason why I've been smiling a lot is because I've been seeing someone who is very nice and I think I really like her a lot."

"Why haven't you told me about her yet?" Jasmine asks.

"I didn't want to tell you until I knew for sure that I really liked her and that she was worth introducing to you," Alex explains. "Those other women I dated didn't work out and I didn't want to mention another woman and then experience the same thing. I felt that would set us both up for disappointment. Can you understand that, baby?"

"Yes sir," Jasmine answers. "I do understand. So when do I get a chance to meet her?"

Alex laughs.

"I'm not sure, but I hope it's soon. Would you like to see a picture of her?" Alex asks.

"Of course I would!" Jasmine replies.

Alex pulls up the picture Vanessa sent him on his iPhone and shows it to Jasmine.

"Oooo, Daddy! She is very pretty. What is her name?" Jasmine asks.

"Her name is Vanessa," Alex answers.

"Did you meet her on the computer too?"

"No, baby. I actually met her the night I went to the Christmas party with Uncle Craig. She was at the same party and we started a conversation and had a great time. We've seen each other a lot since then and have talked and texted quite a bit as well. She is a very nice person," Alex explains.

"I see...so when can I meet her? Does she have any children?" Jasmine asks.

"You'll meet her one day when we feel it's time; and she has one son."

"That's nice. Maybe I'll get a chance to meet him too," Jasmine suggests.

"I'm quite sure you will," Alex says. "In due time, baby."

They continue with the rest of the evening until it's time for Jasmine to go to bed. After he says prayers and tucks Jasmine in, Alex goes to his room and gets on the phone with Vanessa. They talk for what seems like hours. One would think they were a couple of love sick teenagers—lying in bed talking, laughing, and having a good time. The more they talk, they more they learn about each other and begin to develop strong feelings.

After two hours, they realize it's getting late and decide to end the call. After saying goodbye, Alex doesn't go to sleep right away. He still can't believe everything is going so well with Vanessa. He really hopes she likes him as much as he likes her; she seems to. Every time they talk or get together, they take down their guards and lower the walls they both have built up and allow each other into their lives on a more personal level. The more he thinks about her, the more he smiles. His feelings for her are becoming deeper without his intention. After a long time of thinking, he finally drifts off to sleep.

Several days later, while Alex is home one evening doing some work while sitting at his desk, he realizes that there's a possibility that he may not be able to see Vanessa on Christmas Day so he decides to have the gifts sent to her office with the nice card inside. He pulls out the card and writes a message on the inside. Then he takes the gift, which is already wrapped, and puts it all in a box to be mailed off tomorrow at the post office. He looks on the Johnson C. Smith website to find out when their winter break begins to avoid her package sitting at her campus mailbox over the long holiday break. He finds out that he's got plenty of time if he mails it off this week. So the next morning, on his way to work after dropping off Jasmine, he takes the package to the post office.

Two days later, Vanessa gets a knock on her door from her assistant, Tanya.

"Come in!" Vanessa says.

"Ms. León. Sorry to bother you, but this package came for you."

"Does it say who it's from?" Vanessa asks.

"No ma'am," Tanya answers. "It's only addressed to you."

"Thank you very much," Vanessa says as she takes the package. She looks at it and hesitates for a few seconds to open it, but she opens it up and finds a nice, leather-bound journal with her name engraved on a silver plate on the bottom right side of the journal. She notices that there's another box inside of the first box. She opens it and finds a beautiful silver pen and pencil set. Her initial reaction is shock, not prepared to receive anything, but also not knowing who it's from. She looks in the box again and sees a card. She opens it and it reads:

Dear Vanessa,

I know we didn't talk about exchanging gifts for Christmas, but I wanted to do a little something for you to let you know how much I have enjoyed spending time with you. You have brought a lot of sunshine to my life.

Thank you! Please enjoy your gifts and I hope you get back to what you enjoy doing. Hopefully, these little tokens will help get you started.
Merry Christmas!!!
XOXOXOXO
Alex

After reading the card, tears begin to flow down Vanessa's cheek. She realizes that no one has been this kind to her since Guillermo was alive. She never thought she would ever feel this way again. Alex's act of kindness is a little overwhelming at first, but soon turns into a deep appreciation for him and the wonderful gifts. After she regains her composure, she gets on the phone and calls Alex.

"Alex Reed," Alex says when he answers his phone.

"I see that Christmas has come a little early for me," Vanessa says. "One of Santa's elves dropped off my gift today."

"Oh really," Alex replies. "Hopefully, it's something you will like."

"I don't like it at all. I love it! Thank you so much. You really didn't have to do this."

"I know I didn't have to. I wanted to," Alex said. I'm glad you like it. Hopefully, you will get back to writing, and who knows, the next New York Times best seller will be in those pages."

"I don't know about that, but I know I'll have something good to write tonight before I go to bed..." As Vanessa speaks, she begins to cry again and it's apparent to Alex.

"Vanessa, are you OK? Did I do something wrong?" Alex asks with concern.

"No. You haven't done anything. These are happy tears," Vanessa replies. "You have no idea how much your gifts have made my day...my year..." Vanessa starts to cry again. Alex begins to tear up a little.

"I'm glad I was able to make you happy," Alex says. "Are you available for lunch today? I have to get something off my chest."

"Yes I am," Vanessa responds. "Is everything OK?"

"Yes. Everything is fine," Alex says. "I just need to see you face-to-face and it can't wait any longer."

"OK," Vanessa says, with a little hesitation. "Where shall I meet you?"

"I'll come there and I will bring lunch to you. Just let me know what you have a taste for and I'll bring it."

"Ok, I'll text it to you," Vanessa replies.

"Great! I'll see you about 12:30. Is that OK?" Alex asks.

"That's perfect. See you then," Vanessa says.

"Awesome. See you then," Alex says as he hangs up the phone.

After a little while, Alex receives a text from Vanessa stating what she would like for lunch. When it's time, Alex goes to pick up lunch and heads to Vanessa's job. When he walks through the doors of Vanessa's office, Tanya, her assistant, greets him. She looks at Alex, smiles, and says, "Hello sir. How may I help you?"

"Good Afternoon, ma'am!" Alex says. "My name is Alex Reed and I am here to see Dr. León."

"Yes sir. I'll go get her for you. Please have a seat and make yourself comfortable."

"Thank you!" Alex says as he takes a seat.

Tanya goes back to Vanessa's office. "Dr. León, there is a very handsome young man by the name of Alex Reed here to see you. Who is he, where did you find him, and does he have any brothers that look like him?"

Vanessa bursts into laughter.

"Leave me alone," Vanessa says. "I'll tell you about it later. He's my lunch date."

"Lunch date? Well, well. What have we here? Someone has been keeping secrets from me," Tanya jokes.

"I'm not keeping secrets. I'm just not telling anything right now," Vanessa declares. "Now, if you will excuse me, I have a lunch date with a handsome young man out front."

Vanessa and Tanya engage in schoolgirl giggling as they walk towards the front to meet Alex.

"Hi Alex! You can come on back," Vanessa says. "Tanya, if you want to break for lunch you can. I'll let calls roll to voice-mail if need be."

"Thank you Dr. León. I'll do that. It was nice to meet you, Mr. Reed," Tanya says to Alex.

"It was a pleasure to meet you as well, Ms. Tanya."

Vanessa and Alex go into her office and they have a seat while Alex takes food out of the bag to give to Vanessa.

Just before they begin to eat, Alex says a blessing over the food. Before he takes his first bite, he puts down his sandwich and looks Vanessa in the eyes.

"OK. Before I eat, I have to get this off my chest. If what I say offends you or upsets you in any way, let me apologize up front. I want you to know that I have not been this happy with anyone in a long time. The time I spend with you has been absolutely amazing and I don't want it to end," Alex says, as he begins to ramble on about his feelings. "You are a very beautiful woman and I think about you all the time and can't seem to get you out of my mind."

All the while Alex is talking; Vanessa is trying hard not to laugh because she detects how nervous he is. She's also starting to tear up a little.

"...And furthermore, I know I'm putting myself out there and possibly setting myself up for rejection but I'm going to say this anyway. Vanessa, I would love to spend a lot more time with you and ask you if you would like to be in a relationship with me," Alex says, as he pulls out a note from his jacket pocket and hands it to Vanessa. She laughs as she reads the note, which reads:

Will you be my girlfriend?
Yes or No
Please circle one

She grabs a pen, circles yes, and hands the note back to Alex. He looks at the note and smiles from ear to ear. Vanessa comes from behind her desk, sits on Alex's lap, and gives him a long passionate kiss. She gets up, goes back to her chair behind her desk, and begins to eat. Alex is stunned, yet pleased at what just happened. He begins to eat and they enjoy their lunch with great conversation.

As they finish lunch, Vanessa says, "Now that we are officially a couple, you know what has to happen now?"

"What's that?" Alex asks.

"We've got to get introduced to each other's children," Vanessa answers.

"You're right. Jasmine is anxious to meet you anyway."

"Oh really now? You've been talking to her about me?" Vanessa asks.

"Yes I have," he replies. "I spilled the beans one morning a little while ago and she has been bugging me to meet you ever since. I told her it would happen in due time."

"Well, I have to have a conversation with Enrique about it,"

Vanessa says. "I need to know how he will feel about this. I haven't introduced him to any men, so you will be the first."

"I understand. We can take this as slow as we need to. I'm not going anywhere," Alex confesses. "I want to make sure everyone is on board, but I don't foresee that being an issue."

"I sure hope not," Vanessa says. "Thank you very much for the wonderful gifts and lunch. I can't wait until we do this again."

"As long as I keep getting tasty kisses like you just gave me, I'll bring you lunch every day," Alex says, as they laugh and hold hands. "It was my pleasure and I'm looking forward to spending not only my lunches with you, but so much more."

"That sounds good to me," Vanessa admits.

"I'd better let you get back to work and I've got to get back to the office. Let's chat later to see when we can get the kids together," Alex states.

"That'll be great. I'll call you when we get home and get settled. I'll walk out with you."

Before leaving out of Vanessa's office, they kiss once more. After saying their goodbyes, Alex walks to his car and Vanessa goes back to her office and sits in her chair, speechless. Not soon after she sits down, Tanya comes into her office.

"Dr. León, how was your lunch date? I just passed Mr. Reed a second ago."

Vanessa doesn't answer her right away; she seems to be in somewhat of a daze.

"I'm sorry Tanya. What were you saying?" Vanessa says, coming out of her daze with the biggest smile on her face.

"Dr. León, you are glowing," Tanya remarks. "Oh, my goodness. I haven't seen you like this in a very long time."

"I haven't felt like this in a very long time either," Vanessa declares, still smiling from ear to ear. "I am now in a relationship with a wonderful man. I didn't think I would ever find a man as good as Guillermo. He is too good to be true. I think about him and pinch myself because I think the dream will be over with. But then I realize that it's not a dream and I'm blessed to be in the company of a great guy. I can't believe this is happening to me."

"Well, you of all people deserve happiness. I am so happy for you," Tanya tells Vanessa as she gives her a hug. "So when is he going to meet Ricky?"

"I'm not sure yet," Vanessa answers. "We're actually going to talk about that later today. I'm really nervous because I'm not sure how Ricky will respond to another man that's not his father. They were very close and he may be a little overprotective. I just hope he doesn't scare Alex away."

"Ricky is a good kid. I believe he will be very receptive to Alex, especially when he sees how happy he makes you. It's possible that they will have a great relationship."

"I really hope so," Vanessa reflects. "Well, I'd better get myself together for my next class. It's final exam time. We all know how much fun that can be."

Vanessa and Tanya laugh and get back to work.

Later that evening, as Vanessa and Ricky eat dinner, she decides that now is as good a time as any to bring up Alex.

"Ricky, I need to talk with you," Vanessa says.

"What's up Mom?" Ricky looks directly at Vanessa.

"I wanted to get your opinion on something and I want you to be honest with me."

"Ok. What is it?"

"I know you and your father were very close and I know you miss him. I miss him too. We will both always miss him. No one could ever take his place. He'll always have a special place in our hearts. With that being said, what would be your thoughts about me beginning to date again?" Vanessa asks.

Ricky pauses for a minute.

"I've actually thought about that a few times and as much as I miss Papi, I would want you to be happy; and if that means being with someone else, I'd be OK with that. You deserve to be happy."

"So would you have any objections to meeting someone if I met someone who I thought was special?" Vanessa asks.

"I don't think I'd have a problem with it. But I will need to check him out for myself to see what kind of guy he is. The final approval needs to come from me," Ricky says as they both laugh.

"I totally understand. What would you say if I were to tell you that I am dating someone and I wanted you to meet him?" Vanessa asks.

"You're dating someone and didn't tell me, Mom?" Ricky asks, with a grin on his face.

"I am," Vanessa admits.

"Mom, that's great!" Ricky says as he gets up from the table and gives his mom a hug. "Why didn't you tell me?"

"I didn't know how you would respond to it, plus I wanted to make sure he was going to be around for a long time. I didn't want to start bringing a lot of people in and out of our lives. I didn't want that for us," Vanessa explains.

"I can understand and respect that. So...what's his name? Where did you all meet? When will I get the chance to interrogate him?" Ricky asks all at once.

Vanessa laughs.

"His name is Alex Reed, he's an attorney, and we met at the Christmas party Ms. Maria and I went to. You remember how I really didn't want to go? Well I'm glad I did because if I had not gone, I would not have met him. He's really a nice guy."

"You two have already gone out on dates and stuff?" Ricky asks.

"Yes, we have," Vanessa admits, blushing.

"Are there any other secrets you are keeping from me, Mother?" Ricky stands with his arms folded with a frown on his face.

"No secrets here. I'll let you know that he is a football coach and he has a daughter, Jasmine, who is nine years old."

"Oh yeah? I really have to meet this guy now. When do I get the chance?" Ricky asks.

"It'll have to be after Christmas since we are going to Dallas. I'll check with him and we'll get something together."

"Well, I can't wait to meet him. It seems that you really like him and that's all that matters. If you really like him, I'll like him too," Ricky says, as he gives his mother another hug.

During the same time that Vanessa and Ricky are having their talk, Alex and Jasmine are at home and have just finished dinner. Alex is now reading on the couch and Jasmine is doing homework. After a few minutes of reading, Alex stops and begins to talk with Jasmine.

"Jazzy, I need to talk with you for a minute," Alex says.

"What about, Daddy?"

"It's about something very serious."

Jasmine closes up her books and joins Alex on the couch.

"Do you remember me telling you about the lady that I met a little while ago at the Christmas party with Uncle Craig?"

"Yes sir," Jasmine answers. "I remember. Her name is Vanessa, right?"

"Yes. That is correct. Well, I wanted to get your opinion on something. What if I was to tell you that I really like her a lot and that we talk to each other every day and see each other a couple times a week? What would you say?" Alex asks.

"I would think that would be great Daddy!"

"OK. What if I were to tell you that I like her so much that I asked her to be my girlfriend?" Alex asks.

"I would be very happy for you," Jasmine responds with a giggle.

"OK. What would you say if I told you that she wanted to meet you?"

Jasmine hastily jumps off of the couch, grabs Alex's face and with excitement.

"You mean I get a chance to meet her in person?"

"Yes, baby. You get to meet her and her son in person."

Jasmine jumps up and down and runs around the living room. Alex watches her and laughs. After a few laps around the room, Jasmine stops in front of Alex.

"So when? When do I meet her?"

"I'm not sure yet. We are going to talk more about it this evening. She will call me when she gets settled at home. As soon as we come up with a day, I will be sure to let you know."

"I am very excited!" Jasmine exclaims.

"Why is that, baby girl?" Alex asks.

"I'm excited to meet the person who makes you happy. Even though Mama is not here anymore to make you smile, I'm glad that someone you like can do it. That makes me happy and when I'm happy, I smile, just like this..." Jasmine does one of her silly smiles that makes Alex laugh and then they embrace in a hug. After a few minutes, Alex's phone rings. It's Vanessa.

"Hey Vanessa! How are you?" Alex says.

"I'm doing fine, Alex. How are you? What are you up to?"

"Oh nothing," Alex replies. "Jasmine and I were just talking about you."

"Hi Vanessa! Can't wait to meet you!" Jasmine yells loud enough hoping Vanessa can hear her. Vanessa laughs and Alex shakes his head smiling.

"Please tell her hello and I can't wait to meet her too," Vanessa says.

"I will be sure to tell her. Speaking of meeting, did you have an opportunity to think about when we all can meet up?" Alex asks. "How about during the Christmas holiday?"

"I really wish we could. We have plans to be in Dallas for the holidays. We planned this trip months ago. I'm so sorry," Vanessa says apologetically.

"There's no need to be sorry. I totally understand. I knew there was a possibility that you all may be traveling over the holidays. Maybe when you guys come back and before the kids go back to school, we can make the connection. How does that sound?"

"That sounds perfect," Vanessa says. "I'm getting excited already."

"I am too, but I'm also sad that we won't be together for Christmas or New Year's. Next year, we will be together for sure, so go ahead and plan for that," Alex boldly states.

"I'm already one step ahead of you. It's a date," Vanessa responds.

"I'd better get off the phone so I can get Jasmine situated and get some things ready for tomorrow. Shoot me a text when you get in bed. I'm sure I'll be done with everything by then."

"Will do. I'll chat with you later. I love you," The words roll off Vanessa's tongue so smooth and effortlessly.

Immediately, Alex is frozen, not expecting to hear those three words. He stands there for a brief few seconds with his mouth open, speechless. When he comes to his senses and realizes what she said, he responds sincerely, "I love you, too, sweetheart."

They both hang up their phones, with Vanessa blushing and smiling. Both she and Alex go through their nightly routines before going to bed. While in bed, they text, giggle, and laugh just like lovesick teenagers again sneaking on the phone when they're supposed to be asleep. They talk until they get extremely sleepy then they say their goodbyes. It doesn't take Alex long to fall asleep. Vanessa, on the other hand, is now wide-awake and can't seem to fall asleep. Instead of tossing and turning, she takes out the journal and a pen Alex gave her and begins to write:

December 17th

Dear God,

I know it's been a while since I've written. I'm glad we've talked quite a bit though. I don't know what's happening in my life right now but it feels good and I want to thank you. Times have been rough since Guillermo has been gone and I've tried to be strong for Ricky. Then all of a sudden, you allow me to come in contact with this wonderful man and develop these feelings I haven't felt in a long time...and it feels GOOD!!! It was never my plan to pursue another relationship. I guess it's possible that you had a different plan. If this is someone that's going to be in our lives for good, please give me a sign that's crystal clear. I want to be sure that Alex is what's right for me and for Ricky. I want to be happy again and if it's with Alex, I'm OK with that!!!

Vanessa

She closes her journal, turns off her lamp, and drifts off to sleep.

Days go by and Vanessa and Ricky travel to Dallas to meet family while Alex and Jasmine stay in Charlotte spending time getting into the holiday spirit. They play Christmas music throughout the house, make Christmas cookies, and drink lots of hot chocolate. On Christmas morning, Jasmine wakes Alex way earlier than he anticipated, and he is forced to go into the living room to witness Jasmine tear through wrapping paper to open her gifts. She is very excited about her gifts and has a great time admiring all the wonderful things she's received. With all the wrapping paper that's scattered everywhere, there is one bag left under the tree that Alex doesn't recognize. Jasmine eyes it and goes over to the tree to get it.

"This one is for you, Daddy! Merry Christmas!" Jasmine shouts as she hands him the bag containing a box. "Open it! Open it!"

Alex opens the bag and the box and sees a cutout drawing of a Superman logo that was drawn and colored by Jasmine.

"I made this just for you, Daddy, because you are my hero," Jasmine exclaims as she gives him a big hug and kiss on the cheek.

"I love it, baby girl! Thank you and Merry Christmas to you too. Do you like your gifts?"

"Yes sir I do!"

"Good, because I think you may be getting some more things. We're going over to Uncle Elijah and Aunt Corrine's house for dinner," Alex says.

"Yay!" Jasmine cheers with excitement. For the remainder of the morning, Alex sits and enjoys watching Jasmine have a good time with her gifts while also thinking about Vanessa. He doesn't want to disturb her since she's probably surrounded by her family and friends as they enjoy the holiday. Instead of calling, he decides to go ahead and send a text:

Alex: *Hey Beautiful! Merry Christmas! I know you're with family and* *friends but I wanted you to know that I am thinking about you and I miss you. Have a great time and I'll chat with you soon. Love you!!! :-**

A few minutes later, Vanessa replies:

Vanessa: *Hey handsome! I was just thinking about you and was going to text you. You beat me to the punch! LOL! Merry Christmas! I love and miss you too. I hope you and Jasmine are having a great day. I'm sorry I didn't get you a Christmas present. Time just got away from me.*

Alex: No worries. *I was not expecting you to get me one. I'm glad you like your gift and I have you in my life. That's one of the best presents I could have ever received.*

Vanessa: *Awwww! That's sweet! I will chat with you later. Love you!*

Alex: *1-4-3-2*

Vanessa: *Huh?!?!?!?*

Alex: *1-4-3-2...I (1) Love (4) You (3) Too (2)* ☺

Vanessa: *That's cute! 1-4-3-2*

Alex and Jasmine relax a little longer before it's time to go over to Elijah and Corrine's house.

Once they get to the house, they are met by all of their friends. Everyone is having a festive time and exchanging gifts. Craig and Nia are arguing as always, and Corrine and Elijah have prepared a lovely meal for everyone to enjoy. As everyone eats, Alex gets everyone's attention by slightly hitting a glass with a spoon.

"Can I have everyone's attention, please?" He waits momentarily for everyone to get quiet. "Let me first say Merry Christmas to all of you. You all are my family and I love you guys very much. I really appreciate the love and support you have given to Jasmine and I over the past year. Words cannot express how much that has meant to us. There was a point in time I said that I would spend the rest of my life taking care of my daughter and not thinking about getting into any type of relationship. I tried a few times and had horrible experiences and vowed to never get into another situation like that again. Well, when I least expected it, I ended up meeting someone and now, I can proudly say that I am in a relationship."

A simultaneous gasp fills the room, followed by cheers and claps.

"I see someone has been withholding information," Foster chimes in. "What's up with that?"

"OK. Spill the beans, mister!" Hannah yells. "Who is she? Where is she, and where is she from?"

"Is this the same woman you met the night of the Christmas party?" Craig boldly asks. "If so, she is beautiful, bro!"

"OK...OK...one question at a time," Alex says laughing. As he begins to speak further, everyone has his full attention:

"Craig, to answer your question, yes—it's the same woman I met at the party. We've been talking ever since. Her name is Vanessa; she is a professor at Johnson C. Smith; and she is beautiful, smart, and has a high school-aged son. She is absolutely wonderful."

"Is she single or divorced?" Juni asked.

Alex pauses for a minute. "You know what, Juni. I don't know. I just assumed she is single. She hasn't mentioned it and I didn't think to ask. I'll ask her when I see her again."

"When is that going to be and when are we going to meet her?" Alicia asks.

"I'll see her again after the holidays. She is out of town right now, but when she comes back, I'll make sure you all meet her."

"How does Jasmine feel about you dating?" Foster asks.

"Jasmine and I talked about it recently and she says she is OK with it," Alex answers. "As a matter of fact, she has been the one pushing me to date even when I didn't want to. She has been a great support. So I think it's safe to say that she approves of me dating and once she meets Vanessa, she will approve of her, too."

"It's rare to have a daughter to be so receptive of her father dating another woman other than her mother. She must be really special. I really hope there won't be any issues later," Bradley says.

"I don't think there will be," Alex explains. "Jasmine has been a real trooper throughout this entire situation and I am so proud of her."

"And you should be. I'd be proud of her too. In fact, we all are proud of her," Corrine says.

As everyone expresses their happiness for Alex and his newfound love, Elijah and Nia have been very quiet, listening to what everyone has to say. Once the questions and comments die down, Nia chimes in.

"I saw Alex after he came in from the party and I saw something in his eyes that I haven't seen in a long while. He was smiling brighter and was lively and upbeat. I've also seen the disappointment on his face when his dates didn't go as he expected. It broke my heart to see him like that..." Nia begins to cry while talking, and Corrine, Hannah, and Alicia go over to her to comfort her. Some of the others are shedding tears as well.

"All I want is for this good man to find a good woman, and if Vanessa is that one, she has my vote," Nia says.

After a few minutes of comforting Nia, Elijah clears his throat and begins to speak.

"Alex, I want you to know that we are extremely happy for you. I echo Nia's comment in saying that you are a great man who does deserve a great woman. From the way your eyes light up when you talk about her and seeing how big your smile is, I'm willing to bet she is the one God has for you. Take as much time as you need to get to know her and learn to love her. I have never met this woman but I feel deep in my heart that she is the piece that's been missing in your life and her son will add another element to the relationship. I believe the love you all will have for each other will surpass any amount of love you have received in the past, and that's no disrespect to Gabrielle because we all know how much you loved each other. All I'm saying is that with this new relationship, the love will be honest, pure, and on a level you can't comprehend right now. We can't wait to meet her and welcome her into the family."

"Thank you, sir. I really appreciate that," Alex says. "Thank you all for your kind words. I can't wait for you all to meet her as well. Words really can't express how I'm feeling right now. I think if it were anyone else, I would be a nervous wreck, but I'm not. I'm at peace with everything and looking forward to whatever is on the horizon."

For several hours, they all remain at the house playing games, eating, drinking, and having a great time together, as always. When it starts getting late, they all say their farewells before they journey home. Jasmine has had so much fun that she falls asleep on the couch and Alex has to carry her to the car. She stays asleep throughout the entire trip back home, so Alex carries her into the house and puts her in her bed. He goes to his room to change into something a little more comfortable. As he is getting dressed, he receives a call. When he sees that it's Vanessa calling, his smile gets so big and bright, it could light the entire house. They spend the next two hours talking about their day with family and friends and express how much they miss each other. When they both began to get sleepy, they end the call and immediately hit the sack. No one has any problems going to bed this night.

For New Year's Eve, Alex and Jasmine decide to stay home just as they did last year, even though they had invites for quite a few parties. Finger foods, chips, and lemonade are on their menu. The sparkling grape juice to toast at midnight is chilling in the refrigerator. Alex and Jasmine are having a great time together, eating, dancing, and watching all of the broadcasts on television. It's ten minutes before the ball drops in Times Square and Alex gets the sparkling grape juice out of the refrigerator and pours it into plastic champagne glasses for he and Jasmine to toast. He sits on the couch and Jasmine lies on his lap awaiting the countdown.

"Don't get too comfortable, baby girl. I don't want you to miss the countdown like you did last year," Alex says.

"I won't," Jasmine says. "I'm wide awake."

Five minutes later, Jasmine is sound asleep and Alex tries to wake her. She doesn't move. He waits another few minutes and tries to wake her again, unsuccessfully.

"Baby girl, it's almost midnight. We have to do our toast," Alex says, gently shaking her. No movement. Pretty soon, the countdown begins: ten, nine, eight, seven, six, five, four, three, two, one, HAPPY NEW YEAR!!! Alex laughs and whispers Happy New Year in Jasmine's ear and kisses her on her cheek. He reaches for his glass and drinks his and Jasmine's sparkling grape juice. As soon as he's done drinking, he gets a notification on his cell phone. It's a text message from Vanessa:

Vanessa: *Happy New Year my love! May this year be filled with love, happiness and smiles. I miss you!*

Alex: *Happy New Year, sweetheart! I miss you too. Next year, it will not be like this. We will be bringing in the New Year together.*

Vanessa: Promise?

Alex: *Promise!*

Vanessa: *Where's Jasmine?*

Alex: *Asleep...again! LOL!*

Vanessa: *LOL*

Alex: *Where's Ricky?*

Vanessa: *He's playing video games with his cousin. They will be up for the rest of the night.*

Alex: *Will I hear from you later today?*

Vanessa: *Of course you will.*

Alex: *GREAT! Jasmine is asleep on my lap. I need to put her in bed and I'm going to turn in as well. I'll chat with you later. 1-4-3!*

Vanessa: *Looking forward to it. 1-4-3-2!*

Alex takes Jasmine to her room, gets her tucked in, and he goes to bed himself.

Later that day and the days following, Alex and Vanessa have numerous conversations on the phone and in person, enjoying themselves fully as they immerse themselves in their relationship. After some time, the tone of their conversations begins to change.

"You know, we've talked about a little of everything since we've met but there is one thing in particular we've never discussed," Alex notes.

"What's that sweetie?" Vanessa asks.

"I wanted to ask you if you've ever been married before."

There is complete silence from Vanessa; she hesitates to answer the question.

"Hello. Vanessa? Did I lose you? Are you still there?" Alex asks.

"Yes. I'm here," Vanessa responds, but her voice has changed. "I knew the time for this conversation would come. I tried to avoid it as long as I could."

"Is it something you are ready to talk about now or is it something that needs to wait?" Alex questions. "If it's something difficult, we can talk about it when you are ready. I'm in the same boat and I know one day, I will need to talk about it."

"I have a great idea then. Let's just both get everything out that we have been holding in and not keep secrets," Vanessa suggests. "That way, everything is out in the open so we can deal with it and move forward if we choose."

"That's a great idea," Alex says. "Not only does that give us a chance to see each other, but we will be introduced to each other's kiddos and have a chance to grow closer together if you like. When do you want this to happen?

"Let's have dinner at my house this Friday," Vanessa suggests. "I'll cook and we'll all have a great time."

"I can't wait!" Alex says. "Is there anything you want us to bring?"

"Nope! Just bring your handsome self and your beautiful daughter and it's a date," Vanessa says.

"I can do that," Alex replies. "I'll let Jasmine know. She'll be just as excited as I am."

"We're excited as well and can't wait to see you all," Vanessa says.

"What time should we be there?" Alex asks.

"Seven o'clock will be perfect."

"We'll be there with bells on. I even remember where you live," Alex says as they both laugh.

"That's good to know," Vanessa says. "I'll talk with you later. We've got some things to get done around the house."

"Have fun," Alex says jokingly. "Talk with you soon."

They both hang up the phone and go about doing what they need to do for the evening. After the phone call, Alex calls for Jasmine and asks her to come into the living room with him. When she gets there, they both sit on the couch and Alex begins to talk with her.

"Baby girl, I have a surprise for you."

"What is it?" Jasmine asks.

"Well, what's the one thing you have wanted to do for a long time now?"

"Ummm...go to Disney World?" Jasmine answers with some hesitation, not knowing where Alex is going with this.

"Nope!" Alex says.

"Ummm...go ride some horses?" Jasmine tries again.

"Nope!" Alex answers.

"I give up. What is it?" Jasmine pleads.

Alex laughs.

"We are going over to Vanessa's house so you can meet her and her son, Enrique," Alex informs Jasmine, with a smile on his face.

Jasmine's eyes light up like a Christmas tree and she smiles from ear to ear.

"Are you serious? I'm finally getting a chance to meet Vanessa?" Jasmine's eyes get big, filled with hope and excitement.

"Yes. We are going over there this Friday."

"Yes...yes...yes!" Jasmine cheers as she gets up from the couch and does a happy dance. Alex is amused at her reaction to the news. "I finally get to meet Vanessa AND her son! This is so cool!"

"I'm glad you're excited, baby girl. I am too," Alex tells her.

"Can I make something and bring it to her?" Jasmine asks.

"Sure you can. What are you going to make her?"

"It'll be something nice. I'm going to make it now," Jasmine proclaims, getting up to go towards her room.

"OK. Can I see it when you're done?" Alex calls out.

"No. You will see it Friday when I give it to her," Jasmine says as she takes off running to her room to make Vanessa's present. Alex goes to his home office and does some work.

For the next hour, Jasmine runs in and out of his office grabbing things, and getting items out of the kitchen and the living room. He can only imagine what she is concocting. Several minutes later, she comes into his office to see what he's doing.

"Whatcha doin', Daddy?" Jasmine asks.

"I'm doing a little bit of work. Are you all finished with the surprise?" Alex asks.

"Yes sir!" Jasmine replies. "I really hope she likes it."

"I'm sure she will love it because you thought enough of her to make something that comes from your heart," Alex explains. "I only wish I could see it too."

"You will, on Friday like everyone else," Jasmine proclaims as she laughs and goes to her room.

Alex shakes his head, chuckles, and continues to work some more.

Meanwhile, Vanessa and Ricky are in the dining room talking after they have finished dinner.

"Ricky, remember the gentlemen I told you about who I'm dating?"

Vanessa asks.

"Yes ma'am, I remember. Alex, right? What's up? Are you all still dating?" Ricky asks.

Vanessa giggles.

"Yes we are. I wanted to let you know that he and his daughter, Jasmine, are coming over Friday to join us for dinner."

"Cool. I finally get to meet this dude. If I don't like him, this will be a very quick dinner."

"I don't think you will have a problem with him at all. It's possible you will discover how much you all have in common. You never know," Vanessa says with a smirk on her face.

"OK. We will see. I can tell he makes you happy, so I may not be that hard on him," Ricky says with a laugh.

"I appreciate that, son. Just make sure you are on your best behavior."

"Don't worry. I'll be a good boy," Ricky says, but with a sly look on his face.

"I mean it, Enrique Hernando León. You had better be on your best behavior," Vanessa reinforces.

"I will. I will. I promise. I'm just kidding and you know I hate it when you call me by my full name."

"I know you do. I want to make sure you understand what my expectations are," Vanessa says with a serious look on her face.

"Yes ma'am, I do."

Ricky gets up from the table to give Vanessa a hug and a kiss on the cheek before he goes to his room to listen to some music. After he leaves, Vanessa puts some things away in the cabinets and cupboards before turning out the kitchen light. She sits on the couch in the living room and turns on the television. After a few minutes of channel surfing, she gets a text message on her phone. It's Alex. Her heart begins to beat fast and the smile on her face grows bigger by the second. They exchange messages for quite a while before they both end up falling asleep.

Ricky walks into the living room and finds Vanessa sound asleep on the couch. Instead of waking her, he decides to cover her with a blanket. He kisses her on the forehead and goes back to his room.

Jasmine, on the other hand, wakes Alex up when she finds him asleep and tells him to get in the bed. When he realizes what time it is, he gets Jasmine back in her bed and then goes to his room. Before he falls back to sleep, he sends Vanessa a text apologizing for going to sleep on her during their conversation, wishes her sweet dreams, and tells her that he loves her. Soon after, he climbs into bed and falls asleep after a few minutes.

On Friday evening, Alex and Jasmine are getting ready for dinner with Vanessa and Ricky. Alex is visibly nervous and having a difficult time getting things right. He has on two different shoes, socks that don't match, and he's burned a hole in his shirt with the iron. Preparation is not going well at all until Jasmine sees how frazzled he is getting.

"Daddy!" Jasmine says. "Are you OK?"

"Baby girl, I'm not doing so well," Alex confesses. "I can't seem to get anything right; I'm very nervous about tonight and I don't know why."

"Where are the clothes you were going to wear?" Jasmine asks.

"On the bed," Alex replies, "I burned a hole in my shirt, had on mismatched socks, and mismatched shoes. Who knows what can happen next."

Jasmine bursts into laughter.

"Daddy let me help you. Just sit back and relax. I got this," Jasmine confidently declares as she gathers up the clothes he has laid out, including the shirt with the hole, and goes into his closet to pick out some clothes for him. After a few minutes, she comes out with something that matches and doesn't need to be ironed.

"Wow, baby girl!" Alex says, as he looks at the clothes she picked out for him. "You did an amazing job. I really like what you picked out for me. Thank you."

"You're welcome," Jasmine responds. "We don't want to be late, so go ahead and get dressed. I'll be waiting for you in the living room."

"Yes ma'am! I'm on it," Alex responds, shaking his head as he puts on his clothes.

After a few minutes of getting dressed, spraying on some cologne, and making sure everything is in place, Alex meets Jasmine in the living room. There he finds her sitting on the couch with the present she made for Vanessa in hand.

"Are you ready to go, baby girl?" Alex asks.

"Yes I am," Jasmine answers. "You look nice and smell really good too. I'm sure Vanessa will say the same thing."

"Thank you, ma'am. My fashion designer got my wardrobe together for me and I think she did a very good job."

"I think so too," Jasmine says as they both laugh.

They put on their coats, get in the car, and drive over to Vanessa and Ricky's house. Once they arrive at the house, Vanessa, standing in the doorway, greets them. As Alex and Jasmine come through the door, Vanessa gives Alex a hug and a kiss on the cheek.

"I am so glad you all were able to make it. Is this pretty young lady Jasmine?"

"Yes ma'am, it is," Jasmine answers. "It's very nice to meet you finally, Ms. Vanessa."

"It's a pleasure to meet you too, Ms. Jasmine," Vanessa says. Jasmine gives her a hug and a kiss on her cheek. Alex stands off to the side watching them exchange pleasantries.

"I brought you a present, Ms. Vanessa," Jasmine says, as she gives Vanessa the bag with the gift she made. Vanessa opens the bag and unwraps the gift. It is a homemade picture frame with a photo of Jasmine in it. The frame was made out of popsicle sticks, cardboard, and a variety of other decorations all around it.

"Oh, my goodness!" Vanessa says. "This is absolutely beautiful. Did you make this yourself?"

"Yes, ma'am, I did," Jasmine responded. "Do you like it?"

"I love it. Thank you very much," Vanessa answers. "I have a special place I can put it."

"You did a great job with that, baby girl," Alex informs Jasmine.

"This was my first time seeing this too. She refused to let me see it when she was making it," Alex explains to Vanessa.

"Well you should be proud of her doing such a great job," Vanessa says. "Please come in and have a seat. Let me get Enrique so I can introduce you all. Make yourself comfortable."

Vanessa goes into another room to get Ricky. While they are waiting for them to return, Alex and Jasmine sit on the couch and Alex looks around the room. He happens to notice some pictures around the living room. In the pictures, he sees Vanessa, Ricky, and another man. He begins to wonder if this is the man Vanessa never talks about and has been hesitant to discuss in previous conversations. Maybe they will get a chance to talk about it tonight or another time. He will not let anything ruin this evening so he anxiously awaits them to come back. After a few minutes, Vanessa comes back to the living room.

"Alex and Jasmine, this is my son, Enrique, but I call him Ricky for short. Alex gets up from his seat to shake his hand and realizes that Ricky looks very familiar to him, but he can't put his finger on where he may have seen him.

"It's a pleasure to finally meet you, Ricky," Alex says. "I've heard so much about you, I feel like I know you already."

"It's my pleasure to meet you too, sir," Ricky responds.

"This is my daughter, Jasmine," Alex says.

"What's up, Ricky?" Jasmine says as she slaps a high five to Ricky. "You look really familiar. Have we met before?"

"I'm not sure," Ricky says. "Have we?"

"Do you play football?" Jasmine asks.

"Yes I do," Ricky answers.

"Who do you play for?"

"I play for Carver High."

"I KNEW you looked familiar," Jasmine says. "Daddy, this is the guy that we talked about at the Carver High, Central High game we went to with the team last year. Ricky León, right?"

"Yep, that's me," Ricky says. "Oh yeah. I remember you now. You told me that I did a good job that game and Mr. Alex invited me to speak to his players. I remember now. I couldn't talk to you that long because I had to get back to the team and my parents were calling for me. You've got a good memory Jasmine!"

"I remember that day too, Ricky," Alex joins in. "That was one heck of a game you had that day."

"Thank you, sir," Ricky says. "It was a fun game and I'm glad I was able to get the ball as much as I did. It was, by far, one of my best games."

"I'm sure you'll have many more. Maybe one day, I can come to more of your games and we can toss the ball around a bit and I can show you some pointers. I played the same position as you and I'll be more than happy to give you a few tips if you like."

"I'd like that a lot. Thank you," Ricky says. "I'm ready when you are."

"Great!" Alex says. "I'll coordinate everything with your mom and we can make it happen."

"Awesome!" Ricky says.

"All right everyone, it's time for dinner," Vanessa says. They all leave the living room and head towards the dining room. As everyone files into the dining room, Alex takes another look at the pictures again and remembers the day he saw them from a distance waving at Ricky. In Alex's mind, this man may have either been an ex-husband or boyfriend. Now was not the time to ask, but it was something he was going to inquire about.

They all sit down to dinner and Vanessa has prepared a delicious meal consisting of baked chicken breasts, vegetable medley, garlic mashed potatoes, and fresh baked rolls. Vanessa asks Alex to bless the meal so they all grab hands, bow their heads, and Alex begins to pray. As soon as he's finished, they all begin to eat and converse, thoroughly enjoying each other's company.

For dessert, Vanessa brings out homemade apple pie and vanilla ice cream. Everyone's eyes light up when they see it. They enjoy eating it so much, all you can hear are grunts coming from Alex and Ricky (their sign that they completely enjoyed the entire meal). Vanessa and Jasmine looked at them, shake their heads, and laugh. The four of them interact as if they have known each other for years, displaying how comfortable they feel around each other.

"Jasmine, I understand you are learning to speak Spanish," Vanessa says.

"Yes, ma'am," Jasmine responds. "There are some things I learned on my own and I've learned a little bit at school."

"Well, I'm not sure if your dad told you or not but I speak Spanish," Vanessa mentions.

"Really?" Jasmine asks, beginning to get excited.

"Yes. My father was from Mexico and he taught my brothers, my sisters, and me how to speak it when we were very young," Vanessa says. "Let me hear you speak something. Deja para tener una conversación en Español. Comprende?"

Jasmine smiles and prepares to start the conversation in Spanish:

Jasmine: Hola!

Vanessa: Hola Yazmin! That's how you say your name in Spanish.

Jasmine: Como te llama?

Vanessa: Me llamo Vanessa. Como te llama?

Jasmine: Me llamo Yazmin. Mucho gusto.

Vanessa: Mucho gusto.

Jasmine: Como estas?

Vanessa: Muy bien gracias. Como estas?

Jasmine: Muy bien gracias. Adios!

Vanessa: Adios!

"I can also count to 10. Wanna hear me?" Jasmine asks.

"Absolutely!" Vanessa says. "Show me what you got."

Jasmine begins to count in Spanish:

"Uno, dos, tres, cuatro, cinco, seis, siete, ocho, nueve, diez."

"You did a very good job, Jasmine!" Vanessa says. "If it's OK with you, I'd like to teach you some more Spanish and even help you with any Spanish homework you may have."

"I'd love that!" Jasmine yells. "Daddy, is that OK?"

"Sure!" Alex says. "As long as it's OK with Ms. Vanessa, I don't have a problem with it. While you girls are hanging out, Ricky and I can hang out, if he's up to it."

"That sounds like a winner to me," Ricky says. "It'll be good to hang out with someone cool again since dad's not here. I'd like that a lot. Thanks Mr. Alex."

"No problem! I'm looking forward to it," Alex replies.

"Jasmine, do you like to play video games?" Vanessa asks.

"Yes ma'am I do," Jasmine answers. "I bet I can even beat Ricky."

"Oh yeah?" Ricky exclaims. "We'll just have to see about that. Follow me so I can beat you real good."

"In your dreams, mister. I'll have you crying to your mama when I get done with you," Jasmine declares as she and Ricky laugh and head to the room where the video games are located.

"Vanessa, the meal was absolutely delicious!" Alex says.

"Thank you very much, Love," Vanessa responds. "It seems as though Ricky and Jasmine are hitting it off very well."

"It does. Jasmine has always wanted a brother or sister. Ricky seems to be the perfect fit."

"Ironically, Ricky has always wanted a little sister, so I'm sure he's enjoying every second now, hanging with Jasmine," Vanessa says. "Let's go into the living room. There are some things I want to share with you."

They make their way into the living room and sit on the couch facing each other. Vanessa grabs Alex's hand and begins to speak. Her hands are shaky and she is visibly nervous.

"Sweetheart, are you OK?" Alex asks. "Relax. You can talk to me about anything."

"I know," Vanessa says. "I'm OK. I always thought I would be by myself for the rest of my life and never have to share this information with anyone. Then you came along and changed that completely."

"I've wanted to share some things with you as well and now is a perfect time to let it all out."

"Please allow me to go first," Vanessa requests. "I really need to get this out and after I tell you everything, if what I have to say upsets you or you feel it's something you can't handle or deal with, I totally understand and won't be mad if don't want to see me anymore."

"Don't be silly," Alex says. "I love you and whatever you have to say, I can and will deal with. We're a team now."

"Thank you, Love," Vanessa says as she begins to tell Alex what's been on her heart and mind for quite some time. "To start, you asked me a little while ago if I had ever been married before and the answer is yes. I'm sure you've seen the pictures around. I completely forgot to take them down before you all got here. I didn't want to make you all uncomfortable and didn't want Jasmine to have questions about who that man was in the pictures. Guillermo and I were married for eighteen years and we lived a great life. He was an architect and loved what he did and loved his family. He was responsible for most of the renovations around Uptown. He took pride in putting his best foot forward for his clients and thankfully, they all have been completely satisfied. He was a good man and both Ricky and I miss him dearly. I mentioned earlier that Ricky is going to enjoy having Jasmine around because he's always wanted a younger sibling. Unfortunately, I was not able to give him what he wanted. I had a couple of miscarriages and was never able to have another child. Guillermo was devastated but we never had the heart to tell Ricky what happened. We just couldn't bring ourselves to have him devastated too. It's heartbreaking. Ricky takes it hard from time to time that his dad's not here anymore, but he has been a trooper through it all and has been a huge help to me," Vanessa takes a deep breath. "What about you? Were you married before or was there a lucky lady in your life?"

"Baby, I'm so sorry to hear about the miscarriages. I can't imagine what you all went through during those times. To answer your questions, I was married before as well. Gabrielle and I were married for fifteen years and we had a lot of fun together. She was a senior executive at the Federal Reserve Bank and was on the rise to the top. She was a person that never met a stranger. If you had an encounter with her, you immediately became a friend. She would do anything for you; even give you the shirt off of her back if you needed it. She had a heart of gold and Jasmine adored her. They were like best friends. Even though Jasmine was sad when Gabrielle left us, she has been my rock throughout the entire ordeal. She was the one who encouraged me to try to date again and to even go to that Christmas party. She also always told me not to give up hope and the person that's supposed to be in my life would make their way into my life, and you have."

"Awww! That's sweet!" Gabrielle says as she gives Alex a kiss on the lips.

"May I ask what happened to you and Guillermo? Did you all get a divorce?" Alex asks.

"No. Guillermo passed away," Vanessa responds quietly.

"Oh no, baby! I'm sorry to hear about that," Alex says. He momentarily thinks to himself what the likelihood was that he would fall in love with someone who has experienced the same loss that he and Jasmine have gone through.

"Thank you, sweetie. It was a very hard time for Ricky and I and it happened all of a sudden."

"If you don't mind me asking, how did he pass away?" Alex asks out of curiosity.

Vanessa takes a deep breath and begins to tell him the series of events that happened the night of Guillermo's passing. The more she talks about that evening, the more Alex's mouth opens in shock and tears began to flow out of his eyes. Alex soon stops her in the middle of her explanation.

"Wait. I have to ask this question-did this incident happen on the evening of September twelfth?"

"Yes," Vanessa answers, as she looks at Alex with a bewildered look on her face.

"Were you all at an event at the Ritz Carlton that evening?"

"Yes we were. Why do you ask, Alex?" Vanessa wonders how Alex can know to ask her these questions. Where could this be going?

"Was Guillermo pronounced dead at Novant Medical?" Alex asks, as he becomes choked up.

"Yes, but how would you know that?" Vanessa asks, looking at Alex with a wrinkle in her brow.

"I know that because my wife, Gabrielle, and I were in the same accident. Vanessa, you and I both lost our spouses on the same day and in the same way," Alex states with tears in his eyes. "I remember that day vividly and recall seeing you in the midst of all the turmoil. Everything was crazy that night with all of the emergency personnel, fire department, and police officers running all over the place trying to get us all to safety. I couldn't see your face but I saw you being whisked away in the ambulance and remember seeing how distraught you were at the hospital. My heart was breaking right along with yours. I felt sorry for you and didn't know who you were."

Vanessa's eyes now red with tears, she looks at Alex in disbelief.

"I can't believe what I'm hearing," she says with a tremor in her voice. "We were at the same place, at the same time, were involved in the same accident, we both lose our spouses; and here it is a year later, we meet at the same party, fall in love, and find ourselves sitting in my living room talking about this. What are the odds that something like this could ever happen? This must have been divinely orchestrated because no one could ever plan something like this to happen."

"I agree," Alex responds. "Who would have thought that our meeting each other would be the balm we needed to heal the hurts of that horrific day? I never would have imagined it in a million years, but I'm thankful we met each other when we did."

"I am too, my love," Vanessa says.

"Do you think we should tell the kids now or later?" Alex asks.

"I think now," Vanessa answers. "No need to prolong it any longer."

Vanessa calls for Ricky and Jasmine to come into the living room. A few seconds later, they hear what sounds like a herd of wild buffalo running into the living room. It's Jasmine and Ricky and they are racing through the house, making their way to the living room. When they get there, Alex tells them to have a seat because he and Vanessa have some things to share with them. As they tell their stories, Ricky and Jasmine listen intently with a wide range of emotions. They are both stunned, speechless, and at times, confused—wondering how something like this could be possible. They can't believe what they are hearing. One thing for sure, the bond they have begun to form now becomes stronger. Soon, all of them are in tears and embracing one another.

After wiping their eyes and settling back to normal, Alex says, "Now that we all have gotten to know one another, I've got to get you all introduced to the rest of the family."

"What family?" Vanessa asks.

"We have a group of wonderful friends that are like family to us," Alex responds. "We get together once a month and hang out at a place called Petey's. I'd love for you and Ricky to come and meet them."

"That sounds like fun. When are you all going to meet again?" Vanessa asks.

"I'm going to send out a text now and see if they all can meet tomorrow evening, if that works for you."

"You don't think it's too short a notice to try to get everyone together?" Vanessa asks.

"Not at all," Alex says. "We've always done this. It won't be a problem."

"OK. I'll let you work that out. I'm very excited," Vanessa says.

Alex takes out his phone and sends a text message out to all of his friends:

Hey All- I hope all is well. Sorry for the late text but I was wondering if we all can meet at Petey's tomorrow at 7pm for our monthly get together. I have something very important to tell you and it can't wait. Let me know ASAP! Thanks! Alex

After a few minutes, everyone responds to his message and a few of them ask what the urgency is. Of course, he does not respond and leaves them in suspense. Alex shows Vanessa the message and the replies and she laughs.

"You are hilarious," Vanessa says. "I can only imagine what's going through their heads right now. I must admit, I am getting nervous."

"Why?" Alex asks.

"I don't know how they will respond to me. If they loved Gabrielle, and I'm sure they did, what makes you think they will be receptive to me?"

"Because I know my friends and I know they will love you as well. This group wants to see me happy, and when they see how happy I am, they will love you even more. They'll love Ricky also!"

"You mean you want Ricky to come, too"? Vanessa asks.

"Why wouldn't I want Ricky to come?" He's just as important as you," Alex explains. "Trust me, if Ricky is not there and they find out about him later, I'm the one that'll be in the hot seat."

Everyone laughs.

"You are going to love all my aunts and uncles," Jasmine tells Ricky. "They are a lot of fun."

"Well, I can't wait to meet them," Ricky says. "Do we need to get dressed up or anything?"

"Not at all," Alex answers. "Just dress comfortably. We all are just going to hang out and have a great time."

"Cool!" Ricky says. "I'll make sure I look good and smell good. I have to make a great first impression."

They all laugh and all of a sudden, Vanessa jumps up from the couch and runs towards her bedroom.

"Sweetheart, are you alright?" Alex asks.

"I'll be right back!" Vanessa yells back. "Just give me a quick second!"

Everyone is puzzled and can't figure out what happened and why she left the room like that. A few minutes later, Vanessa walks back into the living room, smiling and holding a beautiful gift bag.

"I almost forgot this," Vanessa says. "Not knowing that you were going to give me a beautiful picture frame, I wanted to give you a little gift, Jasmine."

Jasmine's eyes light up when she sees the bag.

"This is for me?" Jasmine asks. "The bag is so pretty."

"Open it and see what's inside," Vanessa says, as she waits patiently for Jasmine to open the bag. Jasmine pulls out an assortment of body sprays, lotions, and perfume.

"Ooooo!" Jasmine yells. "I love it! I love it! I love it! Thank you very much, Ms. Vanessa!"

Jasmine gives Vanessa a hug and a kiss on the cheek. Vanessa takes the perfume and sprays a little on her wrist.

"Mmmm!" Jasmine says. "This smells good."

"Yes it does," Vanessa replies. "Did you see the name of those items?"

Jasmine looks at the bottle and screams. Her name, Jasmine, is on the bottles.

"My name is on the bottles. This is so cool!" Jasmine says. "Where did you find this?"

"I found it at the store the other day. I saw it and immediately thought of you," Vanessa said. "There is a flower called jasmine that is very pretty and smells good. So every time you wear this spray, lotion, or perfume, you will be a beautiful, fragrant flower."

"Thank you, Ms. Vanessa!" Jasmine says. "Hanging out with you is going to be a lot of fun."

"Yes indeed it will," Vanessa says. "I'll make sure of that."

For the remainder of the evening, they continue to enjoy each other's company. After a while, Alex looks at the clock and sees how late it is.

"Again, we've had so much fun that we have let time slip away from us," Alex says. "We'd better let you all get some rest."

"Awww, do we have to leave?" Jasmine pleads. "Can we stay a little longer?"

"No, baby girl," Alex says. "We don't want to wear out our welcome. Plus, we will get a chance to come over another time and they will also come to our house to visit."

"Of course! Trust me, this is not the last time you will see us," Vanessa says. "Remember, we're going to hang out tomorrow night, too."

"Oh yeah. That's right. I almost forgot," Jasmine says.

"What time shall I come by and pick you guys up?" Alex asks Vanessa.

"We'll meet you there," Vanessa says. "I've got some running to do and don't want to hold you up. I'll try not to be too late."

"No problem. We'll look forward to seeing you there," Alex says.

Alex and Jasmine gather their belongings and they all walk to the door. Jasmine hugs Vanessa, Alex slaps fives with Ricky and gives him a hug, Ricky then hugs Jasmine, and lastly, Alex and Vanessa give each other a small kiss and smile at each other. The kids look at them and smile. Alex and Jasmine get into the car and drive off. While still standing in the door watching them leave, Ricky looks at Vanessa and says, "You know what, Mom? I think I really like them."

"I do too, son," Vanessa replies with a smile. "I do too."

As they drive home, Alex and Jasmine talk about their evening with Vanessa and Ricky.

"What do you think about Vanessa and Ricky?" Alex asks Jasmine.

"I really like them, they seem like really nice people," Jasmine answers. "Ricky is really cool too. I can see us hanging out a lot and having fun."

"That's good to hear," Alex says. "I really like them, too; and look forward to spending a lot of time with them."

Jasmine gets quiet for a few minutes with a strange look on her face. Noticing her change in disposition, Alex looks at her and asks, "Baby girl, are you OK?"

"I'm fine. Daddy, can I ask you a question?"

"Sure. What is it?" Alex asks.

"Do you think you like Ms. Vanessa enough to marry her?"

Alex is completely caught off guard and he's almost afraid to answer the question, not knowing what Jasmine's reaction will be.

"You can be totally honest, Daddy," Jasmine says.

"To be quite honest, I don't know yet. I really like her and the way I feel about her, I would like to marry her in the future; but I don't know how she feels about that and I don't want to do or say anything that would mess up what we have now. I'm sure in due time, we will know if that's the route we need to take. Why do you ask?"

"I dunno," Jasmine says. "I was wondering. You look very happy when you are around her and she seems to be happy too."

"You are very observant, baby girl!" Alex says. "I am very happy when I am around her. Let me ask you this. If I were to ask Vanessa to marry me, how would you feel about that?"

Jasmine smiles and says, "I would be the happiest girl in the world."

"Really?" Alex asks.

"Really," Jasmine responds. "I've told you before, I want to see you happy and I would want to see you with someone that makes you happy like Mama did. Ms. Vanessa seems to make you happy like that."

Alex is at a loss for words for a few moments. He gathers his composure in order to reply. "That's very nice of you to say, baby girl. I'm glad that you approve of her. I was always worried that you if I did bring someone around, you wouldn't approve of them."

"I wouldn't approve of them only if I didn't like them," Jasmine says. "But Ms. Vanessa gets two thumbs up."

Once they arrive home, they get themselves ready for bed and Alex goes into Jasmine's room to tuck her in. After they say their prayers, Alex goes into his room. Jasmine looks to make sure Alex is gone and sits up in her bed and says her own prayer:

"Dear God, please allow my daddy to ask Ms. Vanessa to marry him. I think she would be a good wife for him and I would be able to have Ricky as my big brother. And when my daddy asks her, she will say yes and we could be one big happy family together. Please also tell my Mama that we will take good care of Daddy and she doesn't have to worry. Thank you, God. Amen."

After saying her prayer, Jasmine snuggles back under the covers and peacefully goes to sleep. Meanwhile, Alex is in his bed thinking about the wonderful evening they all spent together. He dozes off and on until he gets a text message from Vanessa:

Vanessa: *I'm sure you all have made it home now and are getting settled but I wanted to drop you a quick line to say hello and let you know that we had a wonderful time with you all this evening. Ricky really likes you!!!* ☺

Alex: *Hey Love! I just got Jasmine in the bed and I was just lying here. I was trying to give you some time to get settled before I contacted you. You beat me to it! LOL! We had a great time too, and Jasmine really likes you and Ricky as well. I've never seen her this happy before. If she is happy, I'm happy.*

Vanessa: *I'm glad that she's happy because we are happy. Are you happy? LOL!*

Alex: *I'm very happy. Are you happy?*

Vanessa: *I'm happy! LOL! You are so silly.*

Alex: *I know. Sweet dreams, my love. I'll chat with you tomorrow. Can't wait for you all to meet my friends. They'll love you just as much as I do.*

Vanessa: *Me too. I'm still a little nervous...but I guess I'll be ok.*

Alex: *You'll be perfect. Good night. Love you! :-**

Vanessa: *Good night. Love you, too. :-**

They both put down their phones and go to sleep.

The next day, Alex and Jasmine get their chores done in preparation to meet up with everyone later that evening at Petey's. Vanessa and Ricky spend most of the day running errands. When it's time to get ready to meet up with the friends, Alex has just finished getting dressed when Jasmine knocks on his door.

"Come in!" Alex says.

"Hi Daddy!" Jasmine says.

"Hey baby girl!" Alex says. "Come on in. What's up?"

"Oh nothin'." Jasmine says smiling. "You almost ready?"

"Yep. I'm getting there. I just wish I could get over these nerves," Alex remarks.

"Why are you nervous, Daddy?" Jasmine asks.

"I'm just worried about what everyone will think. Everyone was so used to having your mother around that they might not be too welcoming having someone else come around."

"You don't have anything to worry about, Daddy," Jasmine reassures Alex. "You said so yourself, she will fit right in and they will love her just like they loved Mama."

"You sound very sure about that, baby girl."

"I am, Daddy!" Jasmine says, with her signature smile.

"Ok. I'll take your word for it," Alex says, as he gives her a hug and finishes getting ready.

At the León house, Vanessa and Ricky have made it back home and are scrambling to get cleaned up and dressed for the evening's gathering. They are running around frantically getting themselves together. Unfortunately, Vanessa has a wardrobe malfunction and lets out a loud grunt. Ricky runs to her room to see what happened.

"Mom, are you OK?" Ricky asks.

"I'm OK, son," Vanessa replies. "I have a slight wardrobe malfunction and I have to change clothes."

Ricky notices that Vanessa's hands are shaking and she appears to be nervous.

"Mom, why are your hands shaking?" Ricky asks.

"Sweetie, I am so nervous about tonight. I don't know how Alex's friends are going to receive us. I'm just afraid that we won't be a good fit for them and we won't be accepted."

"I don't think we have to worry about anything," Ricky says. "If the friends are anything like Alex, we will fit in perfectly. Just wait and see. I know what I'm talking about. Plus, they really need to be concerned with fitting in with us. We may not like them."

Both Vanessa and Ricky burst into laughter.

"You have your father's sense of humor," Vanessa says. "I really needed that laugh. It did relax me some."

"In all seriousness, we will be fine," Ricky says. "I honestly believe we will fit in perfectly."

"Thank you, son. I'm more at ease. OK, get out so I can change clothes and we can get out of here."

Ricky gives Vanessa a kiss on the cheek and leaves out of her room. After she changes clothes, they get in the car and head to Petey's. They are running a few minutes behind and she calls Alex to let him know but gets his voicemail, so she leaves him a message.

At Petey's, Alex and Jasmine arrive a few minutes early to ensure there are enough chairs for everyone. As he's doing that, the friends begin to come in. Everyone greets each other as if it's been years since the last time they met. It's always a joyous occasion when they meet and a time for everyone to get caught up on what's been going on in everyone's lives.

Alex is not his usual, talkative self, but is constantly looking at the door to see when Vanessa and Ricky will walk in.

"All right Alex," Hannah says. "Your message sounded pretty urgent. What's going on?"

"Well, I wanted us to get together and fellowship. You all know I love it when we get together," Alex says.

"Yeah, we get that, but I think it's something more to it. What's on your mind? Spill it, buddy," Foster chimes.

Alex is still looking at the door waiting for them to arrive.

"What do you mean?" Alex says, with a smirk on his face. "Why does there have to be more to it? I love hanging out with you guys."

"We love hanging out with you, too, but I'm with Foster, you got something up your sleeves and you need to go ahead and get it out," Corrine demands.

"I bet he got a promotion and he's running his law firm now," Juni says. "That has to be what it is."

"Nope," Alex replies, still looking at the door.

"Is everything going OK with you? You're not in any distress are you?" Bradley asks. "You know if you and Jasmine need anything, we got you covered."

"I know you all do, Brad, and we appreciate that, but that's not it either."

"Well you need to just go ahead and tell us. All this guessing and trying to figure you out is working my last nerve," Nia states as everyone laughs. As they are laughing, Alex looks at the door again and sees Vanessa and Ricky coming into restaurant. He waves his hand to let them know where he is.

"I'll let all know in just a few seconds," Alex says, as he gets up from his seat and walks over towards Vanessa and Ricky. He greets Ricky with a hug and a high five and greets Vanessa with a kiss on the lips. Everyone is amazed. Alex takes Vanessa's hand and they walk over to where everyone is sitting. Jasmine gets up from her seat, runs towards them, and gives Vanessa and Ricky a hug and walks back to the table with them. Once they get to the table, Alex says, "My dear friends, the reason why I called you all together today, in addition to seeing your beautiful faces, is to introduce you to a couple of people who are very special to Jasmine and I. This beautiful woman's name is Dr. Vanessa León and this handsome young man with her is her son, Enrique, but his nickname is Ricky."

After Alex introduces Vanessa and Ricky, Alex then introduces the friends to them. Everyone has a big smile on their faces and appears genuinely happy to meet Vanessa and Ricky and to see how happy Alex and Jasmine are. They are both invited to have a seat at the table. Almost immediately, they start to bombard Alex and Vanessa with questions.

"Is this the same woman I met at the Christmas party that night?" Craig asks.

"Yes sir! She's the one," Alex responds with a big grin.

"Damn, she's still fine!" Craig says, as the group laughs.

"There you go again, stupid," Nia says to Craig. "Why is it that you always have to say something stupid?" She turns to Vanessa and says, "Please excuse Craig's stupidity. At times he just can't help it, especially when he doesn't take his crazy medication."

The group laughs again except Craig.

"I see you got a lot of jokes tonight," Craig says. "You better be lucky we have guests tonight or else I would light you up."

"Whatever fool!" Nia says.

"Alright, alright. You all cut it out," Keiko speaks up. "We have to make a good impression for Vanessa and Ricky. If they see how crazy we all are right away, we might scare them away."

"Yeah," Alicia says. "We have to gradually ease them into our craziness."

Everyone bursts into laughter and proceeds with the evening. As the night progresses, they continue having a great time getting to know Vanessa and Ricky and Vanessa is fitting in very well with everyone.

Alex notices that Elijah has not said too much the entire evening.

"Elijah. Is everything alright with you, big bro?" Alex asks Elijah quietly.

Elijah sits back in his chair quietly for a minute, sits forward again, and begins to speak, "I've been sitting back listening and watching you all the entire evening and I've come to the conclusion that you two are madly in love with each other. It has been a long time since Alex has had a smile on his face like this. It's apparent that you, Vanessa, are the reason for that smile. Whatever you all are doing, don't stop because it looks good on you. We loved his late wife, Gabrielle, like a sister and that's no disrespect to you, Vanessa. I have no doubt in my mind that we will love you and Ricky equally. I think I can speak for all of us in saying, Vanessa and Ricky, welcome to the family. Whatever you need, we all are here for you. Ricky, you have a host of uncles and aunts that will be your biggest cheerleaders in all you do. I don't know what the future holds for you all but know that you have our blessing and we have your back."

Everyone begins to get very emotional in response to Elijah's sentimental speech. A few even have to wipe away tears. Then Nia chimes in.

"I know I've said this to everyone else before the last time we met but I want to tell you, Vanessa, that I knew you were the one the day you and Alex met. The sparkle he had in his eyes was unlike anything I've seen before. The way he talked about you, the way he smiled, the way he lit up like a Christmas tree was priceless and I hoped and prayed you were the one. It was heartbreaking to see how disappointed he was after bad dates. I'm so thankful you and Ricky are in their lives. As Elijah said before, we loved Gabrielle dearly, but we're elated that we've gained another sister and nephew."

"In speaking of Gabrielle, we talked about this yesterday and we all were floored," Alex begins to explain. "You all don't know this, but the very same night Gabrielle passed away, Vanessa's husband passed away as well. Ironically, we all were in the same accident that night. She was the other family across from us in the other part of the waiting area in the emergency room. I believe that our meeting one another was a divine connection. Craig, you remember, I did not want to go to the party but you kinda forced me to go. Vanessa was the same way. Her friend wanted her to go even though she didn't; and with some pressing, she caved in and went. What would have happened if I didn't go? I would have never met this wonderful, smart, and beautiful woman and her awesome son. Then to later discover we've gone through the same trials. What are the chances of that happening?"

Everyone listens attentively to their stories and accounts of what happened in utter amazement, eyes welling up with tears.

"Hearing this proves my point that you two are destined to be with one another," Elijah says. "No matter what you all go through from this point on, you can overcome it together."

"Amen to that," Bradley adds.

"There is a Korean proverb I heard a long time ago that is applicable to you guys today," says Juni. "It says, 'Dance like no one is watching. Love like you've never loved before. Sing as if no one is listening. Work as if you're not looking for money. And live as if today was your last day.' In other words, be the happiest you all can be without any reservations or inhibitions. Live each day to the fullest and love each other like never before. That's a great recipe for a successful relationship."

"Let's propose a toast," Elijah says as he stands. "To Alex, Vanessa, Jasmine, and Ricky. May your future together be bright and your days be pleasant. It is our prayer that God grants you the desires of your heart and that you never lose focus on what's important, and that's each other. Let no one or anything disrupt what you aspire to build. May the roots of your love grow deep so you withstand the winds of change. You will bend, but will not break. Here's to life, love, and happiness. Cheers!"

"Cheers!" everyone says as they take a drink.

"Thank you all so much for your kind words and for welcoming Ricky and me with open arms," Vanessa says. "To be quite honest, I was a bit worried that we would not be accepted. I've heard so many wonderful things about Gabrielle that I felt I couldn't compare to her and that you all could make me feel that way. I see now I was wrong. I appreciate you all for making us feel like we're a part of a family. That really means a lot to us."

"We make you feel like family because you are a part of the family now," Corrine pronounces. "We're honored to have finally met you and to see not only how beautiful you are, but to see firsthand how you make Alex smile. I feel in my heart this is an ideal family unit."

"Thank you so much," Vanessa says. "Ricky and I are looking forward to getting to know you all better and vice versa. This is so exciting to me."

"Before we leave this evening, we have to make sure to get all of your contact information so you will be included on all of our communications. You'll get ours as well tonight," Craig says.

"That'll be great!" Vanessa says.

For the next hour, the group has a wonderful time talking and laughing, with Nia and Craig arguing again, and Vanessa and Ricky feeling right at home. When the evening is complete, they all exchanged contact information and spend a great deal of time saying their goodbyes until the next meeting. After everyone is gone, Alex and Jasmine walk Vanessa and Ricky to their car. Ricky thanks Alex for inviting him and gets inside. Alex walks Vanessa to her door, opens it, and gives her a kiss on the lips.

"Did you have a great time tonight?" Alex asks.

"I had a wonderful time, sweetie," Vanessa replies. "Thank you so much. I really like your friends. They are an awesome bunch."

"Indeed they are," Alex says. "We all can get rowdy at times, but we are a close-knit group and we love each other."

"I can tell, and that's what I like about them. I actually can't wait to hang out with them again."

"That'll happen sooner than you think," Alex says. "You all travel well and call me when you get settled at home. See ya Ricky!"

"See ya, Mr. Alex!" Ricky says. "I enjoyed myself tonight. See ya, Jazzy!"

"See ya later Slick Rick!" Jasmine says, laughing as she goes to him and gives him a fist bump through the window.

Alex closes Vanessa's door and they all wave goodbye as she drives off. Alex gets Jasmine in the car, buckles her in, and drives home. Not too far into the drive Jasmine falls sound asleep. Alex sees her in the back seat through his rear view mirror and he chuckles. When he gets home, he carries Jasmine to her room, tucks her into bed, and kisses her on the forehead. He goes to his room to change and get in the bed. When he gets under the covers, he receives a text notification on his phone.

Vanessa: *Hey handsome!*

Alex: *Hey beautiful! How are you and how's Ricky?*

Vanessa: *We're fine. He talked about you all the way home. I think he really likes you.*

Alex: *That's cool. Jazzy didn't talk about anyone because she went right to sleep. LOL!*

Vanessa: *LOL!*

Alex: *Ricky is a good kid. I like him as well. Looking forward to hanging out with him more.*

Vanessa: *He'd like that a lot. Get some rest. I'll chat with you tomorrow. Kiss baby girl for me.*

Alex: *I already did. Sweet dreams, sweet princess.*

Vanessa: *Sweet dreams, sweet prince. I love you.*

Alex: *I love you back!*

They both put down their phones and fall into a sweet sleep. They get a good night's rest and awake happily the next morning to start a brand new day.

CHAPTER TWELVE

A New Beginning

Still in the month of January, Alex, Vanessa, Jasmine, and Ricky have gotten into a routine of getting together on a regular basis; going to the movies, getting together for dinner, and taking advantage of cultural and church events—and enjoying every minute of it. The more time passes, the more they get to know one other and are developing a genuine love for each other. They always look forward to these times. On occasion, only Alex and Ricky hang out while Vanessa and Jasmine do the same. This weekend in particular, Vanessa and Jasmine decide to have a girls' day out to go shopping and get manicures and pedicures. The guys, on the other hand, decide to relax, watch sports on TV, and toss the football around. Alex also plans to give Ricky some pointers in football.

After a wonderful afternoon of shopping, Vanessa and Jasmine go to Serenity Hair and Nail Salon to take advantage of some more guilty indulgences. Jasmine is shocked at the fact that they are going to a place she is familiar with.

"Are we going to Serenity for our manicures and pedicures?" Jasmine asks.

"Yes we are," Vanessa answers. "Why do you ask?"

"My mom and I used to come here all the time," Jasmine responds.

"Really? I don't think I've ever seen you or your mother here before," Vanessa explains. "I've been coming here for years. That's interesting. We can choose another spa if you like."

"Oh, no. I'm ok!" Jasmine responds.

They both enter the salon and are greeted by Felicia at the reception desk.

"Good afternoon ladies!" Felicia says, with a puzzled look on her face. "Vanessa. Jasmine. What are you all doing here at the same time? How do you know each other?"

"This is my daddy's new girlfriend," Jasmine says, with a big proud smile on her face.

"Yes. Her father and I are seeing each other," Vanessa says, with just as big a smile on her face. "We're just hanging out doing some girl stuff and needed to get pampered today."

"Well, you all have come to the right place," Felicia says, as she gets them signed in. "We will have you ladies back in just a few minutes. Please feel free to have a seat. Can I get you all something to drink?"

"No, thank you. I'm fine," Vanessa responds.

"I'm good. Thanks!" Jasmine answers.

As they are sitting in the waiting area, Jasmine sees Nia in one of the stylist's chairs and runs over to her.

"Hey Auntie Nia!"

"Hey Jazzy! What are you doing here?"

"Me and Vanessa came here to get manicures and pedicures."

Nia looks toward the waiting area and sees Vanessa waving.

"Girl, come on back. I won't bite," Nia yells to Vanessa and they all laugh. Vanessa comes over to where she is and gives her a hug. "I see you all are getting pampered today. I wish I hadda known. I would have hung out with you all."

"It was a spare of the moment thing since the guys were doing their own thing, so we decided we would do something ourselves. Next time, we will be sure to include you too. The more the merrier," Vanessa tells Nia.

"I'd like that very much," Nia says. "Plus, it'll give us a chance to hang out and really get to know one another since you are a part of the family now."

"Well, we have each other's contact info so let's make it happen soon," Vanessa says.

"We will. I guarantee that," Nia responds.

They say their goodbyes as Vanessa and Jasmine get called back to get into their chairs for their pedicures.

"Jasmine, I have a question for you and you don't have to answer if you don't want to. Is that OK?" Vanessa asks.

"Ok. That's fine," Jasmine answers.

"You mentioned that you and your mother came here often. You said it's OK, but I want to make sure. Does it bother you that you're here with me now?" Vanessa asks.

"No," Jasmine answers. "Now I'm making new memories with you!"

"That's sweet, Jasmine," Vanessa says. "I just don't want you to be uncomfortable. If you were, we could definitely go to another place."

"It's fine," Jasmine says, with a smile. "I really like it here and I don't want to go anywhere else. This can be one of our hang out spots now."

"That's good to know and yes, this can be one of our many hang out spots," Vanessa says. They both smile and continue with the rest of their beauty treatments. Once they are done with the manicure and pedicure, they grab a bite to eat. As they eat, talk, and laugh, Vanessa changes the direction of the conversation.

"Jasmine, if you don't mind, tell me a little something about your mother that you'd be willing to share."

Jasmine, with a smile on her face, answers, "My mama was a great lady. She was smart, beautiful, and a really good friend. We had a lot of fun together. There were times we would go out like this and leave Daddy at home. I missed doing things like this. Mama made things fun."

"It seems like you and your mother were very close," Vanessa says.

"Yes we were," Jasmine replies. "We were very close."

"I know how that is because my mother and I were close too. I had two older brothers and I didn't like hanging around them a lot because they always wanted me to do gross boy things that I wasn't interested in. So my mother let me hang out with her and those were the best of times. Whenever my dad and brothers wanted to do boy stuff, my mother and I would do what we wanted to do and that was fun."

"Where is your mom?" Jasmine asks.

"She lives in Texas along with my father and brothers," Vanessa replies. "I don't get a chance to visit them often but when I do, we all have a great time together."

"That sounds like fun," Jasmine says. "I hope you get a chance to see them more."

"I'm sure I will and maybe you can meet them too one day," Vanessa says.

"Really? Can I?" Jasmine asks.

"If you like," Vanessa responds. "Of course you would need to ask your dad, but if he says it's OK, you all can meet them."

"Yes!" Jasmine shouts out with enthusiasm.

"I want you to know this as well," Vanessa says, as she grabs Jasmine's hands and looks into her eyes. "I know your mother has a special place in your heart and always will. I am, in no way, trying to take her place. I could never do that. I love your father very much but I don't know what the future will hold for us and I want to be there for you in any way I can and also be a good friend. Is that OK with you?"

"Yes ma'am!" Jasmine says. "That's fine. You are my friend and I'm glad you're in our lives and hope you are around for a long time. Ricky too!" They both laugh and continue talking and enjoying their lunch.

Meanwhile, Alex and Ricky are in Alex's backyard tossing the football around. Alex is taking Ricky through a number of drills and giving him pointers on how he can take his skills to another level. After a great workout and conversation, the guys go into the house and Alex prepares lunch of homemade cheeseburgers, fries, and a garden salad.

While they eat, Ricky says, "Mr. Alex, I really appreciate you taking the time out to hang out with me."

"It's not a problem at all. It's a pleasure to do this," Alex says, looking at Ricky with a smile.

"My dad and I used to hang out like this quite a bit," Ricky says. "Ever since he's been gone, I haven't done much of anything. My friends try to get me out and even some of their dads have tried to do things with me but it's not the same, especially when they try to do football stuff with me. Most of them have no concept of the game and it's frustrating. I'm glad you know all about football. That's cool."

"I'm glad I can pass along all the pointers I can. You're already a great player. I just want to see you excel."

"I appreciate that, sir," Ricky says.

"That's what I'm here for."

For the next few minutes, they remain quiet while still eating. Alex then asks, "Were you and your dad pretty close?"

"Yes sir, we were," Ricky answers. "We had a great time together and he was always so supportive of me. That's one of the many things I miss about him."

"What else do you miss about him?" Alex asks.

Ricky looks at Alex as if he is afraid to answer the question.

"It's OK to answer the question. I won't be bothered by it."

"Ok. I miss our talks, hanging out, playing jokes on my mom, and stuff like that," Ricky says. "I could go on and on but that's some of the things I miss doing."

"I know it's hard losing a parent. I lost my mother when I was about your age. Thankfully, my grandparents stepped in and took good care of me and helped me get to where I am now. I want to do the same for you. I know I could never replace your father and that's not my goal. I want to be there for you in any way you allow me to. I want to be one of your biggest cheerleaders and I want you to be able to come to me with anything. Nothing is off limits. But most of all, I want to be your friend. Who knows what the future holds for your mother and me. There is no question that I love her and in getting to know you, I'll love you as well."

"I'd like that," Ricky says. "You're a pretty cool guy, Mr. Alex. I like you and I hope you and my mom are together for a long time. I could get used to having a guy like you around."

"Thanks Ricky! I could get used to being around a guy like you as well," Alex replies. "You're a good kid and Jasmine has really taken a liking to you as well. I think she's glad she has a brother figure in her life since she's grown up an only child."

"She is funny and I like being around her too. What would really be great is if we all lived in the same house. That would be so much fun."

"Is that what you want? Is that how you really feel?" Alex asks.

"Yes sir, it is," Ricky answers. "My mom deserves to be happy and so do you. I think you and her make the ideal couple. Plus, in addition to my dad, you're a good person to look up to."

"Thanks. I appreciate your kind words. Do you think your mom is ready for a long-term relationship like marriage?" Alex asks.

"She has not said anything to me but I believe she is." Ricky responds. "I've even seen her look at rings and dresses on the Internet before. She doesn't know that I saw her but that's what she was looking at."

"I won't say anything to her, but can you do me a favor?" Alex asks.

"Sure, what's that?" Ricky replies.

"If you can, find out what kinds of rings she's been looking at. Maybe when the time is right, I can get her what she wants," Alex says.

"I'll be more than happy to help. I can call or text you with anything I find out," says Ricky.

"Perfect!" Alex says. "I appreciate that. Then, I'll need to know what her ring size is."

"I can take care of that as well. You won't have to worry about a thing."

"There is one thing that I'm worried about," Alex says.

"What's that?" Ricky asks.

"I don't know if I would get your blessing if I were to ask your mom to marry me," Alex says.

Ricky can't control his smiles or excitement.

"Are you kidding me?" Ricky shouts. "That would be awesome! Of course I would give you my blessing. It would be an honor for you to be my stepdad. Don't get me wrong. I love and miss my dad a lot, but my mom deserves to be happy and I believe you would not only make her happy, but also take good care of her. Plus, you and I would be able to hang out as often as we would like. That would be wonderful. So, yes, I will give you my blessing."

"Thank you very much," Alex says, shaking Ricky's hand. "I appreciate that. Promise me you will not tell a soul, especially Jasmine. I can't afford to let her get excited and tell everyone."

"I promise," Ricky laughs. "The secret is safe with me and I'll work on getting that information for you."

"Thanks" Alex says.

"Do you know when you're going to propose to her?" Ricky asks.

"I think I do. I need to look at some dates and work some things out. Once I get that all together, I will have a better idea. I do know I want you to be there when I propose. I'll keep you posted."

"This is going to be very exciting," Ricky exclaims. "I can't wait to see the look on her face."

"Yeah! She will be very surprised," Alex notes. "Enough about this proposal stuff, let's finish eating and get back to relaxing. I'm sure the girls will be gone for another few hours. Let's take advantage of the peace and quiet."

"That sounds like a plan to me," Ricky says as they both finish their food and go to the living room to watch television.

After another hour passes, Vanessa and Jasmine come back to the house and find Alex and Ricky sound asleep on the couch. They don't move even though Vanessa and Jasmine come in making a lot of noise. Jasmine goes over to Alex and jumps in his lap, waking him up immediately.

"Ouch!" Alex yells. "What have you been eating, girl? You feel like a bag of bricks."

"Ms. Vanessa and I had so much fun today," Jasmine says, with excitement. "I can't wait to hang out with her again."

"Yes, we did have a great time Jasmine. I'm sure there will be plenty of times we will hang out. I'm looking forward to it as well," Vanessa says to Jasmine.

"Why is Ricky still asleep, Daddy?" Jasmine asks.

"We worked hard today and had a good meal," Alex mumbles, still waking up. "I should be asleep still myself. Thanks to my little bag of bricks dropping on me, I'm wide awake."

Everyone laughs with the exception of Ricky, who's still sound asleep.

"Ricky is hard to get up and there's only one way to wake him," Vanessa says.

"Let me try!" Jasmine says, as she goes over to him. She shoves him, pushes him, pokes at him, and he doesn't budge. Alex even attempts to wake him, but is unsuccessful. Vanessa laughs at them trying to do what seems to be impossible.

Alex says, "I don't know why you're laughing. This is not funny. How in the world do you get him up?"

Vanessa walks over to Ricky, kneels down to where he is, and says in a soft voice, "Ricky, wake up."

Ricky jumps up immediately and says, "Hey Mom, hey guys! What are you all up to?"

Jasmine bursts into laughter and falls out on the floor. Alex sits on the couch in amazement at what he just witnessed.

"What just happened?" Alex asks Vanessa. "How is it that he responds better to your soft voice than anything else?"

"He's always been like that," Vanessa says. "He responds better to that than anything else. He's been like that since he was a baby. Unfortunately, it's carried over into his teens. I sure hope he breaks out of it before he hits adulthood."

They all laugh.

"Alright Ricky, we'd better get going, We've got some things around the house we need to get done," Vanessa says. "I had a wonderful time, Jasmine. You are great to hang out with."

"Thank you, Ms. Vanessa. You are too," Jasmine says as she gives her a big hug. "See you later Ricky."

"Later Jasmine," Ricky tells her, as they fist bump. "Mr. Alex, when can you show me some more pointers?"

"Whenever you like," Alex says. "Just call me and we'll make it happen."

"Cool!" Ricky gives Alex a high five.

"I'll be talking with you later, my love," Vanessa says to Alex and gives him a kiss on the lips.

"Yes indeed you will," Alex says, smiling.

They all walk to Vanessa's car and Alex opens her door. After she and Ricky get in, she starts the car and drives off, waving at Alex and Jasmine as they drive away. Alex and Jasmine stay in the house for the remainder of the day, enjoying each other's company.

Later that evening, Ricky listens to some music in his room while working on a project for school on the computer and Vanessa is in her room doing work on her laptop. After working extensively on the project, Ricky goes to Vanessa's room to check on her.

"Hey Mom! What are you up to?" Ricky says.

"Oh nothing," Vanessa replies. "Just doing some searching online before I turn in. How's your project coming along?"

"It's going good. I should be done by tomorrow, then I can turn it in," Ricky says, as he lies next to Vanessa on her bed. He looks at her laptop screen and notices that she is looking at wedding rings. Ricky remembers what he and Alex talked about earlier that day. "What are you looking for in particular, Mom?"

"Nothing in particular," Vanessa replies. "I was doing some wishful shopping. That's all."

"These are some nice looking rings. How many have you looked at and which one do you really like?" Ricky asks.

"I've looked at a lot of them but this one seems to be the one I like the most," Vanessa says. "What do you think?"

Ricky gets a good look at the ring and tries to remember all of the details about it so he can give the information to Alex. All of a sudden, he smells something burning.

"Mom, do you smell something burning? Do you have something in the oven?"

"Oh my goodness!" Vanessa says, as she jumps out of the bed. "I almost forgot about the cookies I put in the oven."

She runs out of the room and straight for the kitchen.

Ricky takes full advantage of the situation and takes two pictures of the ring and its details with his cell phone. He wonders if he has time to send it now, not knowing when she will be back. He gets the idea to attempt to get one the rings from her jewelry box to see if he can determine Vanessa's ring size, but he doesn't know how much time he has so he just gets back on the bed to avoid getting caught.

"Ricky!" Vanessa yells from the kitchen. "If you want some cookies, come in the kitchen. They're ready and not burned up."

"I'm on my way!" Ricky yells back. Before he goes to the kitchen, he puts the ring in his backpack in his room and goes to meet Vanessa in the kitchen to share some fresh baked cookies and a glass of milk.

Alex and Jasmine are enjoying a bowl of cereal on the couch while watching a movie. "So you and Vanessa had a good time today, huh?" Alex asks, as he looks over at Jasmine.

"We had a great time, Daddy," Jasmine says. "She is very nice and very easy to talk too. It was funny that she goes to the same salon as Mama and Auntie Nia."

"At Serenity?" Alex asks.

"Yes sir," Jasmine answers. "Whenever we go back, Ms. Vanessa is going to call Ms. Nia and the other ladies and we're going to all get together there for a fun girl's day."

"I'm sure you will enjoy that a lot. It's ironic that Vanessa goes to the same salon. There is a great possibility that your mother and her may have come in contact with one another at some point. That's interesting."

"It sure is," Jasmine agrees.

"So, I take it you really like Vanessa, huh?" Alex asks.

"Yes sir. I really do," Jasmine answers. "She makes me happy just like Mama did, and I really like that."

"You don't feel guilty or weird doing things with Vanessa that you and your mom used to do together?" Alex inquires.

"No, not at all," Jasmine answers. "I feel that Mama is telling me that she's OK. Ms. Vanessa is here to make us happy again."

"You really feel that?" Alex asks.

"Yes sir I do," Jasmine answerers, as she resumes eating her cereal and watching the movie.

Alex is taken aback at what Jasmine has just said. It's comforting to him to know that she approves of Vanessa and wants to continue having her around. He smiles and continues with the movie and cereal as well. Several minutes later, he hears a text message notification on his cell phone. He looks at it and sees a message from Ricky:

Hey Alex! Here is the ring mom REALLY likes. Check it out. I also got an old ring of hers to get her size. Gotta get back to her in the kitchen. I'll text you back later! TTYL! Ricky

Alex scrolls down to the picture and sees a beautiful ring setting that not only makes his heart flutter, but puts a huge smile on his face. It would be the perfect ring for Vanessa and he makes a mental plan to look into the specifics when Jasmine goes to bed.

After they have finished their cereal and the movie comes to an end, Alex tells Jasmine that it's time for bed. She goes to her room to get changed into her pajamas. After she is dressed, they go through their nightly ritual. They say their goodnights, Alex kisses Jasmine on the forehead, and Alex leaves out of her room. He immediately goes to his office to get more information on the ring Ricky sent him. He gets online and looks at the ring more in depth. The more he reads the specification and looks at how beautiful it is, the more determined he is to get it for her. Several minutes into his investigation, he gets another text message from Ricky:

Hey Mr. Alex! Did you check it out yet?

Alex: *Yes I did. I'm looking at it now. It's beautiful! Is this the one she really wants?*

Ricky: *I believe so. That's the one she says she really liked and was looking at for a long time.*

Alex: *Ok. I'll contact the store tomorrow to see if they have it in stock. Somehow I need to find out what her ring size is.*

Ricky: *I got it. It's a size 8.*

Alex: *How did you manage to get that?*

Ricky: *While she was looking at the ring again, I told her that I would get it for her and asked her what her ring size was and she told me. We both laughed it off but I made note of it and was going to pass it along to you. Do you know when you're going to give it to her?*

Alex: *I have an idea but I have to work some things out. I'll be sure to keep you posted because I'll still need your help.*

Ricky: *You got it. I'll be more than happy to help. Have a good night.*

Alex: *Good night, man. I appreciate your help!*

Ricky: *No prob!*

The conversation ends and Alex prints a copy of the ring to take to the store and puts it in his work bag. He then prepares himself for bed so he and Jasmine can get up for church the next morning.

The next day, while at the office, Alex takes out the printout of the ring and looks at it some more. He gets on the phone and calls the Tiffany & Co. store at SouthPark Mall to see if they have it in stock. When he calls and speaks with a sales professional and gives her the details, she informs him that the ring in Vanessa's size is in stock. Alex tells her that he will be coming in today to purchase it. After he gets off the phone, he looks at his calendar for possible dates to propose to Vanessa and it immediately hits him when the perfect time to do it is— Valentine's Day. It's on a Friday and all of their friends, Ricky, and Jasmine could be there to witness this special time. Alex logs in to his computer and drafts an e-mail:

Hey All,

I hope this message finds you well. I really need your help. I have something of great importance I need to meet with you all about. I can't really go into details about it on this e-mail but believe me, it is extremely important and urgent. The only day I can get free is February 14th. I know that's Valentine's Day and you probably have plans already and I understand if you can't make it. But if your plans have not been made, please meet with me then. Something has come up and I need to get your honest opinion about it. Let's meet at our normal spot at Petey's around 7pm. I'll see if I can reserve one of the private rooms so it can be a bit more private.

Again, please make it a priority to meet me at Petey's on February 14th at 7pm for this very important meeting. If it wasn't urgent, I wouldn't request this of you. Please reply to this message. I really appreciate and love you guys dearly. Alex

For Alex, the fun part is not only waiting to see who will respond, but also receiving phone calls and text messages from them trying to find out what's going on. He's decided that he will not respond to any of them, but make the big reveal later. With all this excitement, it's hard for Alex to concentrate at work, but he has to try hard to focus and get things done. When lunchtime rolls around, he goes directly to Tiffany & Co. to make the ring purchase. As he talks with the sales professional, he realizes that he needs to also purchase a wedding band. Thankfully, she is able to find a band that will complement the band perfectly. Alex is very happy with his purchase and he hopes Vanessa will be happy as well. After he leaves the store, he goes back to work and completes his day. From time to time throughout the day, he exchanges text messages with Vanessa. As much as he wants to tell her about the purchase, he resists and keeps it to himself.

Once his workday is complete and he is en route to pick up Jasmine from school, he gets a call from Ricky.

"Hey Mr. Alex! How are you?" Ricky says.

"Hey Ricky!" Alex replies. "I'm great. How are you?"

"I'm doing well, thank you," Ricky responds.

"Good. What's up?" Alex asks.

"Nothing much. Mom is not here and I wanted to see if you were able to look into the ring I sent you," Ricky says.

"As a matter of fact, I did, and I made the purchase today."

"That's awesome, sir!" Ricky says.

"I'm glad you called because I want to let you know that I'm going to propose to your mother on Valentine's Day and I need you to make sure she is not planning to do anything. I'll actually ask her out and suggest that we all celebrate together along with our friends. I think she will like that," Alex explains.

"That sounds like a great plan," Ricky says. "I'll make sure she doesn't plan anything."

"Actually, I will call her tonight and let her know that I'm making plans for all of us to hang out on Valentine's Day and to not make any plans. Please, please make sure you don't tell anyone, not even Jasmine. I want her to be just as surprised," Alex says.

"Don't worry, sir," Ricky says. "I will not tell a soul."

"Thank you. Hey, I've got to let you go because I'm at Jasmine's school. I'll touch base with you later."

"Ok. See ya," Ricky says, as he hangs up the phone.

Jasmine gets in the car and they drive home engaged in their usual conversation about how each other's day was. After dinner, they enjoy the remainder of the evening until it's time to go to bed.

Once Jasmine has gone to bed, Alex calls Vanessa and they begin a long conversation. After several minutes, Alex says to Vanessa, "You know what I was thinking?"

"No, sweetie, what were you thinking?" Vanessa asks.

"I know Valentine's Day is still a few weeks away, but I was thinking we should get together with the other couples and have a nice couple's night out and Jasmine and Ricky could come along," Alex suggests. "What do you think about that?"

"That sounds like a wonderful idea," Vanessa says. "I was just wondering what we could do that day. I'm glad you were already thinking about it. It'll be fun to get together with the gang again. They are an interesting group."

They both laugh.

"Yes, indeed, they are, but they are really good people that I have grown to love, admire, and respect over the years. Hopefully you will feel the same."

"I'm sure I will," Vanessa says with confidence.

They continue to talk into the wee hours of the night.

"I hate to cut this wonderful conversation short, but I've got to get some sleep. I have several lectures tomorrow," Vanessa says, almost asleep.

"I understand," Alex explains. "I have a couple big meetings tomorrow myself. I have to make sure I stay on my A-game."

"I'm sure you won't have any problems with that."

"Thanks for your support, baby."

"No problem. That's what I'm here for. Have a good night, my love. I love you," Vanessa says.

"I love you more. Sweet dreams, princess," Alex utters, and they both hang up the phone. They both lie in bed looking at the ceiling and smiling. Shortly after turning off their lamps, they fall fast asleep.

Valentine's Day arrives and Alex gets dressed for his evening with Vanessa, Ricky, Jasmine, and their friends. He is so nervous that he is pacing the floor, talking to himself. Jasmine notices his behavior and she asks, "Daddy, are you alright?"

"Yes, baby girl, I'm fine. Why do you ask?"

"Because you are walking back and forth and talking to yourself," Jasmine says.

Alex laughs.

"I'm fine, baby. Really," Alex assures Jasmine. "I'm just making sure everything is perfect for this evening."

"Ok. I was just checking," Jasmine says.

"Well, thanks for checking. Hey, would you like your Valentine's gift now or later?" Alex asks.

"Hmmm...I think I'll get it later," Jasmine replies.

"Ok. Later it is. Are you ready to get this party started?"

"Yes sir I am," Jasmine exclaims as she jumps up.

Alex gets on the phone and calls Vanessa to let her know that he and Jasmine are on the way to pick up her and Ricky. Once they get to the house, Vanessa and Ricky get in the car and they all drive to Petey's to meet up with the rest of the gang. When they arrive, they are the first ones there and they are escorted to the private room where it is beautifully decorated. After a few minutes, everyone else begins to arrive. They all greet each other with hugs, kisses, and handshakes as they take their seats and carry on with conversation and laughs. Drinks and dinner are ordered as the fun continues. Towards the end of dinner, Craig gets everyone's attention.

"Alright Alex. What's so important and urgent that you had to call us all together on Valentine's Day? I had a number of beautiful ladies ready for Mr. Cupid to shoot his arrow tonight."

Everyone laughs except Nia.

"Oh Lord. Here we go again with his fairy tales," Nia states. "There's no telling what dog with fleas he was going to be rolling around with."

"Come on you two. Cut it out," Corrine says. "Let's find out what Alex has to say."

"First of all, let me wish everyone a Happy Valentine's Day to you all and I thank you for taking time out of your schedules and maybe even rearranging them to meet with me tonight. I just want you all to know how much you mean to me. I know you might say that you know this already, but I feel that I have to tell you again. It's not every day that a man can have a group of friends that are like family who have stood by me through the thick and the thin and have never disappointed me. You've always managed to come through for me whenever I needed you and I want to thank you. So today, to show how much I love you all, I'm picking up the tab for everyone."

Everyone rejoices with excitement and thanks Alex for his generosity.

"That's not all. Valentine's Day is a day for lovers. I salute all of you that have special people in your lives and allow your love to shine bright every day no matter what situations and circumstances you may face. I realize that not every day is perfect but I salute you all for staying in there and fighting the good fight and keeping your relationships strong and vibrant. Thank you for being ideal role models for me."

Everyone claps in response to Alex's speech.

"That's not all either," Alex says again. "To my baby girl, Jasmine. You are an amazing little woman. You never cease to amaze me. You have been my rock and my inspiration. I love you so much and I want you to have this special gift."

Alex hands Jasmine a large gift bag with a lovely wrapped gift inside of it. When she tears the wrapping off of the gift, one of the biggest smiles comes across her face and her eyes light up when she sees the mahogany jewelry box that plays music when it is opened.

"Daddy, I love it! Thank you so much!" Jasmine says, giving Alex a hug and a kiss.

Again, everyone claps.

"And that's not all either," Alex says. "Vanessa, my love. Words cannot express what I'm feeling right now. I never thought in a million years that I would be standing here expressing to someone how much I love her. From the moment I laid eyes on you, I knew there was something special about you. As much as I tried to look away or as much as I wanted to walk away and leave, something didn't want me to leave and I'm so glad I didn't. That night at the Christmas party was the turning point in my life where I realized that I could love again and that our lives could be complete again. Thank God it can be complete with you. I want you to know and I wanted to express to my family how much you mean to me, and that I love you with every fiber of my being. I can't imagine my life without you. I don't want to go another day without you in it and there is only one way that I can think of that would make that possible."

Alex reaches into his jacket pocket and pulls out a blue box, opens it, and shows Vanessa a beautiful Tiffany & Company Grace™ ring—a platinum band with beautiful round diamonds complementing an exquisite princess-cut diamond at the center. Everyone gasps in amazement at what they are witnessing. After Alex shows her the ring, he gets on one knee.

"Vanessa, I have asked the man of the house if it was OK to have your hand in marriage and he said 'yes.' Now I will ask you, Vanessa, will you marry me and become my wife?"

Vanessa is in tears along with everyone in the entire room, who are quietly waiting on her response.

"Alex you know how to completely catch someone off guard," Vanessa says, tears rolling down her cheeks. "I have long dreamed of a day like this when my knight in shining armor would come and rescue me from my pain and agony. I've dreamed of the day when someone would learn to love me for me and not because of who I am or where I'm from. I've longed for someone to see past the hurt and directly into my heart and soul. You have done that, and have made me feel like a brand new woman. I thank you for loving me in your own special way. It comes naturally and I can feel that it's genuine. I want to experience that for the rest of my life. Yes. Yes I will marry you. Yes!"

Alex gets up from his knee and places the ring on her finger and they exchange in a long passionate kiss as everyone cheers and claps, still in tears.

"It's a perfect fit and this is the exact ring I wanted. How did you know?" Vanessa asks Alex, looking at him intently.

"Let's just say I had an inside scoop that gave me all the details," Alex responds as he gives Ricky a fist bump and a hug.

"You little stinker. I'm going to get you," Vanessa says to Ricky as she puts him in a headlock, rubs his head, and kisses him. Everyone bursts into laughter.

"Wait. So does this mean that Ricky is going to be my big brother?" Jasmine asks.

"Yes it does!" Vanessa says.

"Yes, yes, yes!" Jasmine says as she hugs Ricky and Vanessa, jumping up and down.

"Well, since we all are in the celebratory mood, I would like to present my fiancé and my soon-to-be daughter their gifts," Vanessa says with a smile on her face. She reaches under the table and pulls out two wrapped gifts. She gives one to Jasmine and says, "Happy Valentine's Day Jasmine. I saw this and thought of you. I hope you like it."

Jasmine tears into the wrapping and opens the box, which reveals a beautiful silver heart necklace with her name engraved in it. She takes it out of the box, holds it up, and smiles from ear to ear.

"This is so pretty! I love it!" Jasmine says. "Thank you so much Ms. Vanessa!" Jasmine gives Vanessa a tight hug and kiss on the cheek.

"You are so welcome, sweetie! I'm glad you like it," Vanessa says. "Would you like for me to help you put it on?"

"Can you?" Jasmine asks.

"Absolutely," Vanessa replies, as she takes the necklace from Jasmine's hands and fastens it around her neck.

She takes the second wrapped box and gives it to Alex.

"There were so many things I saw that I wanted to get for you and I couldn't make up my mind. But when I saw this I knew you would like it. Go ahead, open it," Vanessa states.

Alex tears off the wrapping paper and opens the box to find a black and gold Montblanc™ fountain pen. His eyes open wide and his mouth drops.

"This is absolutely amazing, baby!" Alex says with excitement. "I've always wanted to get one but never got around to getting it. Thank you. I love it!"

"You are so welcome, my love," Vanessa says. "I was hoping you would. So, every time you have to sign documents or wherever you go, you can look at it and know it's from me, and that I'm always with you. Plus, it has your fraternity colors on it and I knew you'd really appreciate that."

Everyone laughs.

"I really love it. Thank you again. This has been an awesome day," Alex says.

"Yes it has, and I just had a great idea," Vanessa says.

"What's that, love?" Alex asks.

"I know the announcement of our engagement is so new and we have not had a chance to talk about specifics, but I think it would be a splendid idea if you all will be a part of the wedding party," Vanessa suggests.

Everyone is quiet, stunned at Vanessa's suggestion.

"I think I can speak for all of us when I say that we are flattered that you would want us to be in the wedding, but don't you have any other close friends you would want to be in it?" Corrine speaks up.

"There is one person that will definitely be in it and that's my best friend, Maria. Other than that, I would much rather have you all stand with us. I see how much love you have for Alex and Jasmine and how you've shown so much love for Ricky and me, it's the least I could do and would be honored to have you all there with us; as long as Alex doesn't have a problem with it," Vanessa says.

"I have no problem with that. I was going to ask the fellas anyway so that works out fine," Alex says. "This is going to be a glorious day and we'd be happy if you all will accept."

Everyone looks around for a minute and then Elijah says,

"I think I can speak for everyone in saying that we will be honored and privileged to be a part of your wedding in any capacity you need us. But let me say this. Today marks a very special moment in your lives. This is the beginning of a wonderful lifetime together. In the midst of adversity and pain, you both were able to find each other in the most unexpected way. Just think, if either of you would have decided not to go to that party, we probably would not all be here today. God knew exactly what he was doing; make no mistake about that. He knew exactly what you needed in a mate and you're sitting next to each other. Even in pain, God continues to strengthen and mold you into the people you need to be for each other. That's something you can't do on your own. I applaud you all for staying true to yourselves and not compromising your values and beliefs. God will honor that in ways you can't begin to imagine. I'm so happy for you guys and I pray God's continued happiness for you now and forever."

Alex and Vanessa go over to Elijah and give him a hug. Everyone else is crying happy tears.

"Wow!" Bradley says. "This started out as an urgent meeting, then an engagement party, now we may as well make this into a wedding-planning party."

Everyone bursts into laughter.

"We will need to do some extensive planning outside of here," Vanessa says. "Ladies, let's meet up sometime soon. I haven't planned a wedding in a long time. I may need a little help."

"We will be more than happy to assist," Alicia says.

"Don't forget to include your best friend. Plus, we would like to meet her and have her included in all the planning meetings," Keiko says.

"I couldn't forget her," Vanessa says. "As a matter of fact, she is going to flip out when I tell her we're engaged now. I'll call her when I get home."

"When you are ready to get the ball rolling, just send out a group message and we will be there for you," says Alicia.

"Thanks ladies. I really appreciate you all and I'm looking forward to this experience." Vanessa gives a big smile.

"Alright fellas, we've got to get together too," Foster states. "We've got to make sure our man, Alex, is together."

"Yep and make sure he has the best bachelor party he's ever had,"

Craig adds. "I'll take care of that."

"Oh Lord!" Hannah says. "You all may end up in another state dealing with Craig. You may want to reconsider that, Alex."

Everyone bursts into laughter again.

"I will be sure to keep that in mind, Hannah," Alex says. "Guys, I'll be getting with you once Vanessa and I sit down and do some initial planning. I'm quite sure she will want us looking debonair so I'll keep you posted."

"There is no need to worry, my dear," Vanessa says to Alex. "You and the guys will be the best looking ones attending the wedding. Of course you will be the best looking of them all."

Vanessa then gives Alex a nice, long kiss and everyone pokes fun at them.

Juni strikes her spoon on a glass to get everyone's attention. "Could I have everyone's attention please? I'd like to propose a toast. There is a Chinese proverb that says, 'When there is love in a marriage, there is harmony in the home; when there is harmony in the home, there is contentment in the community; when there is contentment in the community, there is prosperity in the nation; when there is prosperity in the nation, there is peace in the world.' When we look at you, we see love; because we see love, we see harmony; we see harmony because we see contentment; we see contentment because we see the prosperity in you; and because we see the prosperity in you, you will be a blessing to the nation and to the world. Great things are going to happen to you all. Old dreams will be resurrected, new ideas will spring up, and the love you all share will be unbreakable. As long as you continue to work together as a united front, nothing will ever get in your way. So we lift our glasses in honor and recognition of Alex and Vanessa, we pray God's richest blessings upon you and your extended family. We all are your family. Whatever excites you excites us, and whatever hurts you hurts us. Whenever you need someone, look around this room. You don't need to look very far. To Alex and Vanessa."

"To Alex and Vanessa!" everyone says in unison as they toast their glasses and take a sip. As they converse and offering more congratulations, Craig notices that Nia is crying.

"Nia, are you alright?" Craig asks.

"Yeah, I'm fine. I'll be OK," Nia says.

"No, Nia, something is wrong. What's going on?" Craig says again as he sits next to her and puts his arm around her.

"Really, I'm fine," Nia says, still crying. Craig and others continue to try and comfort her. "I'm just happy for the both of them. I've said this before and I'll say it again. Vanessa, I'm so thankful that you came into Alex and Jasmine's lives. All of us have always wanted the best for them because we love them so much. When he came home after the encounter with you at the party, I knew he found his soul mate. There was something about him when he walked through that door and it was how his face lit up as he was telling me about you. I didn't say any-thing, but I prayed you were the one for him. I didn't want to see him disappointed or heartbroken anymore. I wanted to see that sparkle in his eyes again and a smile on his face. I wanted him to have faith that he would find love again and he has with you. As a result, I now be-lieve in love again and hope one day I'll be as happy as you all are. I love you guys."

"We love you too, Nia," Vanessa says, as she goes over to where Nia is and gives her a hug. Craig gives her his handkerchief to wipe her tears.

"You know, to be quite honest, seeing the love you all display has reignited my desire to find love again too," Craig says, to the total shock of everyone. Even Nia looks at him with a puzzled look.

"I'm serious. I know I have not been the ideal man for any woman for a long time, I can admit that. I've done a lot of wrong to so many women I should be ashamed of myself, and I am. But when I see you all, I think to myself that if I were to get myself together, I could have that too. I've got some growing up to do and I've got to sit down and discover what I want in a potential partner and work hard at doing the right things. It's a process that I'm willing to undertake and looking at you, Alex and Vanessa, and all of the other couples here, I have great role models and thank you all for keeping it real with me even though I haven't always listened."

"Wow Craig," Alex responds. "That was very mature of you to say. I'm proud of you, bro. We knew you had it in you. It just needed to come out one day and I'm glad today is it."

"Yeah, me too," Craig says.

It's beginning to get late and everyone says their goodbyes and head for their cars. As they are leaving out of Petey's, Craig said to Nia, "Hey. I'll walk you to your car."

"Ok," Nia says. "You know, that was pretty profound what you said in there. I was shocked to hear those words come out of your mouth."

"Yeah. I was just as shocked as you were," Craig says as they both laugh. "Seriously, knowing what they have gone through and somehow still find a way to find true love and happiness, there must be something I can do to have the same thing."

"I agree. I settled on being by myself for a long time and just do my thing. But when I saw Alex that night, I knew being by myself was not the answer and I couldn't waste my life sitting around doing nothing. Someone is looking for a woman like me that has a lot to offer. One day he will find me."

"I'm sure he will," Craig responds. "He'll show up before you know it."

"You think so?" Nia says, smiling.

"I know so," says Craig, smiling back.

"Ok. We will see," Nia says as she opens her car door. "Thanks for walking me to the car. I really appreciate it."

"No problem. Shoot me a text when you get home to let me know you made it safely."

"I will do just that," Nia says as she gives Craig a hug and they both say goodnight.

On the ride home, Vanessa sits in her seat smiling and looking at her ring, not saying a word. Alex chuckles as he looks at her from time to time.

"I take it you really don't like your ring, huh?" Alex asks, sarcastically.

"Oh sweetheart, I absolutely love it," Vanessa says.

"I'm glad you do. It's a beautiful ring for a beautiful woman."

"That's sweet. Thank you," Vanessa responds.

After a few minutes, they arrive at Vanessa's house. Jasmine has fallen asleep in the back seat, but Ricky gets out and says his goodbyes before going into the house while Alex and Vanessa talk a little bit outside the car.

"I thoroughly enjoyed myself tonight and I can't seem to stop smiling. My cheeks are going to hurt tomorrow," Vanessa jokes.

"I had an outstanding time myself," Alex replies. "This was a perfect evening to get engaged to the perfect person."

"Well I'll tell you now, I'm far from being perfect," Vanessa admits.

"Trust me. I'm not perfect either," Alex confesses. "But you are perfect for me and we're perfect for each other."

"Amen to that," Vanessa says, as they both laugh. "I love you, future husband Reed."

"I love you more, soon-to-be Mrs. Dr. Vanessa Reed," Alex says before they engage in a long passionate kiss.

Afterwards, he walks her to the front door, they wave goodbye, and Alex gets back in the car and drives off. All the way home Alex smiles; proud of how well the evening went. When he gets home, he gets Jasmine out of the car and gently puts her in her bed. He goes to his room to change clothes and gets comfortable.

Meanwhile, Vanessa gets on the phone and calls her friend, Maria. "Hey Maria! How are you? Is it too late to call?" Vanessa asks.

"No. Don't be silly," Maria says. "I'm doing fine. What are you up to?"

"Nothing. Are you busy right now?" Vanessa asks, as if she is in a panic.

"No. Are you all right? You don't sound too good," Maria comments.

"How quick can you get over here?" Vanessa asks. "I really need to talk to you."

"Vanessa, you're scaring me. Is everything all right?" Maria asks.

"Yes. But please get here as fast as you can and please don't get a ticket," Vanessa explains.

"Ok. I'm on my way," Maria says as she hangs up the phone.

Vanessa waits for Maria to arrive but she can't sit still. She sits for a few minutes, and then paces the floor for a few more minutes. After about fifteen minutes, Maria rings the doorbell and Vanessa opens it almost immediately.

"Maria!" Vanessa yells as she gives her a big hug. "I'm so happy to see you!"

"I'm happy to see you, too," Maria says. "What is going on? Are you all right?"

"I'm fine. I'm fine," Vanessa says with a bright smile on her face, holding both of Maria's hands.

"You sounded like you were in a panic and something was wrong. What's so urgent?" Maria asks.

"Remember when I told you things between Alex and I were going extremely well?" Vanessa asks.

"Yes..." Maria says with hesitation.

"And remember when I said that he was a wonderful man, the perfect gentleman, and he was great with Ricky?" Vanessa asks.

"Yes... What about him?" Maria asks.

"Well, he expressed to me this evening that he does not want to date me anymore," Vanessa says with a smile.

"Vanessa. I am so sorry to hear that," Maria says. "I thought you all were the cutest couple and was hoping he would be around for a long time. Maybe he was not the one for you. Don't worry, your Prince Charming will come. Why do you have a smile on your face? I thought you would be sad about something like this."

Vanessa continues to smile while doing motions with her left hand, "I should be sad but I'm not. I've got so much to be thankful for," Vanessa says. "I'm smiling because I'm happy. I choose to be happy and I will continue to stay that way. Is it hot in here to you? Maybe I need to turn on a fan or something." Vanessa begins to fan herself with her hand trying to get Maria to notice her engagement ring.

"What are you talking about? It's not hot at all in here," Maria says, still not noticing her ring. "Maybe you are having hot flashes at your old age."

"I don't know, it seems pretty hot in here," Vanessa says, still fanning with her hand as she sits closer to Maria so she can get a closer look. All of a sudden, Maria stops, looks at her hand, and stares at it for a brief moment.

"Vanessa, what is this on your finger? Is this what I think it is?" Maria asks.

"What do you think it is?"

"It looks like an engagement ring. Is it?"

"Yes it is!" Vanessa says.

Maria jumps up in excitement. "Oh my goodness, oh my goodness, oh my goodness!" Maria screams. "Are you telling me that you and Alex are getting married?"

"Yes," Vanessa says in a calm voice. "Alex and I are getting married."

Maria screams, starts crying, grabs Vanessa, and gives her a big hug.

"You're getting married, but I thought you said you all broke up today?" Maria inquires.

"I didn't say we broke up," Vanessa explains. "I said Alex expressed he didn't want to date me anymore. Instead, he asked me to marry him and I said yes. Are you happy for me?"

"I am beyond happy for you and for Ricky," Maria says, still in tears. "I knew Alex would be the one. I felt it deep in my heart when I met him that night at the party. You all will be very happy together. I just know it."

"Thank you, my dear friend. The other reason I wanted to invite you over here was to ask you for a favor."

"Anything for you. What is it?" Maria asks.

"I would be elated if you would be my Maid of Honor." Vanessa says.

"Oh, Vanessa, I would be honored to stand with you," Maria responds, as she reaches out to hug Vanessa. "We have not talked specifics yet but everyone wants you to be included in all the meetings."

"Everyone like who?" Maria asks.

"All of Alex's close friends," Vanessa responds. "I asked them to be a part of the wedding party. I can't wait for you to meet them. They are a great group who have really been there for Alex and love him dearly. They have really embraced Ricky and me and they are really cool to be around. Just wait and see."

"If you say they are great to be around, I'll take your word for it. I can't wait to meet them as well. I am so excited for you. You deserve to be happy and I see that you are."

"I will let you know when the meetings will start so you can get yourself prepared."

"Trust me. I will be more than ready," Maria says, and then she gets quiet and looks at Vanessa for a few seconds.

"What's wrong, Maria?" Vanessa asks.

"I have to ask you a very serious question," Maria says.

"Sure. Go right ahead. You can ask me anything."

"Well, let me just say again how happy I am for you and I only want the very best for you but I have to ask, have you talked to Alex about Guillermo and if you have, do you have closure with the fact Guillermo is gone and you're about to embark on a new marriage?" Maria asks.

Vanessa pauses for a brief time and answers.

"Maria, Alex knows all about Guillermo and I know about his wife as well, because we all were involved in the same accident that night of the awards ceremony."

"WHAT?!?!?!" Maria screams. "You never told me that. Are you serious?"

"I am very serious," Vanessa replies as she tells Maria the entire story and how, as a result of them talking about it, they became close.

"I cannot believe what I am hearing," Maria states, in disbelief. "This is something you would never think would happen. It's almost like you two were destined to be together. That is absolutely amazing. Do you think you have closure with Guillermo's passing and have you been to visit his grave?"

"I have not been able to go to the gravesite. Ricky and I have never been brave enough to go out there. We just can't get ourselves to go, mainly because we weren't ready or willing to go there. Maybe we should and see how things go. I don't know. All I know is that I love Alex and he loves me. I don't want to do anything to mess that up."

"I don't think you will mess anything up," Maria says. "If he loves you as much as you say he does, he will be supportive of you going and not have any problems with it. Just try to go when you're ready."

"Maybe I will. You always give such good advice. That's why I keep you around as my best friend," Vanessa says as they both laugh and exchange another hug.

"You better. You will never find another friend like me," Maria declares, laughing. "Let me go. Keep me informed on when the meetings start so I can attend and meet everyone else."

"I will. Thank you so much for all your support. I love you so much."

"I love you too," Maria replies. "Try to get some rest. I see you're still on cloud nine and won't come down for a long time. I'm outta here."

"Thanks again, sister. Text me when you get home," Vanessa says. She waves as Maria gets in her car and drives off.

For the rest of the evening, Vanessa spends a great deal of time admiring her ring and thinking about how wonderful it is to be in love again. She never imagined she would be head over hills in love with someone so soon. She thought something like this would happen when Ricky was in college or even married himself. Now she's in love with a man who loves her equally and will be married to him in the very near future. The more she thinks about it, the more nervous she becomes. She then begins to consider details about the wedding-what time of year she wants the wedding to be, the type of dress she should wear, where the locale should be, and so on. It all begins to overwhelm her.

She stops thinking about it and picks up the phone to text Alex:

Vanessa: *Hey Love! Are you awake?*

Alex: *Hey baby! Yes. What are you doing? I thought you may have fallen asleep.*

Vanessa: *No. Right now I'm wide awake. Maria just left a few minutes ago and I was thinking about wedding stuff and stressing out.*

Alex: *Don't stress yourself out. It's too early for that. LOL!!! Try not to think about it so much and just wait until we get together and talk about it. I hope we can make this as stress free as possible. How is Maria doing anyway?*

Vanessa: *She is fine. She is happy for us and elated that she is going to be my Maid of Honor.*

Alex: *I bet she is.*

Vanessa: *I must admit that I'm getting a bit nervous.*

Alex: *Why?*

Vanessa: *I don't know. I was thinking about all the things that need to be done and just got overwhelmed. That's all. Can we just elope and get married?*

Alex: *LOL! Nope. You just asked all our friends to be in the wedding and now you want to elope? That ain't gonna fly. Try again. LOL!*

Vanessa: *I know. It was worth a shot! LOL! Get some rest and I'm going to try to do the same.*

Alex: *Don't worry about anything. We will be fine. We have a great support system and they will be there to make this entire wedding come off without a hitch. I'm confident of that.*

Vanessa: *I love your confidence and I love you.*

Alex: *I love you back!*

Vanessa: *Good night, sweet prince.*

Alex: *Sweet dreams, my love.*

They end the texting and try their best to fall asleep but it does not happen. They both lie in the bed replaying the evening's series of events over and over in their heads. All they can do is smile. After several minutes, they finally fall asleep and rest well for the remainder of the night.

In the following days, Alex and Vanessa get together and talk about the details of the wedding. They make a list of everything that needs to be done, discuss potential color schemes, look at invitations, set up meetings with their pastors, ideas for dresses and tuxedos, and most importantly, the day and time of the wedding. As they talk and look at the calendar, they decide the wedding will be Saturday, June fifteenth, at 3 o'clock in the afternoon. The plan is to make some calls to several venues to check availability and cost to make a final decision on where the wedding can take place. Once everything is written down on what needs to be done, Alex sends out a group e-mail to everyone letting them know the details:

Hey All,

I hope all is well. Vanessa and I had a chance to talk and get some things on paper and we wanted to get the ball rolling and fill you guys in on what needs to be done. If you all are free this coming Thursday at 7pm, let's all meet at my house and go over all the details. Please let us know if you will or will not be able to attend. Thanks again for agreeing to be a part of our special day.

Love Ya!!!

Alex

After a few minutes, responses begin to come in and everyone will be in attendance, so Alex and Vanessa discuss more items and finish for the day.

When Wednesday comes around, everyone gathers at Alex's house and begins talking in detail about the plans for the wedding.

Everyone's excitement level is rising. Vanessa and the ladies selected a day to look at and try on dresses and the guys set a time to get fitted for their tuxedos. All of the friends agree to help make this entire process stress-free for Alex and Vanessa-whatever needs to be done, they are willing to assist.

They are able to secure a photographer, DJ, florist, cake designer, and the locale-the Omni Hotel and Resort in Charlotte. They decide to have the wedding and reception there to take advantage of all the amenities that come with the package, including food and drinks. For the last remaining piece, they are able to meet with Bishop Palmer and Pastor Mendoza to ask them to both officiate the ceremony. They both graciously accept and walk through what the day will look like and consist of, relating to their parts.

As the days and weeks go by, things are going according to plan; all of ladies have been fitted for their dresses, the guys have been fitted for their tuxedos, and responses are flowing in from guests who are planning to attend the wedding. Everything is falling into place.

Two weeks before the wedding, Alex and Vanessa are having dinner together. Alex notices Vanessa is not eating or talking a lot.

"Is everything OK, sweetie?" Alex asks. "You're very quiet and have barely touched your food. What's on your mind?"

"There is something that's been on my mind that I should have taken care of months ago," Vanessa confesses. "I want to talk to you about it but don't want to upset you."

"What makes you think you're going to upset me?" Alex asks.

"I don't know," Vanessa replies. "It's so close to our wedding day and I don't want to cause any stress to the situation."

"What do you mean?"

"Let me ask you this," Vanessa proceeds. "Have you had any closure with Gabrielle's death since she's been gone?"

Alex pauses for a few seconds and asks, "Why do you ask?"

"I've asked myself that question as well and I think I could answer the question for the both of us, but I want to make sure. I don't want there to be anything getting in the way of our future, so I just want to make sure."

"What do you propose we do?" Alex asks.

"Have you been to Gabrielle's grave site since she's been gone?"

"No, I haven't," Alex replies. "Jasmine and I have not been able to bring ourselves to get to that point. It's always been too hard."

"I totally understand. Ricky and I are the same way. We have yet to go," Vanessa continues. "I have an idea. Let's all get the courage and go this one time so that if there is any closure that needs to take place, then it can be over and done with and we can move on with our lives together. How does that sound?"

Alex pauses for a few seconds and says, "That is probably one of the weirdest requests I've ever heard of in my life, but yet, the most ingenious at the same time," Alex responds. "Where is Guillermo buried?"

"He's at Forest Lawn Cemetery," Vanessa answers. Alex's mouth opens. "What's wrong, honey?"

"Gabrielle is buried there, too," Alex responds.

"No way."

"Way," Alex responds. "At what end of the cemetery is he buried?"

"He's on the south end," Vanessa answers. "What about Gabrielle?"

"She's on the north end."

"We all can load up this weekend and make it happen," Alex suggests. "I think it will be good for all of us."

"I agree. Consider it done," Vanessa says, as they continue with dinner.

Once they get to their respective homes, Alex and Vanessa sit down with Jasmine and Ricky and talk about the plans to visit the gravesites. There is some hesitation from both Jasmine and Ricky, but once it is fully explained, the idea doesn't seem as bad as either of them thought and they end up agreeing to go through with it.

That Saturday afternoon, they all load up in Alex's car and take a trip to the cemetery. Once they arrive, Alex parks his car on the side of the pathway and they all get out the car. Jasmine and Ricky do not go with their parents but decided to stay at the car. Alex and Vanessa don't press the issue or try to force them to go. Instead, Alex and Vanessa engaged in a kiss before departing towards the grave markers of their deceased spouses in opposite directions.

Once they find the grave markers, they sit down and begin to talk with their spouse.

"I know I haven't been here to visit you. I'm sorry but I just could not bring myself to do it. It was bad enough I have to live with the fact that you're not here anymore, you were taken from me way too soon, and the last time I would ever see you is in a coffin, that was a bit much for me. Imagine how difficult that was for our child. It was never brought up and I didn't want to force it either; so I just let it be. Nonetheless, you have been missed. Even in the midst of reliving that dreadful day when I lost you each and every day, comfort found its way into my life through another person. At first, I felt guilty about getting involved with another person, but as I spent time with them and got to know them better, the guilt went away and feelings developed. As time went on, those feelings grew into something I never thought I would ever experience again. Love. Love entered the picture and changed everything for me. I was happy again and felt alive. And to see how my being happy made our child happy, that meant the world to me. To be quite honest, I'm in love with this person and we plan to marry. Ironically, we all were involved in the same accident that night and the spouse of the other person is on the other side of this cemetery. Go figure. We both want to make sure we have closure with your death before we move forward. It wouldn't be fair to get into another relationship and not have closure. So the reason why I'm here today is to not only visit you but to also get a sign from you or God or someone that what I'm about to embark on is OK. I need a sign."

When Alex and Vanessa are done speaking, they lay a flower on the grave marker, bow their heads, and close their eyes. A few minutes later, a cool breeze blows throughout the entire cemetery and causes the leaves on the trees to blow. When they both look up, they see a dove fly out of the trees and disappear into the cloudy, blue sky. When the breeze stops, they both feel a sense of relief and comfort that they have gained approval from Gabrielle and Guillermo. They both begin to weep tears of joy. After several minutes, they get up from the ground and walk back to the car. Once they see each other, they embrace with a hug and kiss. They invited Jasmine and Ricky to join in. In their hearts, they both feel as though they received confirmation that they are indeed marrying the right person. After embracing, Alex says to Jasmine and Ricky,

"I know you guys have not been here to visit your parent's grave, but if you feel it's something you need to do at any time, please let us know. We will be more than happy to bring you out here. Don't worry; Vanessa and I are fine with it. You don't have to feel like you're going to hurt our feelings, because you won't. We understand you love them just as much as you love us and we want you to still remember them however you see fit. We support you in whatever you decide."

"Yes sir. Thank you," Ricky responds.

"Thank you Daddy," Jasmine says. "But I believe Mama and Mr. Guillermo are happy that you are happy and want you to be that way forever."

"We believe that too, Jasmine," Vanessa says, as she gives her a tight hug. "All of us will be one big happy family."

They all get back in the car to go home. For the remainder of the day, they work on some last minute things regarding the wedding and still find some time to relax.

For the rest of the days leading up to the wedding, a lot of things need to be done in a short period of time: final fittings for the ladies' dresses and men's tuxedos, final meetings with hair stylists and makeup artists, appointments need to be made with barbers at the same barbershop, dress rehearsal has to take place at the Omni Hotel, and lastly, the rehearsal dinner. The rehearsal dinner was the last 'event' per se, before the ceremony.

During the rehearsal dinner, everyone is having a great time, and can't help but to notice that Craig and Nia are not at each other's throat as much as they have been in the past. Instead, they are talking, laughing, and being very cordial. No one says anything to them, but it is obvious that there is something different about them, with no drama at all.

This is a perfect end to what seemed like a whirlwind few months with the planning and preparation of the wedding. Thankfully, everyone lent a hand and made the process enjoyable and less stressful. Before everyone leaves, Alex and Vanessa present gifts to everyone in the wedding party, including Jasmine and Ricky.

"We just want to show our appreciation and thank you all for being such great friends," Vanessa says. "Alex has always known this, but I'm thankful to see it for myself. Thank you for allowing Ricky and I into your worlds and welcoming us as part of your family. Words cannot express how appreciative we are. Thank you and we love you."

"Vanessa said it all," Alex adds. "You guys have always been awesome and I can't think of a better group of people to call my family. You all have been there through thick and thin and I'm grateful that you are still here, not only to witness but to be a part of something great as Vanessa, myself, and our children, unite to become one. We are blessed beyond comprehension and we thank God for you."

Everyone thanks them for the gifts as they finish dinner and dessert. Once the evening has come to a completion, they all say their goodbyes in excitement and anticipation of the big event on Saturday.

That night, Alex and Vanessa both toss and turn most of the night. The thoughts of getting married and starting a new life are heavy on their minds, making it difficult to fall asleep. Just as Alex is about to pick up his phone and text Vanessa, his phone rings. It's Vanessa.

"Hey love!" Alex answers, "What's up?"

"Nothing. Did I wake you?"

"No. Not at all," Alex says. "I was lying here tossing and turning. I can't seem to fall asleep."

"Me either," Vanessa says. "I've been trying but I can't seem to do it. My nerves are shot and I'm very nervous."

"I know the feeling," Alex says. "But just think, in less than twenty-four hours, you will be known as Dr. Vanessa Reed. That has a nice ring to it."

Vanessa laughs.

"Wait a minute. I thought you were going to be known as Attorney Alexander León," Vanessa remarks, as they both erupt into laughter. "Can you believe we are about to be married?"

"I've had to pinch myself to make sure I am not in a dream," Alex notes. "Then I realized this is no dream, but a dream come true. We both have experienced a great deal of loss, and through patience, time, and with the help of God, we have been able to find each other and gain back what we lost-plus so much more."

"I agree" Vanessa responds. "We are definitely a match made in Heaven. I'm elated and honored to be the future Dr. Vanessa Reed."

"And I am elated and honored to be the future Attorney Alexander León, as well," Alex says, and they laugh again. "Get some sleep, my love. We have a very busy and important day in the morning.

"Yes we do," Vanessa says. "Thank you for always making me laugh when I need it. I love you so much."

"I love you, too. Good night," Alex says.

"Good night, my love."

They hang up and fall fast asleep. After getting a good night's rest, they both wake up the next morning; ready to take on the day.

CHAPTER THIRTEEN

It's Time to say 'I Do'

June fifteenth has finally arrived. The day everyone has been anticipating for a long time; the wedding of Alex and Vanessa. The day starts out early for the ladies since they all have appointments at the beauty salon beginning at six o'clock in the morning. The guys can sleep in just a little later since their appointments at the barbershop don't begin until seven o'clock. Either way, everyone is up, ready, and excited about what the day is going to bring. Once the guys are finished with their haircuts, they head to the tuxedo shop to pick up their tuxedos. Afterwards, they all go to eat breakfast together. It's been made perfectly clear to Alex by the ladies that he is not to see Vanessa before the ceremony and that he better show up at the Omni on time. All of the guys agree to make sure of it, so they are staying on a tight schedule.

Once the ladies are finished with their hair appointments, they get manicures and pedicures and then grab a bite to eat afterwards. Once everyone is finished with their meals, they all arrive at the Omni separately and are escorted to their respective dressing rooms.

Everything they can possibly need is in the room. The hotel has done everything they can to make sure everyone is comfortable and well taken care of. If Alex or Vanessa need anything, all they have to do is communicate it through the friends or to the staff, and it's done.

About an hour before the ceremony is going to take place, there is a knock on the door to the men's dressing room. Alex answers it.

"Bishop Palmer! Pastor Mendoza! Please come in. It's so good to see you both," Alex says, as he shows them in. "Gentlemen, you all remember Bishop Palmer and Pastor Mendoza from the rehearsal, right?" Alex asks. The guys all come over to them to shake their hands and thank them for officiating the ceremony.

"We just wanted to stop by to say hello and to make sure you don't have cold feet," Bishop Palmer says jokingly.

"Yeah. We were hoping that we wouldn't come in here and the guys tell us that you went to the bathroom and never returned. That wouldn't look good," Pastor Mendoza says, as they all burst into laughter.

"No sir!" Alex says. "I'm not going to run away. I can guarantee that. Plus, these guys wouldn't let me do it even if I wanted to."

"Ricky, you are looking mighty fine there, young man," Pastor Mendoza says. "How are you holding up?"

"I'm doing fine, sir," Ricky replies. "Today is going to be a great day and I'm very excited."

"And you should be excited," Bishop Palmer comments. "You and your mother will have a great guy and sweet little angel in your corner. I've known Alex for a long time and I know him to be a great person and an outstanding father. Trust me, you are in good hands."

"Yes sir. I know we will be. I really appreciate what he has done for my mom and me. We have a lot in common and I look forward to hanging out with him a lot more and getting to know him better," Ricky says.

"I feel the same way, man!" Alex says, as he gives Ricky a hug.

"We will see you all in a little bit," Bishop Palmer says. "We are going to check on Vanessa and the other ladies before the ceremony."

"Thanks for stopping by. I really appreciate it. Oh, will you please do me a quick favor?" Alex asks.

"Sure. What's that?" Bishop Palmer says.

"Could you have them send Jasmine over? I have something to give her," Alex says.

"No problem," Bishop Palmer replies. "I can take care of that."

The pastors leave and go over to the ladies' dressing room. When they get there and knock on the door, Mrs. Palmer answers it.

"Hello gentlemen," she says. "How can I help you?"

"We are here to check on the ladies to see how they are and to offer any counsel to the bride if she needs it," Bishop Palmer states.

"They are fine-they don't need anything right now, but thanks for asking," Mrs. Mendoza says, looking over Mrs. Palmer's shoulder and closing the door on the pastors. All the pastors hear on the other side of the door is laughter and giggles. A few seconds later, Mrs. Palmer opens the door and lets them in. The ladies are still laughing as they walk through the door.

"I'm glad we can provide entertainment on such a glorious day," Pastor Mendoza responds. "How are you ladies doing today and how's the bride-to-be?"

"We're doing fine sir, but I must admit, I am a little nervous," Vanessa says.

"That's to be expected," Pastor Mendoza responds. "This is one of the biggest days in your life."

"That's true," Vanessa says.

"But she will be perfectly fine," Mrs. Mendoza adds. "This is the day she has dreamed of and it's now about to come true."

"We have no doubt in our minds that you are ready to take this step," Mrs. Palmer says to Vanessa. "From the short time I've gotten to know you, not only has it been a pleasure but I feel like we've known each other for years. I'm going to love getting to know all of you. I'm so happy for you all."

"Thank you, ladies!" Vanessa says. "I really appreciate your kind words and support. Between you and these wonderful ladies I have around me, I feel I'm in the best of hands."

"That's because you are in the best hands," Maria says. "We would not be here if you weren't special to us."

Everyone acknowledges their agreement as they begin to wipe away tears.

"Before I forget, Jasmine, your father wanted to see you before the ceremony. He says he has something for you," Bishop Palmer says. "Come on. I'll take you over there."

"Yes sir!" Jasmine says, as she grabs his hand and walks over to the men's dressing room. Jasmine knocks on the door and Ricky opens it.

"Hey Ricky!" Jasmine shouts.

"Hey Jasmine!" Ricky says, as he gives her a hug and lets her in. All of the guys comment on how beautiful Jasmine looks. She blushes while telling everyone thank you.

"Hey baby girl!" Alex says as they embrace in a hug. "You look so beautiful today."

"Thank you, Daddy! You look mighty handsome as well," Jasmine says as she adjusts his tie. "Bishop Palmer said you wanted to see me."

"Yes I do," Alex says. "Have a seat for a minute."

Alex gets up and goes over to where his duffle bag is located and says to Jasmine, "Close your eyes and don't open them until I tell you."

Jasmine closes her eyes and puts her hands in her lap. Alex has a box in his hands and takes out a pair of earrings. He takes out the ones that are in her ears and replaces them with the new ones. Once he has them in her ears, he grabs her hand and leads her to a mirror and says,

"Open your eyes."

She opens her eyes and sees the shiny new earrings in her ears. "Daddy! These are so pretty."

Jasmine turns her head back and forth looking at the earrings. "Where did you get these?"

"This is a pair of your mother's earrings," Alex says. "Since your mother is not here to see you looking so beautiful, I figured you would want to have a part of her here with you even though she will be alive in your heart forever. I'm sure she would have given them to you at some point in time. I believe that this is a great time to pass them along. I really hope you like them."

"I love them, Daddy, and I love you! Thank you!" Jasmine says as she gives Alex one of the biggest hugs she has ever given him. There is not a dry eye in the room. Alex gets a tissue and wipes the tears from Jasmine's eyes and gives her a kiss on the cheek. She and Bishop Palmer leave the room and go back to the ladies' room.

As three o'clock rapidly approaches, everyone begins making sure everything is perfect while doing last minute adjustments. Both the men and women engage in a short prayer and take their places until they get further instructions from the wedding coordinator and her team. Once the ceremony is about to begin, everyone, with the exception of the bride and maid of honor, is lined up and paired. All of the married couples are paired with each other and Craig and Nia are paired as well. They hold hands the entire time.

Three o'clock has arrived, music begins to play, and the ceremony begins. The pastors and Alex proceed inside and take their places at the front of the beautifully decorated room that is filled to capacity with friends and family. All of the couples proceed into the room after the pastors and Alex and go to their assigned sections. After everyone is in place, ushers unroll the runner down the aisle. Immediately, Jasmine enters the room and the door closes behind her when she steps in. She begins sprinkle rose petals as she walks on the runner all the way to the front of the room and then she stands with the rest of the ladies. The door opens again and in comes Maria, the maid of honor. She walks in gracefully down the aisle and walks to her position in the front. As she takes her spot, the music changes and Pastor Mendoza asks everyone to stand for the entrance of the bride. Everyone stands in anticipation of Vanessa's entrance, waiting for the door to open again. After a couple of minutes, the door finally opens and Vanessa and Ricky emerge together. The entire room gasps as they see how beautifully dressed she is in her off-white chiffon halter dress. Ricky is handsomely dressed in a black tuxedo and bow tie. Alex tries hard to fight back tears with a smile so bright it could light up a dark room. The closer Vanessa gets to Alex, the more his heart begins to race. When Vanessa gets to the end of the runner, Alex gave Ricky a hug, takes Vanessa's arm, and they turn and face the pastors. Bishop Palmer asks the guests to take their seats as the ceremony begins.

Bishop Palmer proceeds, "Dearly beloved. We are gathered here today to witness Alex and Vanessa unite as one in holy matrimony. Marriage is honorable and well respected amongst most and should not be entered into lightly, without sound advice, or with any hidden agendas; but should be entered into with reverence, the full knowledge of what each other's expectations are, and the fear and admonition of God. It is God's intent for marriage to be enjoyable, fruitful, and long lasting. Marriage is for those individuals who have unconditional love for each other and are willing to put in the work to make it successful. Whatever it takes, they will fight for it. And being in council with these two standing before us today, I know without a shadow of a doubt that they are in this for the long haul and will fight to ensure their marriage will last and will be well equipped to weather the storms as they come. I require and charge you both to disclose anything that could possibly be a detriment to your marriage. For if there is something that needs to be disclosed, please do so now, for if it is found out later that there was something, your marriage will not be valid."

Alex and Vanessa look at each other acknowledging that there is nothing that needs to be disclosed by either of them. Bishop Palmer proceeds with his portion of the ceremony.

"We see there is nothing. Who gives this woman to be married to this man?"

"I do!" Ricky says.

"Thank you, young man!" Bishop Palmer says, as the congregation chuckles. "Alex and Vanessa have decided to say their own vows to each other."

Alex and Vanessa turn to face one another. They hold hands as Vanessa begins to say her vows.

"My dearest Alex, first of all, I thank God for you. Secondly, I want to personally thank you for saving my life and being my hero. You came into my life when I was at my lowest and you picked me up and put me on solid ground. You are and have always been a perfect gentleman and there's never been a day that you haven't made me smile or feel loved. It almost seemed as though you knew immediately what I needed in my life without even asking. My life up to this point has been wonderful. The rest of my life is going to be magnificent. From this day forward, I promise to love you unconditionally and be your biggest cheerleader. No one or thing will ever come between us. My love for you is wider than any canyon and deeper than any ocean. I vow to be the wife and friend you need to accomplish any endeavor you set your heart to do. No matter where you are in this life, trust and believe that I will be with you every step of the way. Together, we can move mountains and slay dragons. I love you more than words can express and I'm honored and privileged to become your wife toady."

Alex clears his throat, looks into Vanessa's eyes and says,

"Vanessa, my love, when I think about you, all I can do is smile. That was not always easy to do at one point. Coming from a place of darkness and brokenness, I thank you for resurrecting my faith in love. Just when I was about to throw in the towel, you came along and gave me hope; hope to trust again; trust to love again; and trust to be myself again. I am a new man because of you. Never in a million years did I think I would ever fall in love again. Then I met you and all of that changed. I love you with an everlasting love. You are one of the best gifts from God I could ever receive and it's my job to take really good care of it. I can't promise that I won't make mistakes and say or do stupid things; but I will promise to love you forever, protect you, cover you, and be an awesome father figure in Ricky's life. No matter what life throws at us, both good and bad, my promise to you is that I'll be there no matter what and nothing will get in the way of the love I have for you. God knew what He was doing at the beginning of time. He allowed us to experience all that we have to shape and mold us for this very hour. We are exactly what we need for each other and were divinely orchestrated that way. I'm looking forward to spending eternity with you."

"May we have the rings, please?" Pastor Mendoza says. Maria and Elijah both give the rings in their possession to Bishop Palmer. Pastor Mendoza begins to speak:

"These rings are an outward expression of the inward love they share for each other that will continue forever. These rings are made of the strongest metal on Earth and signify the unbreakable love they share that will withstand the tests of time."

He gives Vanessa's ring to Alex and instructs him to place it on her left ring finger and asks him to repeat, "With this ring, I seal this marriage to you. In the name of the Father, the Son, and the Holy Spirit. Amen."

He then gives Alex's ring to Vanessa and instructs her to do and say the same thing, "With this ring, I seal this marriage to you. In the name of the Father, the Son, and the Holy Spirit. Amen."

"All of us are a part of one, big family-God's family. Today as Alex and Vanessa have publicly expressed their love and commitment for each other by exchanging rings, they want to publicly make a commitment to their children. Jasmine and Enrique play significant roles in this marriage being celebrated today. They will now join their parents as individual people coming together as a blended family. This is symbolized by the pouring of this colored sand into this crystal vase. As each individual pours the sand into the vase, it is a sign of unity and they all will be joined together as one. These grains of sand may never be able to be separated again, and the bond of this family will never be broken. From this day and beyond, you are no longer one couple and two individuals anymore, but are now one united, loving family that loves one another very much. As they pour the sand into the vase, I will recite a poem by an unknown author entitled, 'What is Family?'

> *A family is...*
> *The sweetest feelings*
> *The warmest hugs*
> *Trust and tenderness*
> *Unconditional love*
> *The stories of our lives written on the same page*
> *The nicest memories anyone has ever made*
> *Treasured photos*
> *Thankful tears*
> *Hearts overflowing with all the years*
> *Being there for one another*
> *Supporting and caring*
> *Understanding, helping, sharing*
> *Walking life's paths together*
> *And making the journey more beautiful because...*

We are a family...and a family is love.

As Pastor Mendoza recites the poem, Alex, Vanessa, Jasmine, and Ricky take turns pouring their container of colored sand into the vase. Once the sand is poured and the poem is complete, Pastor Mendoza announces that Alex and Vanessa would like to have a private moment to take Communion. So for the next few minutes, as the pastor's microphone is turned off, he administers the Communion elements to Alex and Vanessa and they partake of them. When they are done, Bishop Palmer concludes the ceremony.

"Now that Alex and Vanessa have come together today and have expressed their love and have shown their love by exchanging rings, by the authority vested in Pastor Mendoza and myself as ordained ministers of the Gospel, we are excited to pronounce you as husband and wife. What God has brought together, let no man or woman put it asunder. In the name of the Father, the Son, and the Holy Spirit. May God forever bless you and keep you in His care. Alex, you may now kiss your bride."

Alex faces Vanessa, pulls her close to him and gives her a kiss and whispers, "I love you".

"Ladies and gentlemen, my I present to you Mr. and Mrs. Alexander and Vanessa Reed!" Bishop Palmer and Pastor Mendoza say simultaneously as the room full of guests jump to their feet cheering and clapping their hands.

Everyone proceeds to the banquet hall, where music is playing and the wedding party begins to take pictures. Guests mingle and laugh as they wait for Alex and Vanessa to make their entrance. Once they arrive, there's a sound of rejoicing, clapping, and whistling. Dinner is served and everyone has a seat. After a few minutes, friends from the wedding party begin to make their toasts to the couple before it's announced that it's time for the couple to have their first dance as husband and wife.

As the song plays, all Alex and Vanessa can do is close their eyes, smile and dance slowly to the music. A few minutes into the song, they receive a tap on the shoulder. It's Jasmine and Ricky. They all embrace in a hug and begin to dance, Jasmine with Alex and Ricky with Vanessa—a picture-perfect moment witnessed by everyone.

The celebration continues with the cutting of the cake and the catching of the bouquet and garter. As the evening is drawing to an end, guests begin to express their congratulations to the bride and groom before they leave.

The bridal party remains to spend the last few moments with Alex and Vanessa. While they are all sitting and standing around, Alex takes the time to thank his friends.

"Words cannot express how much we really appreciate you guys. You have helped this day be a total success and we thank God for you. We can never thank you enough."

"Exactly," Vanessa says. "You all were the perfect people to stand with us on this special day. We wouldn't have wanted it any other way. The love you show us is amazing and for me, that means a lot because you didn't have to accept me. But because you have, I've gained a family who I love very much. My husband and I are truly blessed to have you."

Vanessa puts an emphasis on husband with a big smile on her face.

Everyone exchanges hugs before they leave, allowing Alex and Vanessa to have private time as husband and wife before going on their honeymoon. Jasmine goes with Nia and Ricky with Maria. This was the perfect end to a perfect day. They spent the entire day with friends and family and ended the day as husband and wife. What more could they ask for?

The following day, they awake and head to the airport to go on their honeymoon to the Virgin Islands. They've both always wanted to go somewhere tropical so they made the decision that their honeymoon would be the perfect time to try something new as they begin their new journey together.

Six months later, when everyone has settled back into their routines, Alex is back at work and sends out a strange   e-mail to all of his friends:

Hey All!!!

Hope all is well. The first person to solve this puzzle and reply back to me will receive a prize. Oh, by the way, the prize will be given at our get together at Petey's this Saturday at 7pm. Be there or be square!!! LOL!!! Here is the puzzle...

pvtannaegsesrapis
Good Luck,
Alex

As the days go by, Alex is amused that no one has replied with the answer to the puzzle and when Saturday arrives, no one has given an answer. He, Vanessa, Jasmine, and Ricky are the first ones at Petey's. When everyone else arrives, they all see an easel at the end of the table with the letters of the puzzle on a poster board.

"OK. Since none of you smart people could figure out the puzzle, I'm going to give you another chance to win this lovely prize we have for you," Alex says after everyone is seated. "I'm going to give you five minutes to figure it out. If you happen to solve it before time is over, raise your hand and don't yell it out."

"Right," Vanessa says. "Also, before the reveal of the answer, there will be a short presentation that will hopefully give you some insight on what the answer is. So your time starts...now!"

Everyone looks at the puzzle trying to figure it out. After about three minutes, Maria screams and covers her mouth. Alex goes over to her and she shows him what she wrote on a piece of paper, which is the correct answer.

"Alright, everyone! Maria has the right answer so she will win the prize," Alex announces as everyone grunts and laughs.

"Before we give Maria her prize, my lovely wife and I would like to make a special presentation at this time."

"Would Jasmine and Ricky please come forward?" Vanessa says as she reaches into a bag and pulls out two beautifully wrapped gifts and gives one to each of them. "Please open them up."

They unwrap the gifts and pull out t-shirts. The one Ricky pulls out has the words I'm the big brother on it and Jasmine's has I'm the big sister. They both stand there looking slightly puzzled.

"What does this mean?" Jasmine asks. "How can I be a big sister?"

"Maria, what is your answer to the puzzle?" Alex asks.

"Vanessa is pregnant!" she yells, as Alex turns the poster board over revealing the answer that Maria correctly guessed. Alex then gives the gift to Maria. When she opens it, she sees that it's a framed picture of the ultrasound of the baby with the caption, 'It's a boy!!!' Everyone is elated including Jasmine and Ricky.

"Man, this is awesome!" Craig says. "We are so happy for you guys and we're looking forward to seeing our nephew in the future. It makes the news Nia and I were going to share not that important. Maybe we need to announce it at a later time."

"No way, man!" Alex says. "If you got something, spill it!"

"Well, if you insist," Craig says while holding Nia's hand. "As you probably have seen lately, Nia and I have not been at each other's throat like we usually are. The more I have gotten to know her and get over my past hurts and insecurities, I have begun to see what a beautiful woman she really is. Honestly, everything I've ever wanted in a woman was right next to me all along. So we've been hanging out and really getting to know one another and eventually, we fell in love. Yes, I said we're in love. The time I've spent with her has been wonderful and I don't want to lose that. So I turned in my player card and got a ring. I can't let this good thing pass me by."

Nia then shows everyone her ring and declares, "We're engaged now!"

Everyone is shocked and happy at the same time. It takes a few seconds for everyone to react, and then they begin to clap, cheer, and pass out hugs of congratulations. These were the last two people they thought would even consider marriage, and especially not even marrying each other as often as they fought.

"Craig really is a wonderful man," Nia says. "We have had our arguments and said some awful things to one another in the past. We were both hurt and felt it was easier to attack the person closest to us. But deep down inside, he really does have a heart of gold and is a strong and loving person who was yearning for genuine love. Now he has it and I've got plenty to give him."

"Have you all set a date yet?" Corrine asks.

"Not yet," Nia says. "We are tossing some dates around but of course all of you are invited."

"We had better be," Elijah says, as everyone bursts into laughter.

"I will be getting with all you men to get some sound advice on marriage and relationships. I've been a little rusty," Craig says.

"We got you covered, bro," Alex says, "I'm proud of you, man."

"Thanks Al!" Craig says, as he gives Alex a hug.

The remainder of the evening is spent with a lot of love and laughs. When the fellowship comes to an end and everyone goes their separate directions, Alex and Vanessa sit back and think about their journeys that brought them to get to this point and the pain and hurt that they've endured. But through it all, they were still able to find what once was lost, which was love and the loves of their lives. Now, a new chapter is beginning with new experiences and new developments. No one knows what's on the horizon for Alex and Vanessa. But whatever it is, they are more than ready to face it head on and come out on top as champions.

THE END (for now).

ABOUT THE AUTHOR

Jovan Williams, a St. Louis, Missouri native, is a talented musician, singer, video gamer, and family man. He also enjoys writing, traveling, and relaxing. Jovan is also an ordained minister and attends Restoration Church of Northwest Arkansas where he serves as Executive Director of the Membership/Guest Services Ministry, alongside his wife, Sheronda. Jovan's passion is to be a blessing to others through community service. Jovan is a proud member of Alpha Phi Alpha Fraternity, Inc.

Jovan's mission in life is to inspire everyone he comes in contact with to live out their potential and not lose hope when things are going wrong. He lives by the scripture - Proverbs 3:5-6.

Jovan obtained his Bachelor of Science in Management and Masters of Business Administration degrees from National-Louis University. He also studied music education at Jackson State University in Jackson, Mississippi. Jovan resides in Arkansas with his wife, Sheronda, and together they help raise five children.

CPSIA information can be obtained
at www.ICGtesting.com
Printed in the USA
FFOW04n1822240516
24414FF